IMAGES
of America

LANGLEY

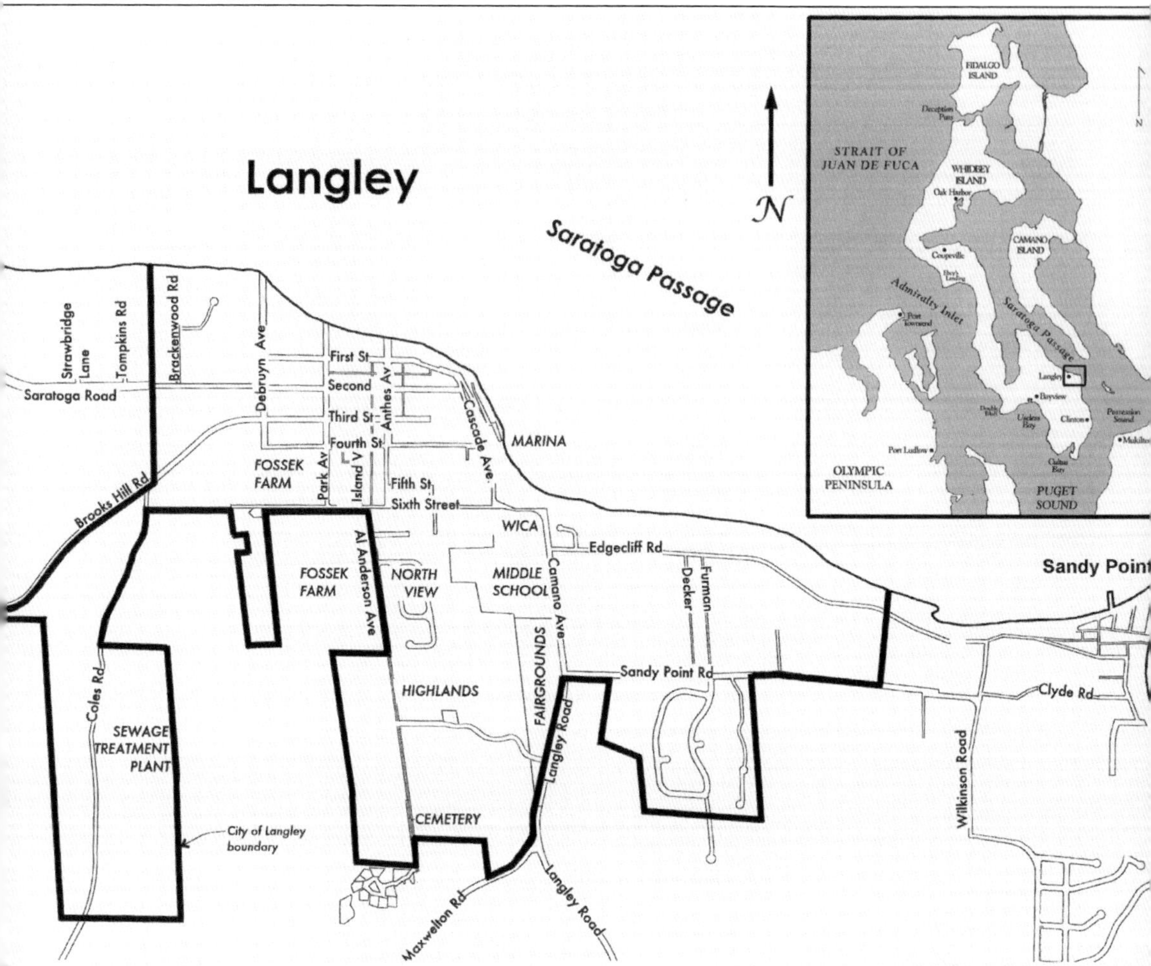

The city of Langley, Washington, is located on the southeastern edge of Whidbey Island in Puget Sound (see insert.) The map shows present-day Langley; the bold line demarcates the city boundary. (Courtesy of Robert Waterman.)

On the Cover: The Dog House Tavern (left) on First Street, seen here around 1940, is a Langley icon listed in the National Register of Historic Places. Built in 1908 as a sporting venue known as the Olympic Club, its occupants over the years have included a mercantile store, confectionery, tavern and pool hall, gymnasium, and a variety of other businesses. It has also hosted several community events and served as a residence. (Courtesy of the South Whidbey Historical Society.)

IMAGES
of America

LANGLEY

Robert E. Waterman
and Frances L. Wood

ARCADIA
PUBLISHING

ISBN 978-0-7385-9600-6

Published by Arcadia Publishing
Charleston, South Carolina

Printed in the United States of America

Library of Congress Control Number: 2012940640

For all general information, please contact Arcadia Publishing:
Telephone 843-853-2070
Fax 843-853-0044
E-mail sales@arcadiapublishing.com
For customer service and orders:
Toll-Free 1-888-313-2665

Visit us on the Internet at www.arcadiapublishing.com

To all the citizens of Langley, past and present, whose lives and hard work made the "Village by the Sea" grow and prosper.

Contents

ACKNOWLEDGMENTS

Thanks go to the founders and board members of the South Whidbey Historical Society, who strive to preserve the history of South Whidbey Island. A special debt is owed to the society's past president, Lorna Cherry, whose three-volume *South Whidbey and Its People* provides a rich collection of information. We are especially grateful to the many people who have contributed photographs, stories, and memories for the writing of this book and for the ongoing collecting of Langley's history. We wish we could list you all here.

The following abbreviations have been used in this book:
SWHS: South Whidbey Historical Society
ICHS: Island County Historical Society
PSMHS: Puget Sound Maritime Historical Society
MOHI: Museum of History and Industry

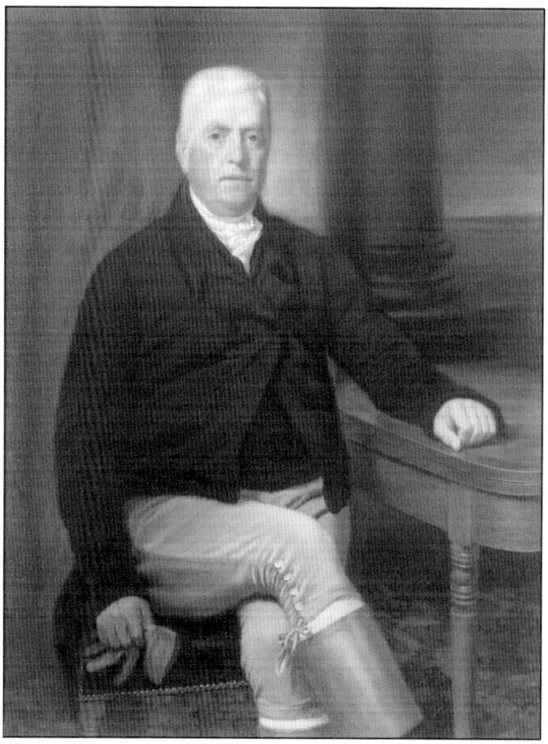

Joseph Whidbey was likely one of the first white people to visit the area on Whidbey Island where Langley is now located. This portrait hangs in the Institution of Civil Engineers in London, England. (Courtesy of the SWHS.)

INTRODUCTION

The city of Langley, Washington, is perched on a low bank near the southeastern corner of Whidbey Island, a 45-mile-long island snaking through the northern half of Puget Sound. On a clear day, Langley enjoys a picture postcard view north across Saratoga Passage toward Camano Island and the Cascade Mountains. The town is protected from prevailing southwest winds and enjoys proximity to the Clinton ferry, which connects it to the mainland and, 30 miles farther south, the city of Seattle.

Approximately 12,000 years ago, the Vashon Glacier retreated from Puget Sound by scraping its way north into Canada, leaving behind the basic landforms of Whidbey Island and its neighbors, Camano and Gedney (Hat) Islands. Lodgepole and white pine forests first colonized the southern part of Whidbey Island, followed by Douglas fir, western hemlock, red cedar, and red alder that filled in the landscape and created a dense forest.

Humans arrived about 10,000 years ago, some migrating down the coast from Alaska, others spreading west from the interior of the continent. Those people who settled at the mouth of the Snohomish River on the western shores of Puget Sound relied on salmon as their most abundant and reliable food source. They moved easily by canoe beyond the mouth of the river to the southern ends of Camano and Whidbey Islands, where they established camps. The population of these outlying villages fluctuated seasonally as the native people fished, collected clams and berries, and hunted deer. One such beach camp, *TSEHT-skluhks*, meaning "ragged nose," was located at Sandy Point, one and one-half miles east of Langley.

During his 1792 voyage to Puget Sound, British captain George Vancouver sent Joseph Whidbey, master of the ship *Discovery*, to explore and circumnavigate the large island, which Vancouver later named in Whidbey's honor. On May 29, 1792, Whidbey anchored near present-day Mukilteo and took the ship's launches to explore what we now call Saratoga Passage. At Sandy Point, Whidbey noted in his journals that they were met by several hundred people, who received them in a friendly manner both in canoes and by walking along the shore. During the following century, illness killed off many local natives, and in 1855, laws restricted the Snohomish peoples to their reservation, near the mouth of the Snohomish River.

So it was a raw, dense forest that greeted the first white settlers to South Whidbey in the 1880s. Logging camps and a few scattered homesteaders and squatters began taming the wilderness. Among them was Jacob Anthes, who wrote about his first year. "We didn't make money but we had a good time living on game, clams, and fish. We cleared a few acres of land on which we grew all the vegetables we could use and sold several tons of spuds to the logging campsite the following year."

When Langley's founder, Anthes, went looking for land to purchase, it was those glacier-created landforms that helped influence his decision. He chose land for the practical reason that the long north/south valleys ending at the water's edge would allow future commerce with surrounding farms and towns, and his wharf would open the commerce to the rest of Puget Sound.

Jacob Anthes first purchased land here at the age of 15 and helped plat the town in 1891, naming it for Judge James W. Langley, the president of the Langley Land and Improvement Company.

Anthes, Langley, and a handful of others hoped to benefit from the anticipated economic boom created by the arrival of the railroad to the region, a promise that never materialized. Initially based on logging, the character of the town changed as farming followed the removal of trees. Stumps were cleared and fruit orchards and berry crops appeared.

The town grew as new families arrived. General stores, hotels, a tavern, barbershop, meat market, blacksmith shop, livery stable, bank, and real estate offices were built. A wharf provided the essential link to the "outside world." The town remained one of South Whidbey's main ports from its formation in 1891 until 1929, when car ferry service serving Whidbey shifted from Langley to Clinton.

Throughout its history, Langley has been a magnet for creative people. In 1917, Peter and Margaret Camfferman established the Brackenwood artists compound that, for more than two decades, attracted students and early modernist painters, including members of Seattle's "Group of Twelve." In 1920, Langley was governed by an all-woman town administration led by Margaret Camfferman's aunt, Helen Coe.

Completion of the Deception Pass Bridge in 1936 at the north end of the island provided an alternative to ferry transport and ushered in an increasing number of vacationers, some of whom built summer cabins in and around the town. Fishing resorts, such as Langley's Sunrise Beach, were popular during the 1930s, 1940s, and 1950s, but this seasonal influx of tourists couldn't support a town languishing from the effects of the Great Depression, World War II, and a lack of industry.

However, it was the quiet, off-the-beaten-path character of Langley, combined with the natural beauty and cheap housing, that attracted the next wave of inhabitants. During the 1970s, young, educated, and disenchanted individuals and families began arriving, some from Seattle, others from California or the Midwest. Shaped by the increasingly unpopular Vietnam War, new feminism, and alternative lifestyles, they radically altered the character of the town by creating a vibrant, artistic, and close-knit community.

As the country's economy became stronger, Langley's quaint artistic nature and proximity to the metropolitan Seattle area oriented the town toward tourism and away from a primarily locally supported economy. Construction of upscale tourist lodging and bed-and-breakfast operations in the 1980s and 1990s accommodated the influx of tourists. Gas stations, hardware stores, and lumberyards closed or moved out of town, to be replaced by restaurants, art galleries, antique shops, and other establishments catering primarily to visitors.

Today, with a population of around 1,200, Langley remains the only incorporated city on South Whidbey. It supports a community of local businesspeople, artists, writers, off-island commuters, and retirees. Still offering stunning views of natural beauty and retaining the look and feel of its past, Langley remains a quaint "Village by the Sea."

A note to readers: The spelling of the name Whidbey has changed over the years. Recorded as "Whidbey's Island" by Vancouver, it is identified as "Whitby's Island" on some early maps and was also spelled "Whidby" for many years. In the late 1940s, the official spelling became "Whidbey." The spelling will vary with the time period being discussed. Although street names have also changed over the years, current street names are used to avoid confusion.

One

Founding of the Town
Pre-1900

If ever a town had one indisputable founding father, it was Langley's Jacob Anthes—that is, if one can count a 15-year-old as a founding father. Anthes, along with childhood friend George Miller, left Germany to escape registration for military service but also to seek adventure. They sailed to New York and traveled by train, stopping in Kansas. Anthes continued to San Francisco before heading to Seattle, where he was hired by a local man to hold down his homestead. Five days later, in September 1880, Langley's founder arrived on South Whidbey.

The following year, Anthes purchased 120 acres of forest a half-mile west of present-day Langley, built a log cabin, and cut cordwood to supply steamers plying Saratoga Passage. In 1886, when he was finally old enough to homestead, he acquired 160 acres adjoining what became the town of Langley. In 1890, Anthes interested Judge James Langley in forming the Langley Land and Improvement Company. The town site was surveyed, platted, and named for the primary investor.

Anthes built the town's first general store and residence on the corner of First Street and Anthes Avenue, where he lived with his family for the next 18 years. He established a post office and became the first postmaster. To attract commerce, Anthes built a 999-foot dock at the base of Anthes Avenue. Soon, up to 35 cords of wood per day were sold to steamers plying Saratoga Passage. However, the economic downturn of 1893–1894 halted most steamer travel along Saratoga Passage, and the town's growth lagged.

By 1898, the town's economy picked up, with Alaska's gold fever bringing new life to the Puget Sound area. Seattle was expanding its harbor, and much of the brush used for fill came from South Whidbey. That same year, Langley established a school district and built its first school building.

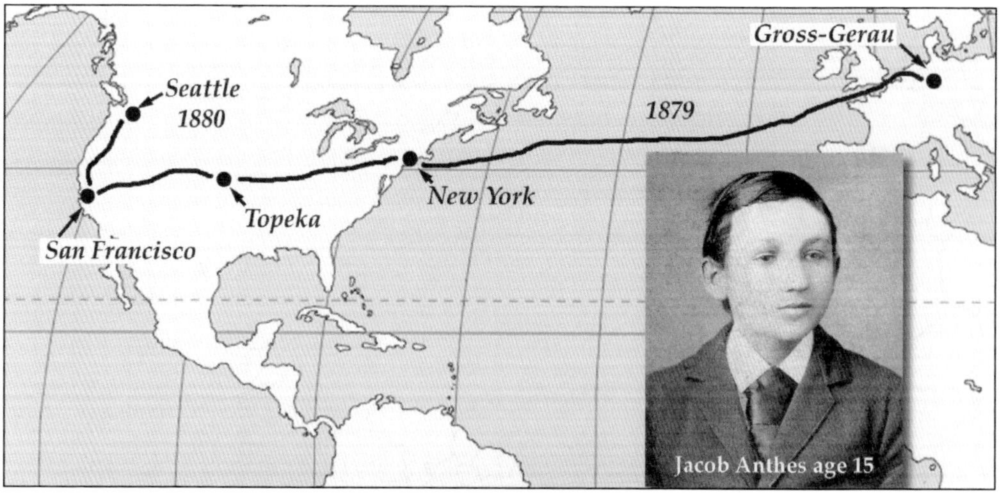

In 1879, fourteen-year-old Jacob Anthes left his home in Gross-Gerau, Germany, and sailed to New York with a friend. After a brief period in Topeka, Kansas, Anthes left his friend and made his way to San Francisco, then up the coast to Seattle, arriving on Whidbey Island in the fall of 1880. He bought land, built a cabin, and sold cordwood and potatoes. (Courtesy of Helene Ryan.)

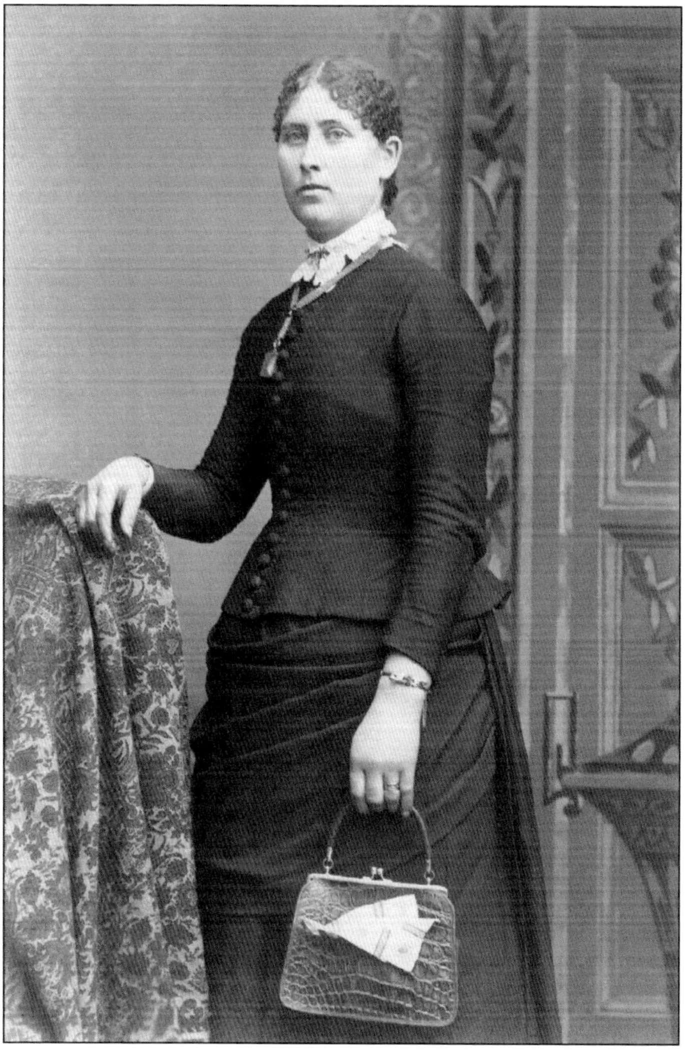

Jacob Anthes met Leafy Weeks in 1887. She persuaded Anthes to start a small tobacco business near the Seattle waterfront. He lost his wares in the 1889 Seattle fire but married Leafy a few months later, and the newlyweds left for a trip to Germany to introduce Leafy to his relatives. (Courtesy of Helene Ryan.)

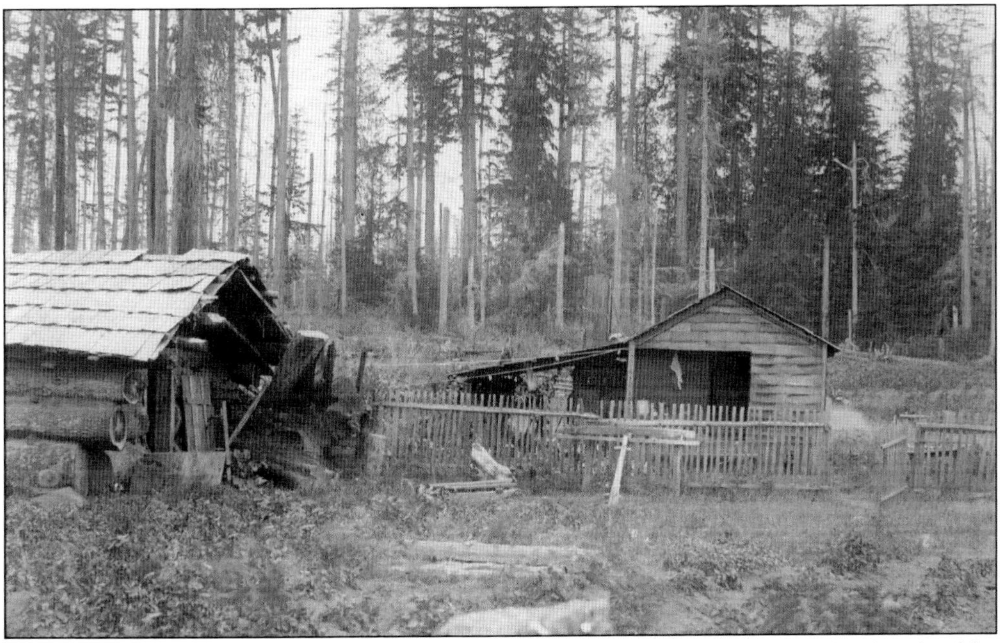

Jacob Anthes built this cabin in the woods west of present-day Langley on the first land he purchased in 1880 at age 15. He brought his bride, Leafy, here in 1890 after returning from Germany to introduce her to his family. She cooked bread outdoors in a Dutch oven. Their first child, Mabel, was born here on December 13, 1890. (Courtesy of Helene Ryan.)

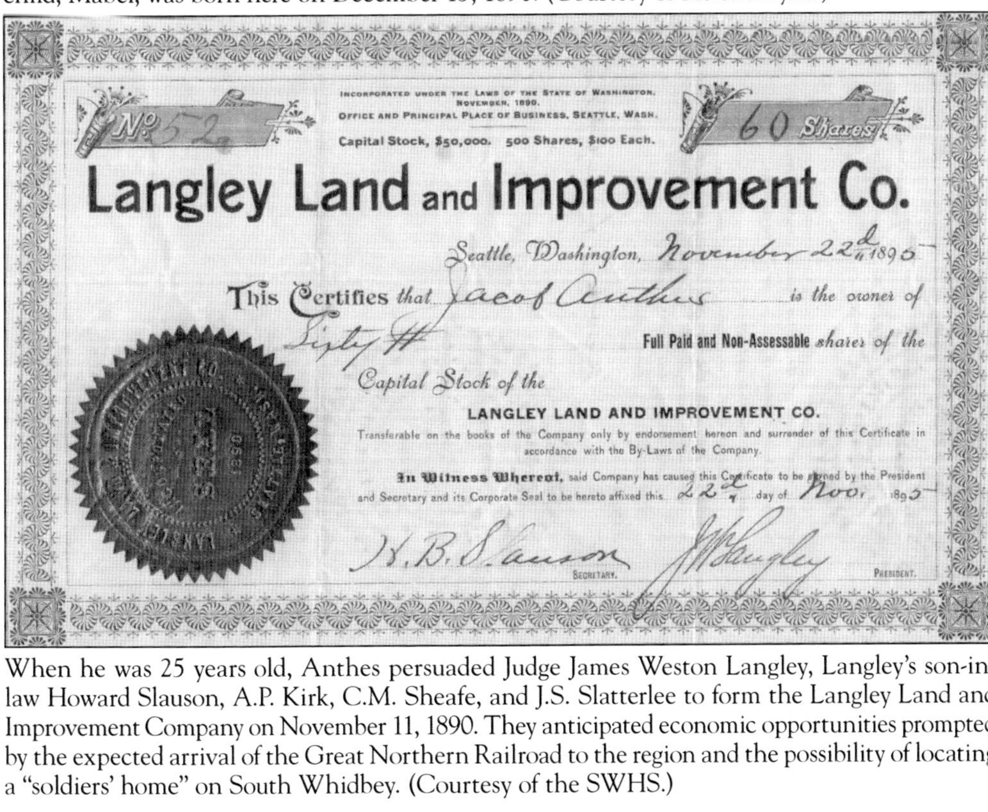

No. 52

Incorporated under the Laws of the State of Washington, November, 1890.
Office and Principal Place of Business, Seattle, Wash.
Capital Stock, $50,000. 500 Shares, $100 Each.

60 Shares

Langley Land and Improvement Co.

Seattle, Washington, November 22d 1895

This Certifies that Jacob Anthes is the owner of Sixty Full Paid and Non-Assessable shares of the Capital Stock of the

LANGLEY LAND AND IMPROVEMENT CO.

Transferable on the books of the Company only by endorsement hereon and surrender of this Certificate in accordance with the By-Laws of the Company.

In Witness Whereof, said Company has caused this Certificate to be signed by the President and Secretary and its Corporate Seal to be hereto affixed this 22d day of Nov. 1895

H. B. Slauson
Secretary.

J W Langley
President.

When he was 25 years old, Anthes persuaded Judge James Weston Langley, Langley's son-in-law Howard Slauson, A.P. Kirk, C.M. Sheafe, and J.S. Slatterlee to form the Langley Land and Improvement Company on November 11, 1890. They anticipated economic opportunities prompted by the expected arrival of the Great Northern Railroad to the region and the possibility of locating a "soldiers' home" on South Whidbey. (Courtesy of the SWHS.)

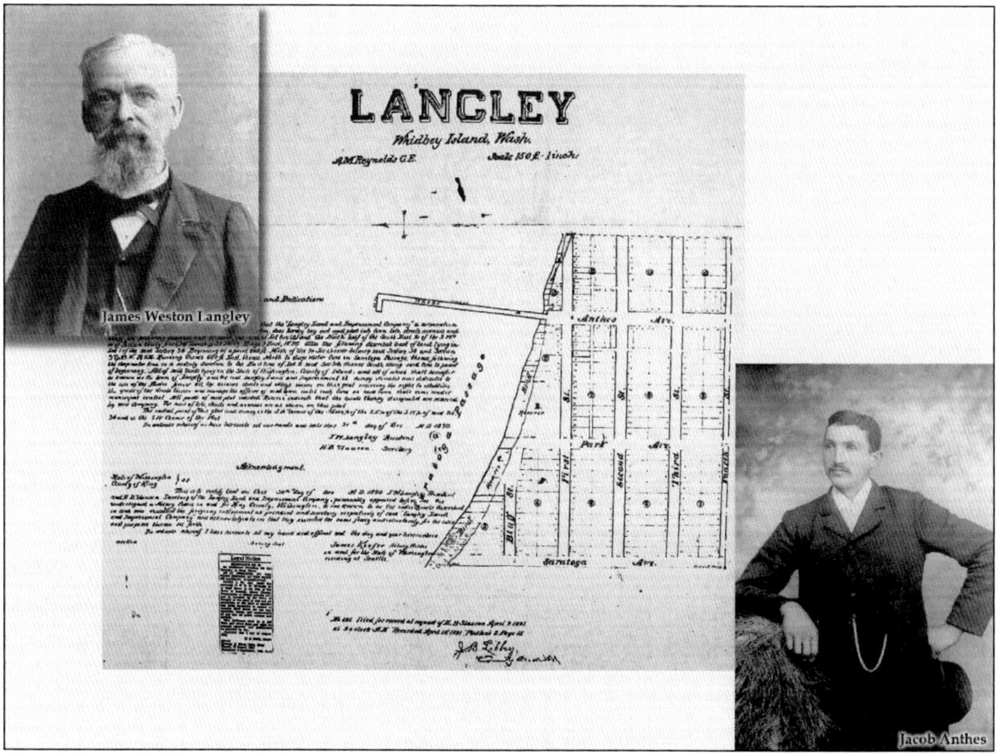

A town site named for Judge James Weston Langley was platted by the Langley Land and Improvement Company on December 30, 1890, and filed in Island County on April 9, 1891. A large reserve on the north side of First Street was set aside for a future park. (Photograph of Judge Langley courtesy of Kenneth Slauson; photograph of Anthes courtesy of Helene Ryan; plat mat courtesy of SWHS.)

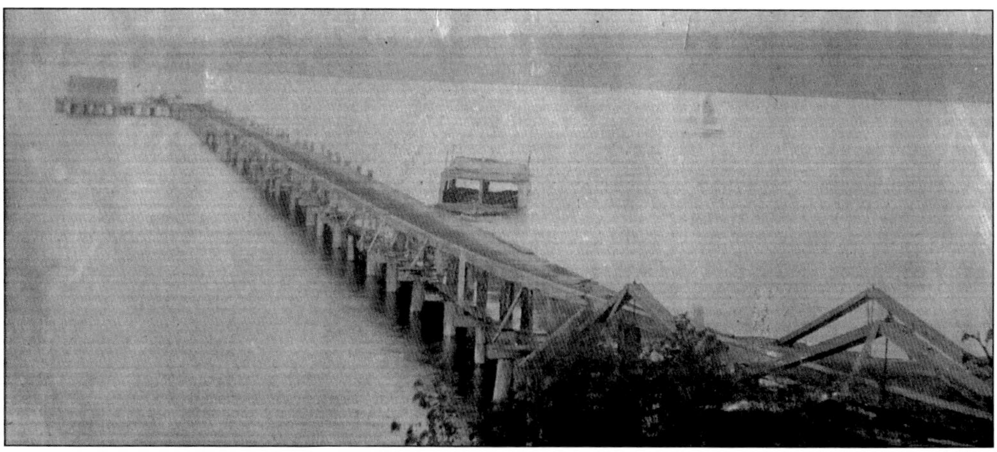

The first thing constructed in Langley was a wharf at the foot of Anthes Avenue in 1890–1891. It extended almost 1,000 feet to reach deep water and cost $5,000. It was essential for bringing people and produce to and from the town. Because of its location, it was severely damaged by a spring storm in 1894 and needed to be repaired. (Courtesy of Helene Ryan.)

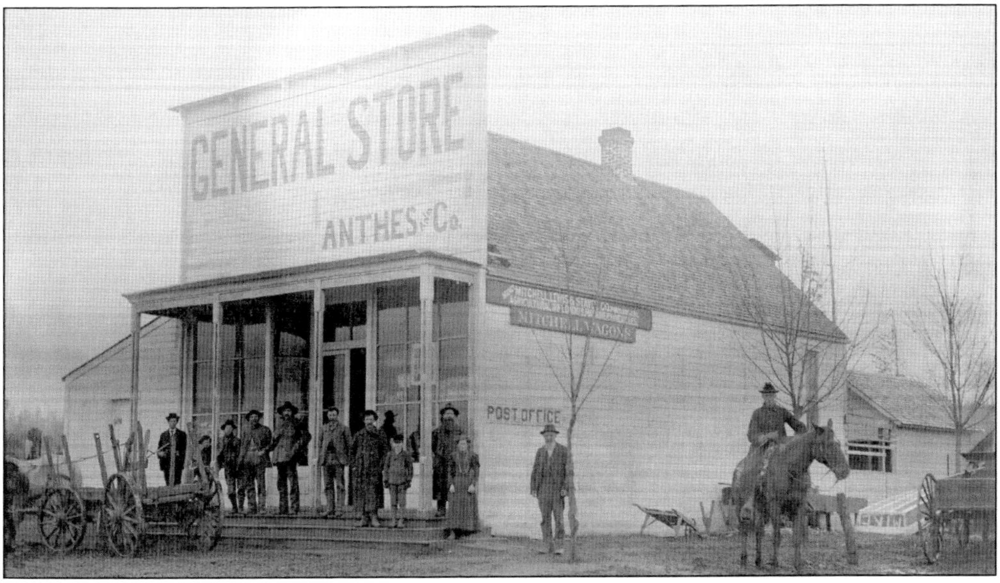

This store, built by Jacob Anthes in 1891 at the southeast corner of First Street and Anthes Avenue, was the sole commercial building in Langley for several years. He planted rows of maple trees along Anthes Avenue and on the south side of First Street that became prominent features for many years. Anthes also served as Langley's postmaster from 1891 to 1904. (Courtesy of Helene Ryan.)

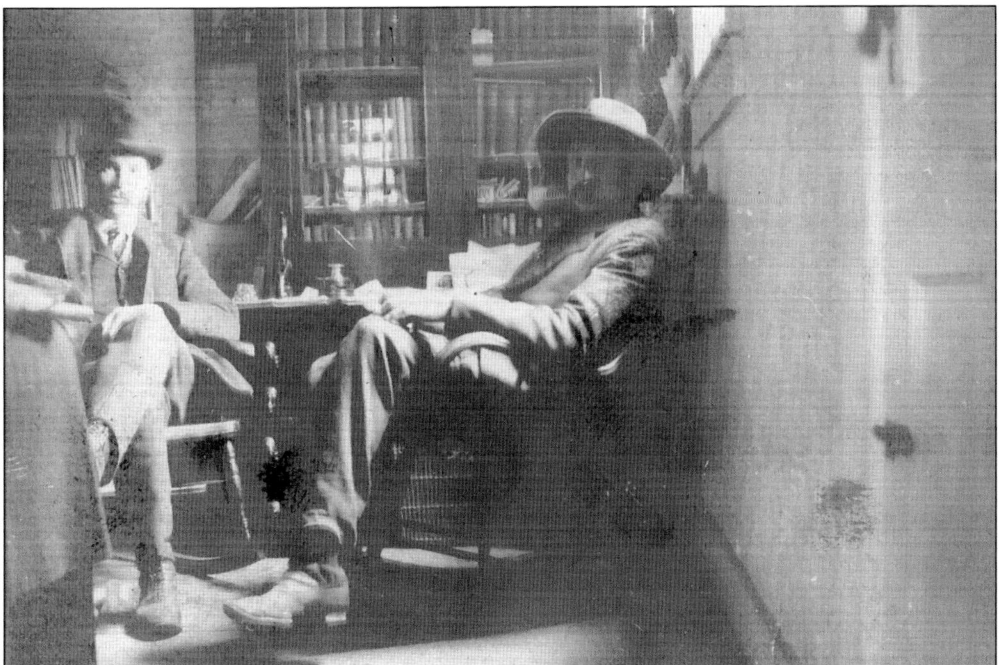
Jacob Anthes (right) and an unidentified man are pictured in the "library and den" of the home Anthes built behind his store. A nearby creek supplied water. Anthes was an avid reader. As a schoolboy, he was especially fond of James Fenimore Cooper's novels. A telephone line connected his store with the wharf. (Courtesy of Helene Ryan.)

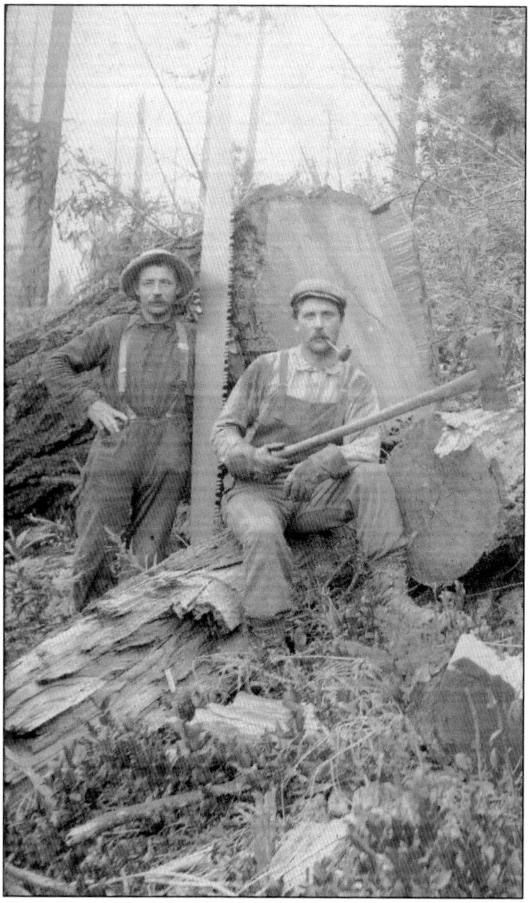

Loggers helped to clear the town site. They made a living selling cordwood to the steamships of the "Mosquito Fleet" that plied Saratoga Passage. Anthes recalled that sales averaged 35 cords per day from 1891 to 1893. He employed some 25 men and seven teams of horses and built a bunkhouse on Second Street to house them. (Courtesy of Helene Ryan.)

Some early loggers came with families and lived in rough log cabins, such as the one shown here located along a skid road. These hearty folks were self-sufficient. The woman near the center is holding a spindle for making yarn. A sow and piglets (right) lie next to the road. (Courtesy of Helene Ryan.)

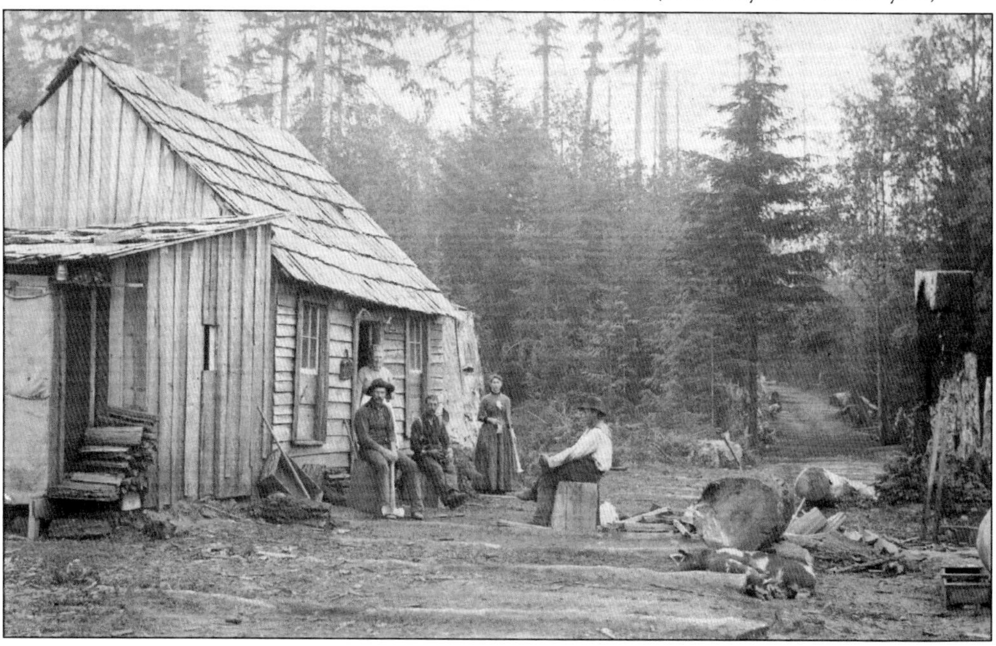

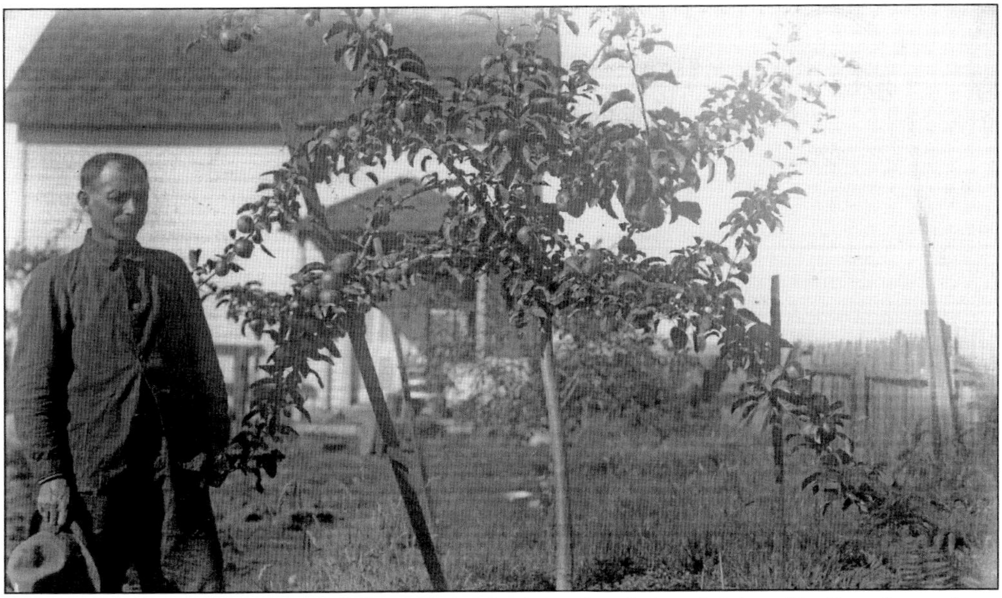

Early residents of Langley included Jacob Anthes's boyhood friend Adam Voelker, shown here behind his house in Langley in 1911. Voelker emigrated from Germany in 1881. He came to Langley in 1887 at Anthes's request and became his right-hand man, supervising many of Anthes's building projects. (Courtesy of Helene Ryan.)

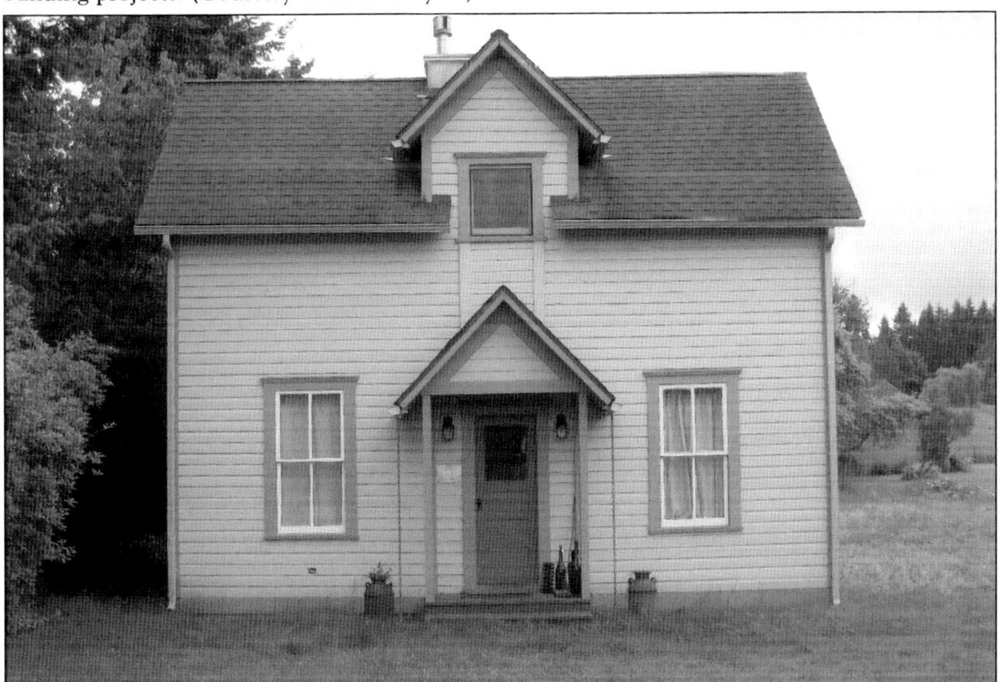

Adam Voelker built a small house on the hill at the west edge of town, where he lived until his death in 1940. His house on Third Street, shown here in 2004, was known as the Prairie Schooner. Voelker and Jacob Anthes were known as "Mutt and Jeff"—Voelker was short and bowlegged, Anthes tall and slender. (Courtesy of Robert Waterman.)

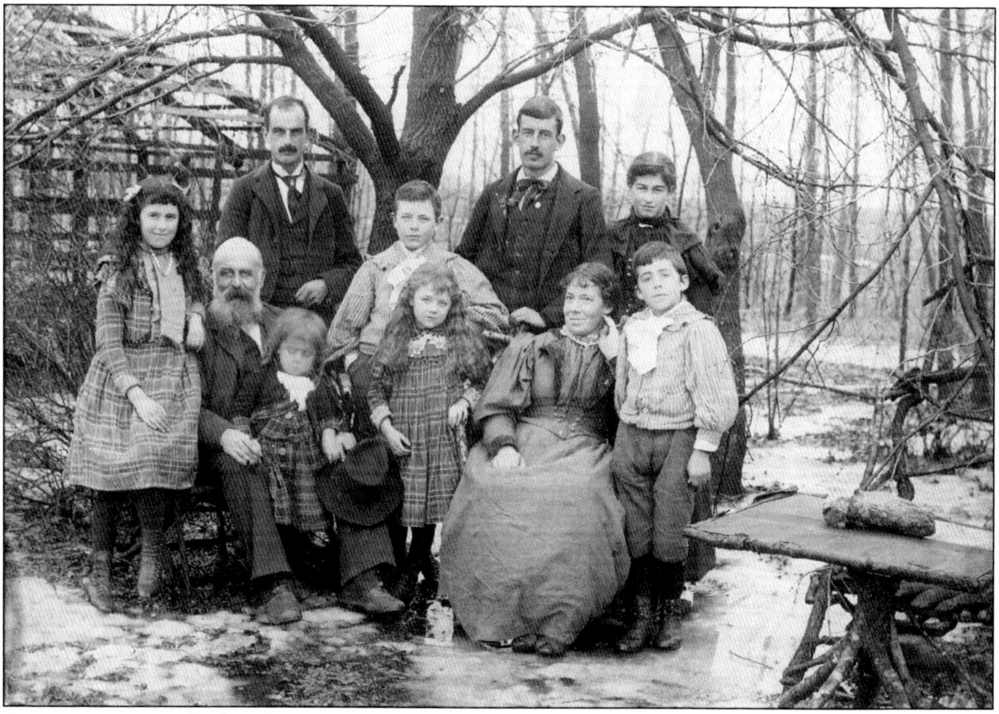

An important early family in Langley was that of Johan Frederick Hunziker (shown above in Minnesota prior to coming to Langley). Born in Switzerland, he served as a missionary in Patagonia from 1860 to 1864. He then went to the Falkland Islands, where he met his first wife, Martha Felton, with whom he had five children. When she died, he married her sister, Madeline, and they had three children. In 1886, most of the family traveled to Minnesota, where John raised sheep. In 1899, John, Madeline, and five of their children traveled to Everett, then to Langley, where he purchased five uncleared acres and a four-room house on Sixth Street from Oliver Cogean. The photograph below shows Nora (left), Madeline (center), and Walter Hunziker standing in the front yard of that house. (Both, courtesy of Mary Campbell.)

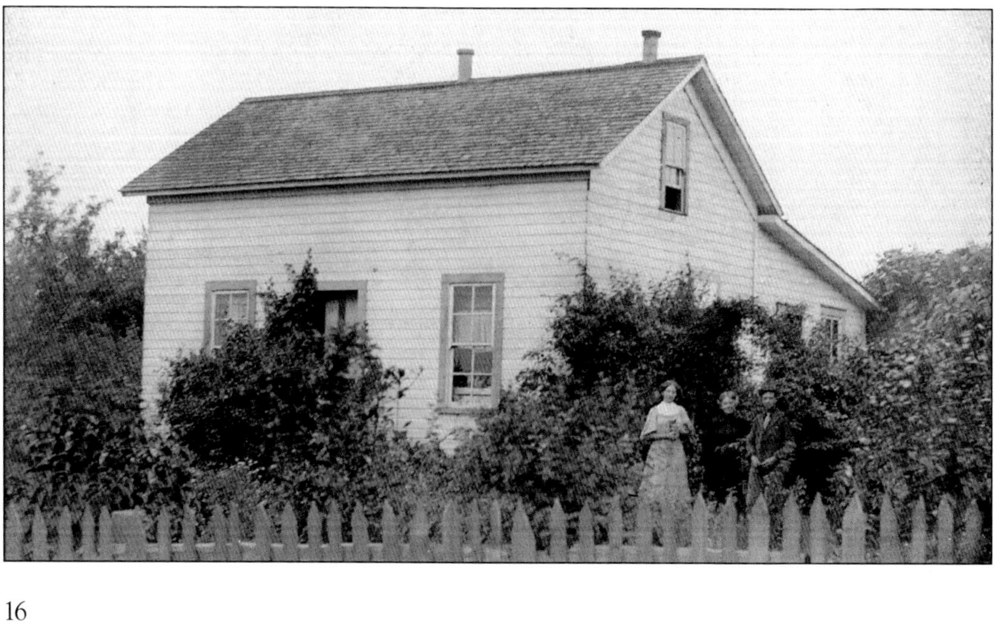

Two

The Town Grows 1900–1910

At first, Langley hosted transient loggers, fishermen, and workers, but by 1896, residents arrived to stay. The 1900 census counted 18 families in the greater Langley area, including Bayview, Lone Lake, Saratoga, Maple Cove, and Brown's Point (later renamed Sandy Point). In 10 years, the tally reached 142 families. The temperate climate, recommendations of friends and relations, and advertisements that Anthes published attracted these settlers.

Oliver Joseph Cogean and his wife, Ellen Bradshaw, arrived from Missouri in 1890. Eight years later, the Cogean house on Sixth Street was sold to John and Madeline Hunziker. Helen Coe, a teacher and "lady of culture," arrived in 1896 from Minnesota. Frank and Anna Furman, Zillah Skidmore, and members of the Cattron and McGinnis families claimed land to the east of Langley, along the road to Sandy Point.

New buildings sprouted along First Street and Anthes Avenue at the turn of the century. Edward and Clara Howard arrived in 1900 and opened a general merchandise store on First Street across the street from Anthes's store. A wheeler-dealer in various businesses, Edward Howard also built the Howard Hotel and replaced Anthes as postmaster in 1904. Hugh McLeod, an attorney, real estate agent, and later the justice of the peace, came in 1902, the first of his Scottish clan to settle in Langley. Members of the Lenz, Skidmore, Mortenson, Anderson, and Monson families also played important roles in Langley's early history.

When storms destroyed the original wharf, a new, U-shaped wharf was built in a sheltered cove east of town. The nondenominational Friends Community Church was established, followed by a Methodist church. In 1906, the town added telephone service, and a couple of years later, the Olympic Club, the iconic Langley building, later called the Dog House (pictured on this book's cover), was built at the corner of Anthes Avenue and First Street. Roads connected Langley to neighboring settlements, encouraging more growth. The Langley Land and Improvement Company sold its assets to Jacob Anthes in 1902, but, disillusioned with the direction in which the town was headed, he moved to Everett in 1908.

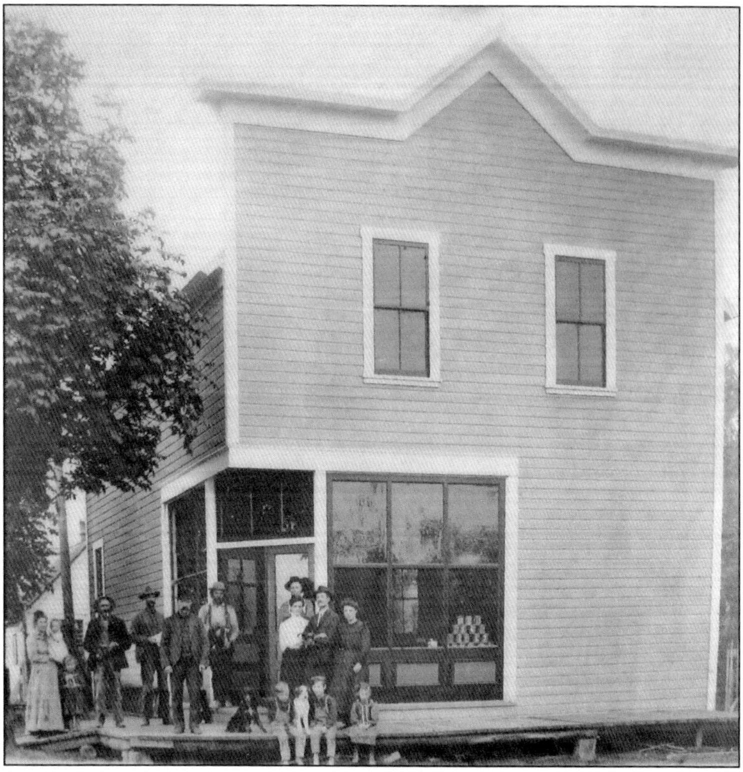

Edward Howard arrived in Langley from Nebraska in 1900 with his wife, Clara (far left), and their six children. He built a general store at the southwest corner of First Street and Anthes Avenue, across the street from the Anthes store. Howard (center, in bowler hat) was an energetic entrepreneur who posed a threat to Jacob Anthes's vision of the town. (Courtesy of the SWHS.)

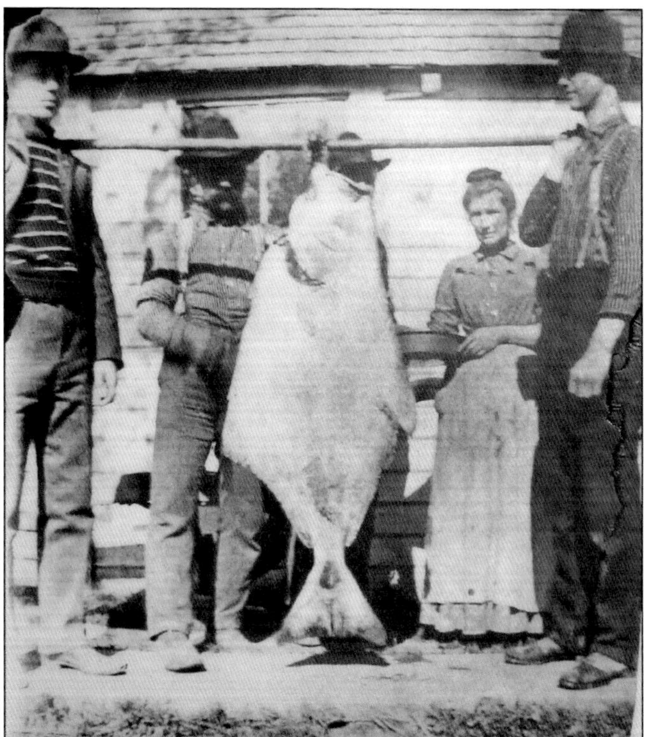

Edward Howard (second from left) was short, slightly bowlegged, and tough and had a finger missing on one hand. Howard's wife, Clara, is second from right. Howard, Murdoch McLeod, and Howard's brother William, editor of the *Island County Times* newspaper in Coupeville, had all served together in the Nebraska National Guard. In 1908, Howard created a home near the west end of First Street by placing two one-story houses together. (Courtesy of the SWHS.)

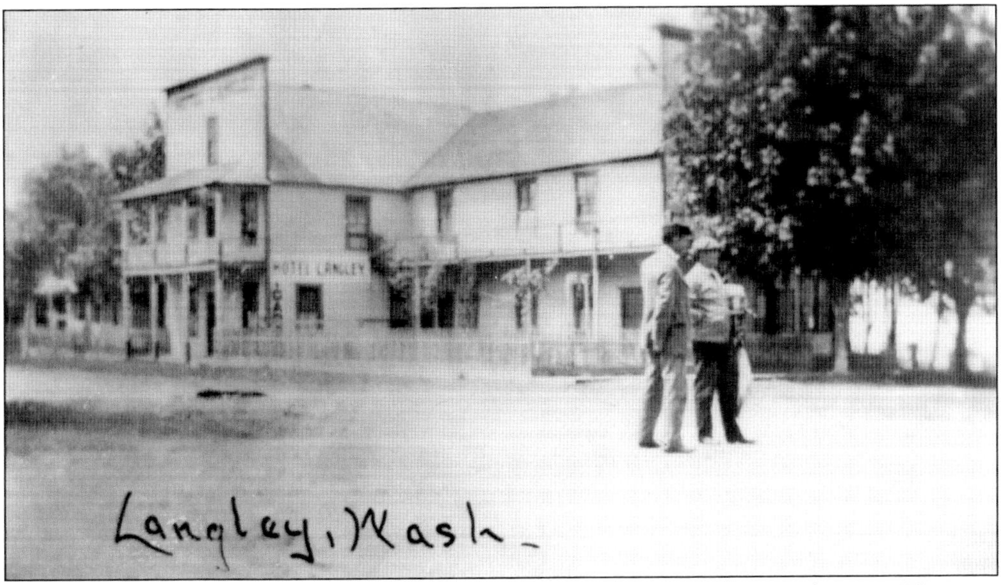

In 1901, a Mr. McCarter built a tourist hotel across First Street from Howard's store. This new hotel had a large porch on the ground level and a balcony above affording a magnificent view of Saratoga Passage. It served the community for two decades under different names until it burned down in 1921. (Courtesy of the ICHS.)

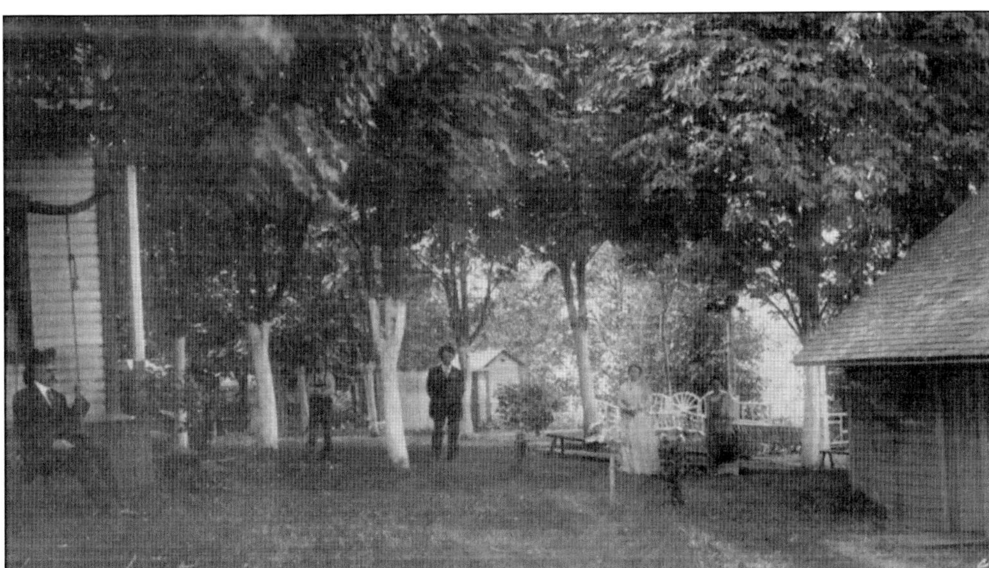

The hotel had a "Tourist Park" with trees and benches on the lawn behind it. The bank extended about 100 feet further toward the water than today. Many early families arriving in Langley stayed at the hotel while building homes. The small cottage (right) served at times as a residence. (Courtesy of the ICHS.)

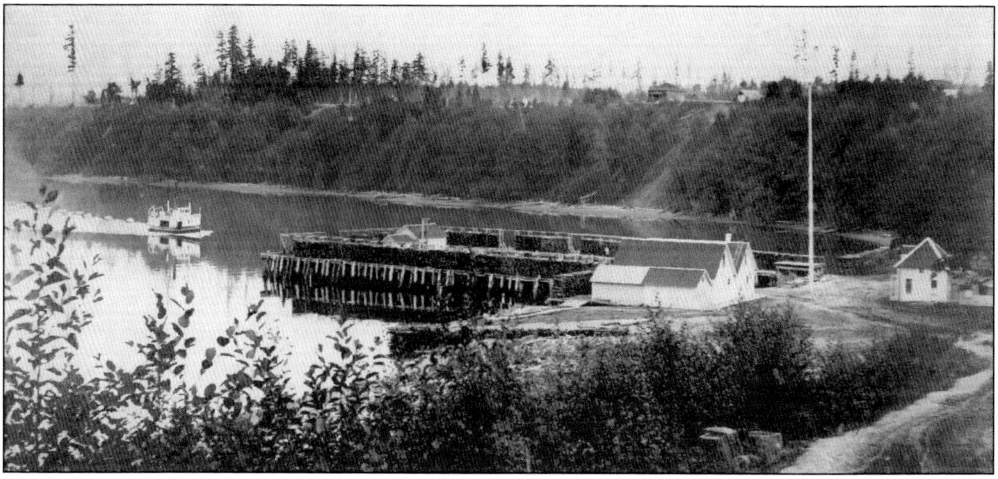

Because of the vulnerability of the original wharf, a new, U-shaped wharf was constructed in 1902 about a half-mile to the east. A road was graded out of the bluff, and several small warehouses and a small house were built. Cordwood was stacked along the wharf to supply the steamships of the "Mosquito Fleet" such as the *Hattie Hansen*, seen here approaching the new Langley wharf. (Courtesy of Helene Ryan.)

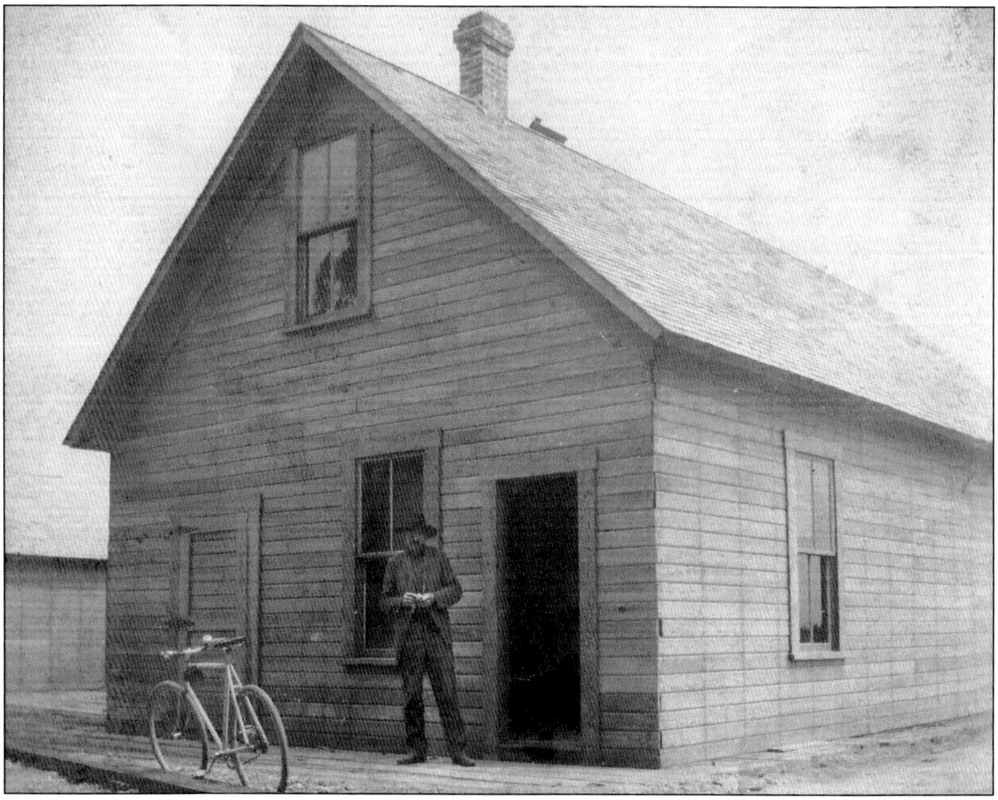

Jacob Anthes stands in front of the first warehouse built at the wharf. The first floor served as a waiting room for passengers. Relocating the wharf from the foot of Anthes Avenue constituted a major change for the town, since it separated the commercial activity related to boat traffic from the rest of the town. (Courtesy of Helene Ryan.)

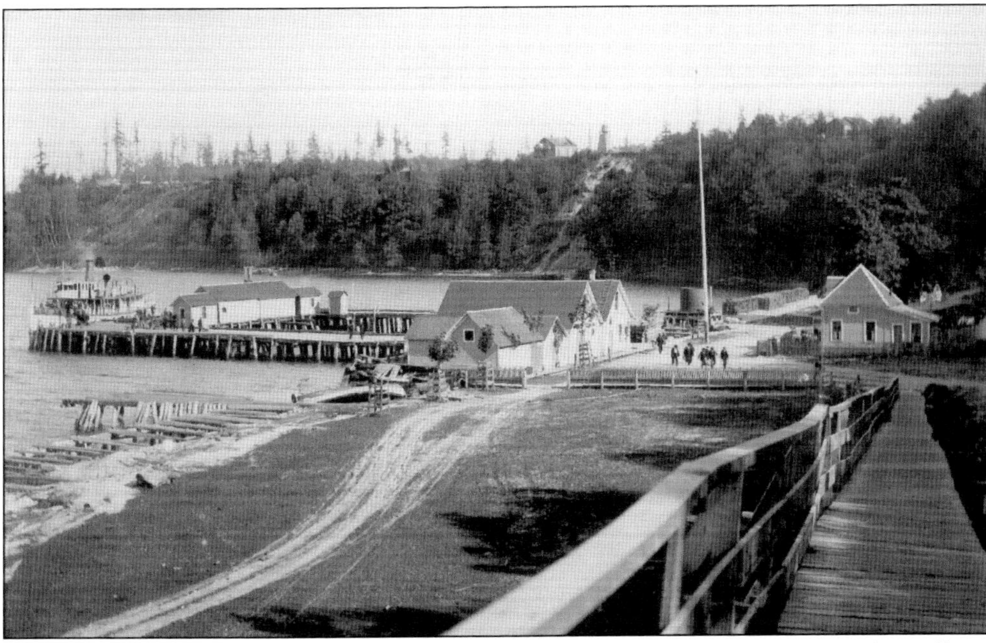

By 1911, new warehouses were added on the end and at the foot of the wharf. A wooden walkway was constructed next to the road. A large water tank on a platform held water for the steamships. The small house (right) became home to the Phillip Simon family in 1910. John Cattron's home and water tower perched on the bluff. (Courtesy of Maureen Duryee.)

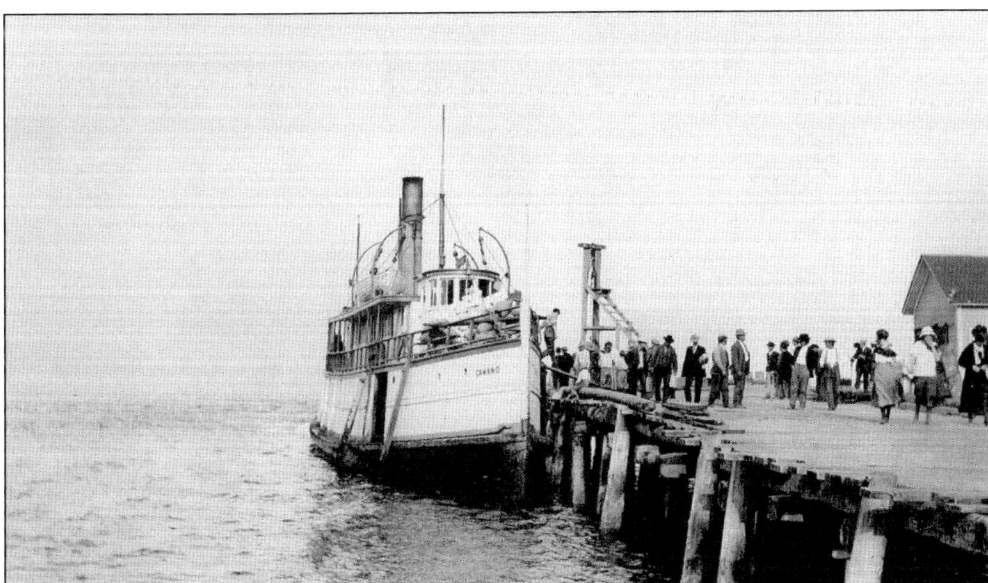

Passengers and freight were delivered by boats of the Mosquito Fleet such as the *Camano*, seen here disembarking passengers at the Langley wharf around 1909. Traffic between Langley, Everett, and Seattle, as well as other communities along the shore of Saratoga Passage, helped spur the growth of the town. (Courtesy of Helen Hulbert.)

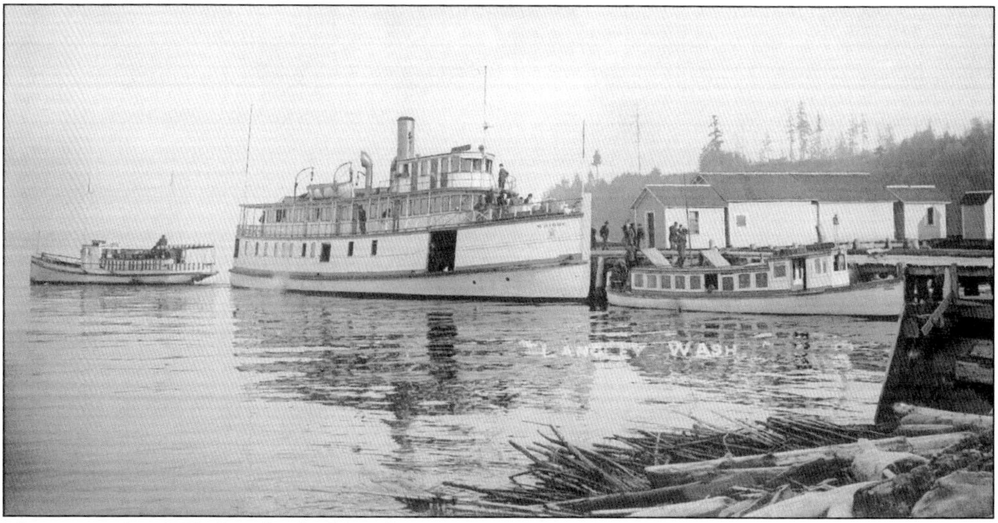

The steamship *Whidby*, flanked by the gas-powered *Wolverine* (left) and *Norine*, illustrate the variety of crafts that frequented the Langley wharf in 1909. The *Whidby* burned in Oak Harbor in 1911. Its boiler was salvaged and placed in a new boat, the *Calista*, which took its place. The *Calista* in turn was rammed and sank in 1922. (Courtesy of the SWHS.)

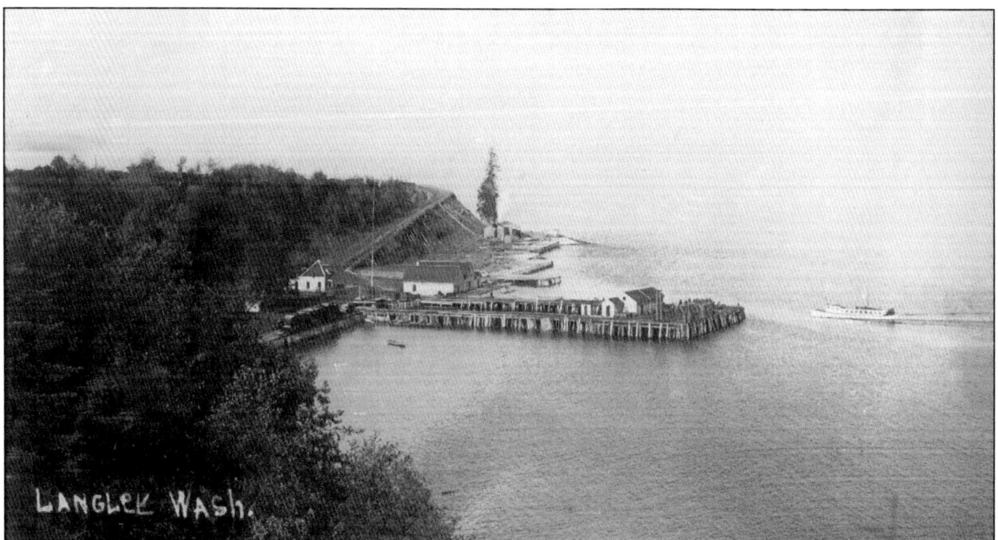

The Langley marina was a busy place in 1911, serving not only the needs of Langley but the surrounding farms and communities as well. Using brush and dirt fill, land was created adjacent to the wharf and warehouses, and this area became the site of many community picnics and clambakes. (Courtesy of Helene Ryan.)

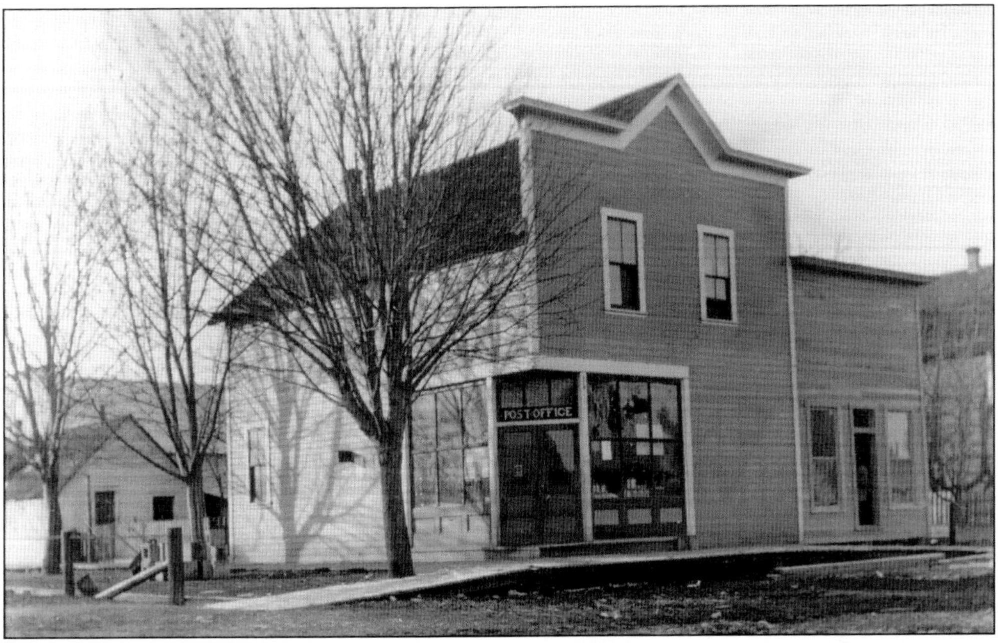

Edward Howard replaced Jacob Anthes as postmaster in 1904. Anthes was so upset that he took the mail across the street and dumped it on the floor of Howard's store, shown above. Relatively new to the area, Howard enlisted the help of his daughter Alice and her suitor, Walter Hunziker, to help sort and deliver the mail. (Courtesy of Mary Campbell.)

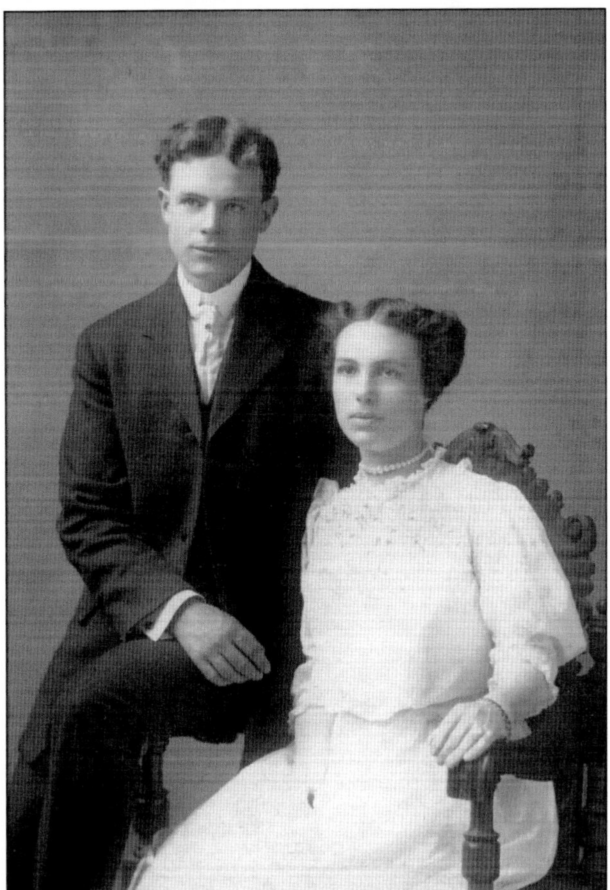

Walter Hunziker and Alice Howard were married in 1906. They built a house at the corner of Sixth Street and Al Anderson Avenue in 1908. Hunziker delivered the mail to the south end of the island and became Langley's postmaster from 1922 to 1934. (Courtesy of Jim and Ardeth Bolin.)

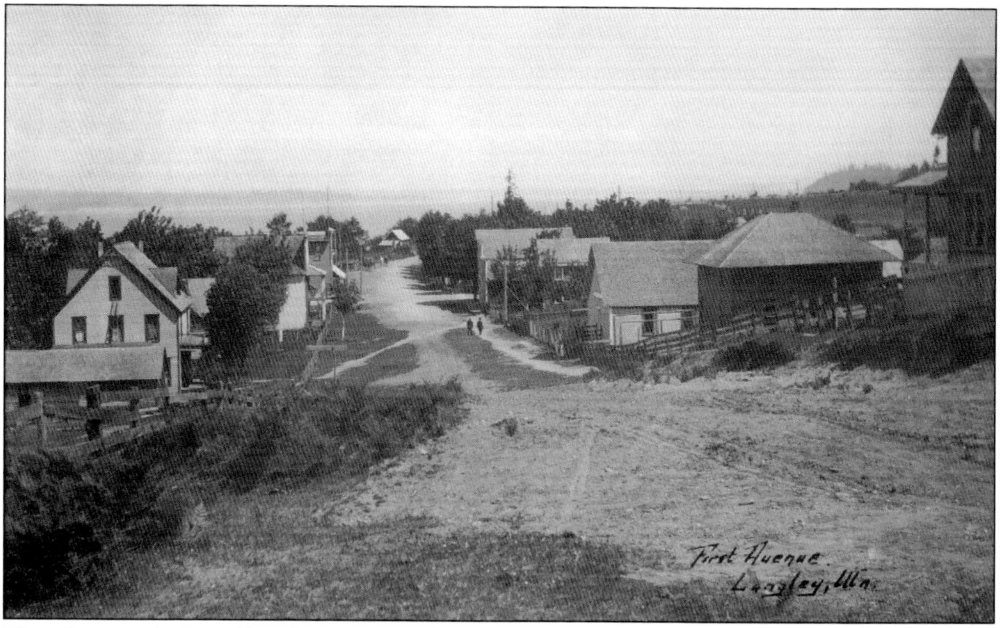

This photograph shows First Street in 1908 looking east. Roderick McLeod came to Langley in 1905 with his wife, Sarah, and their three children. With his brother-in-law, Edward Howard, he built a hotel (left) west of the original hotel and a home between the two hotels. The nondenominational Friends Community Church, constructed in 1900, and an adjacent parsonage with hip roof (right) are across the street. (Courtesy of Maureen Duryee.)

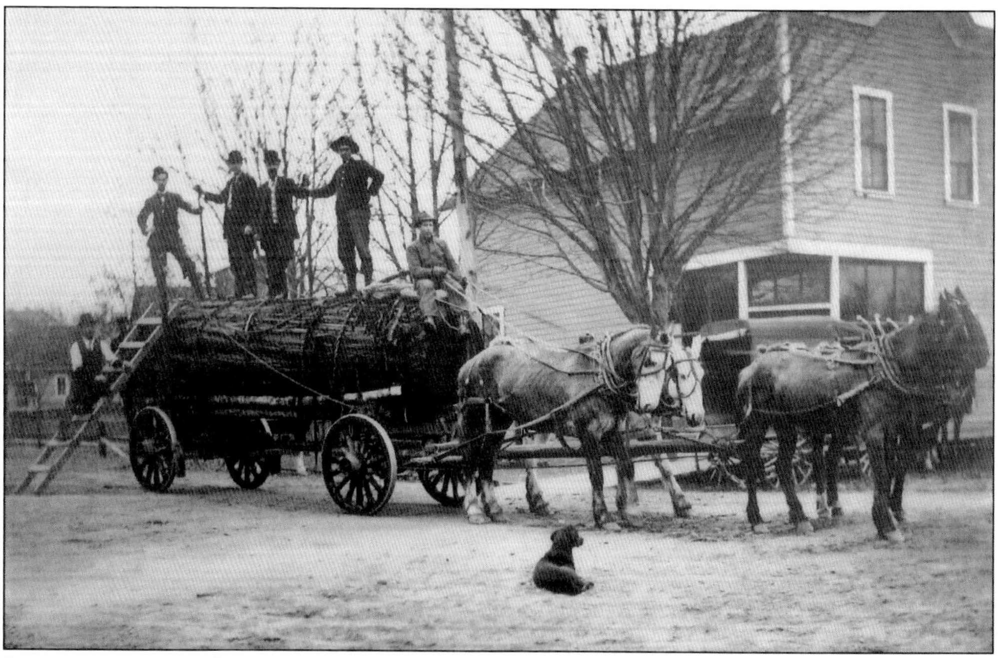

Logging was a major business. Teams of oxen and horses were common sights on Langley's streets and kept the blacksmith busy. Loggers pose in front of Howard's store and post office in 1908. The names George Swain, W.J. Hunziker, Edward Howard, William Foster, and William Howard are listed on the back of the photograph. (Courtesy of the SWHS.)

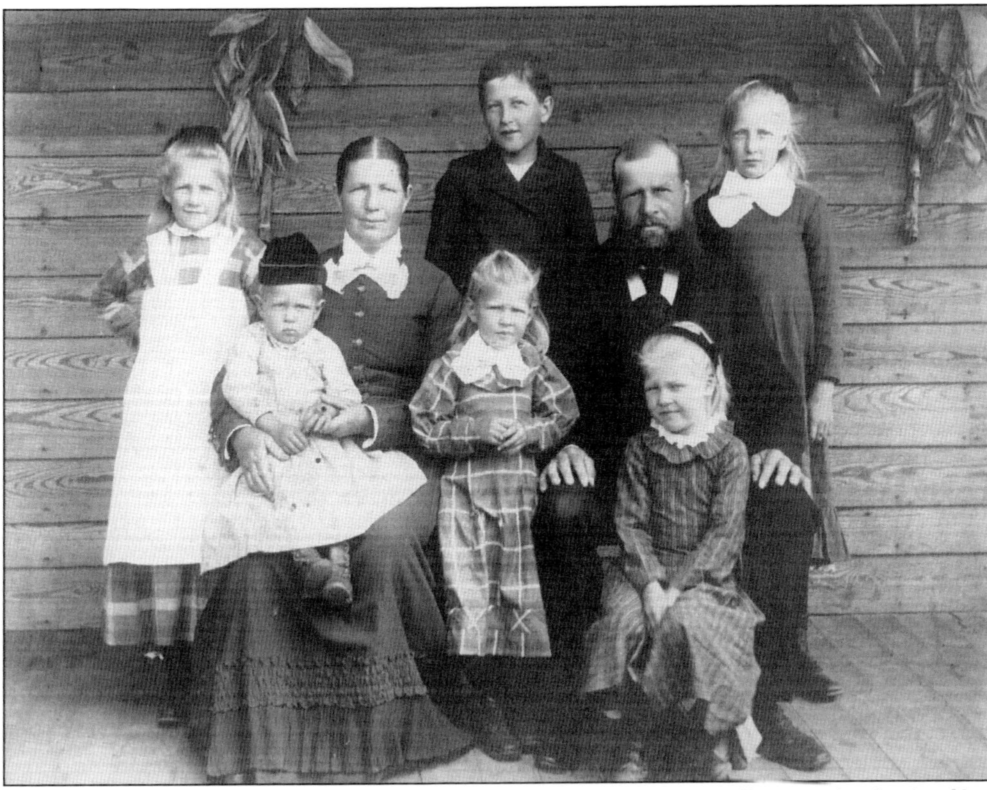

Louisa Lenz (third from left) is shown with her family in Virginia. Following the death of her husband, Wilhelm, Louisa and her children came to Whidbey Island in 1907. She purchased 10 acres on Third Street and lived in a 16-by-20-foot cabin. (Courtesy of the Fossek family.)

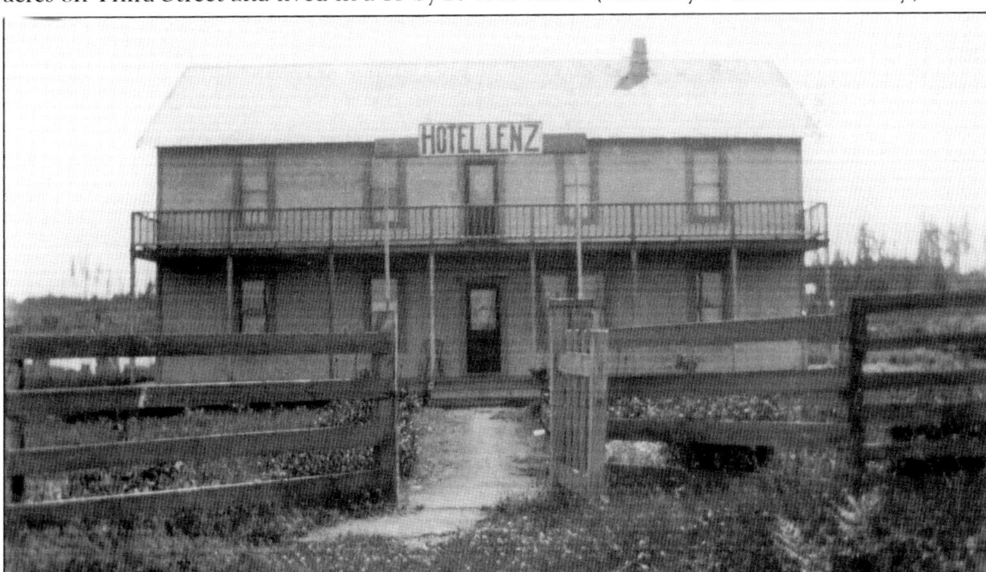

Around 1908, Louisa built the Hotel Lenz at the southwest corner of Third Street and DeBruyn Avenue. It served as both a hotel and as living quarters for the family until it burned down in 1930. (Courtesy of the Fossek family.)

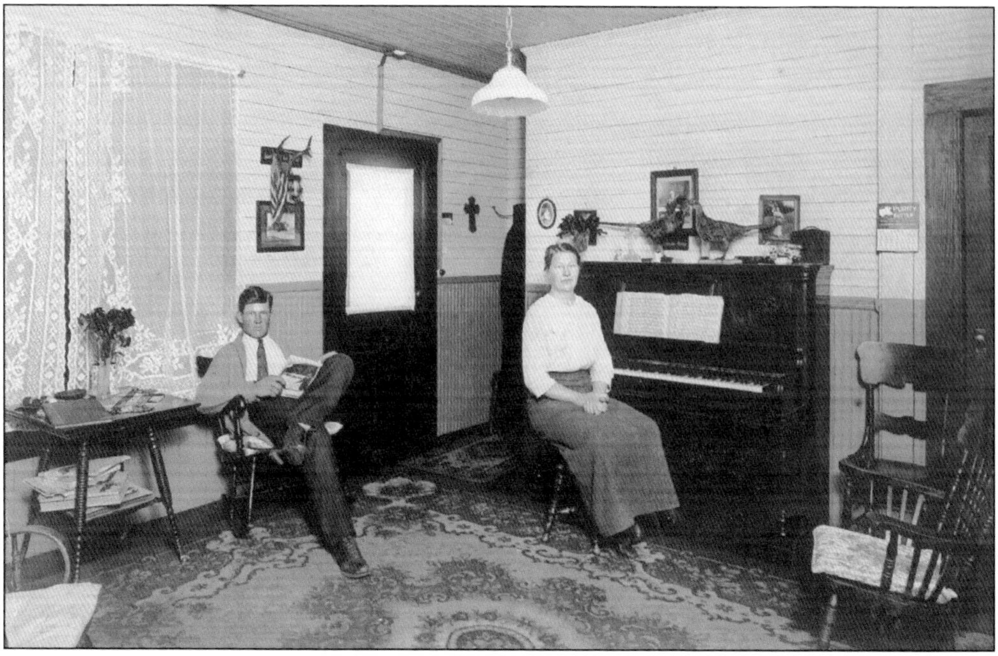

Two of Louisa Lenz's children, Fredrick (left) and Marie, are shown inside the Lenz Hotel in 1916. They both married and left Langley. When the hotel burned down in 1932, Louisa was carried out in a chair. Later, Louisa Lenz built a new house, assisted by her grandson Raymond Fossek. In 1934, Fossek bought the house and farm from her. (Courtesy of the Fossek family.)

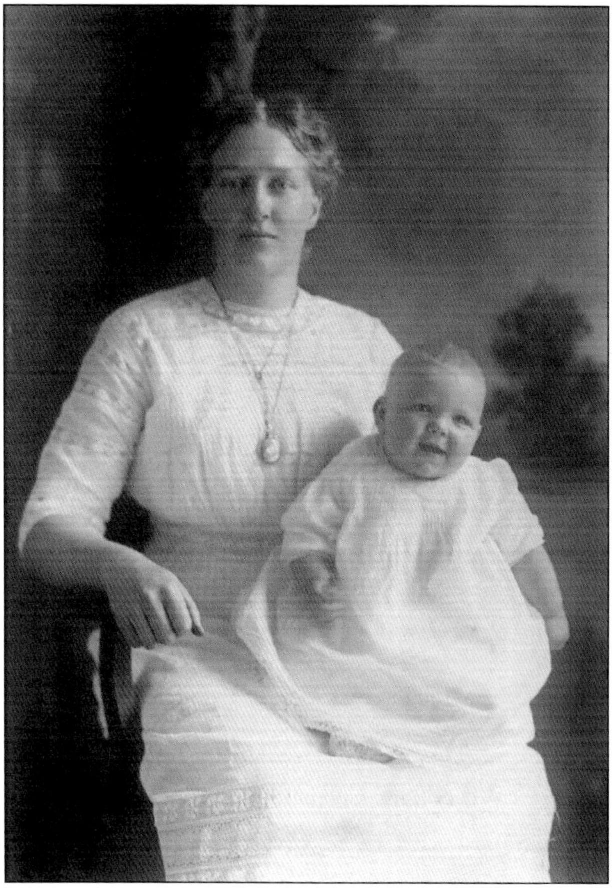

Emma Lenz married Emil Fossek, and their son Raymond was born in 1913. His parents soon divorced, and Raymond spent much of his time in Langley. When Raymond was 12, Emma married Joe Reuter on September 16, 1925. Raymond stayed in Langley with his grandmother Louisa Lenz and his uncle Carl Lenz, eventually becoming one of the town's leading citizens. (Courtesy of the Fossek family.)

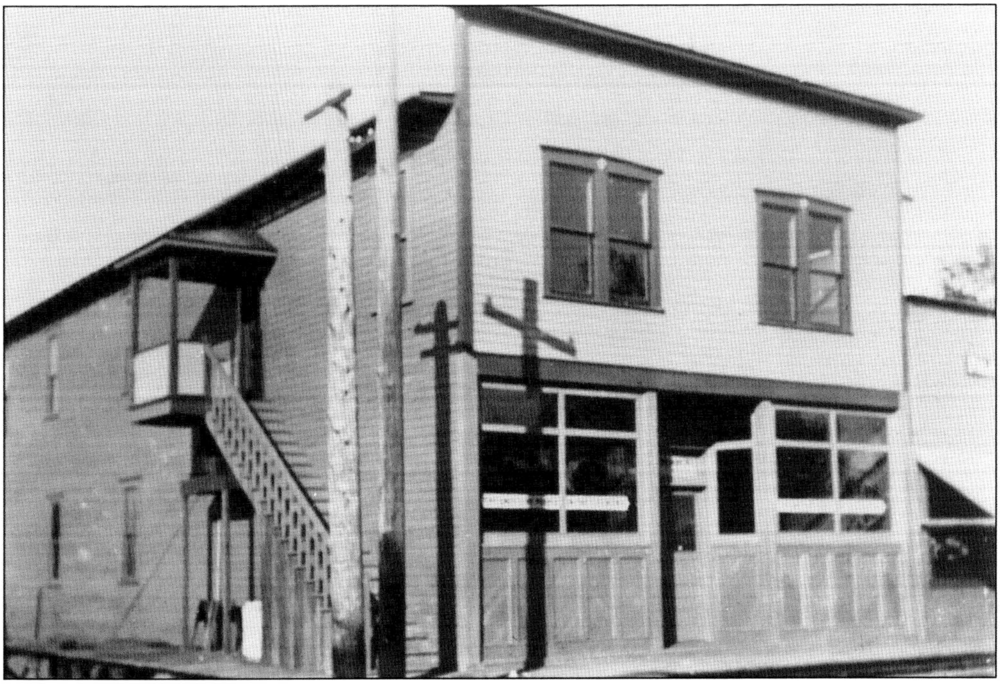

A meat market, barbershop, blacksmith shop, and livery stable appeared on the north side of First Street, east of Anthes Avenue, between 1904 and 1908. In 1908, the Olympic Club (shown here) was built at the northeast corner of Anthes Avenue and First Street as a venue for sporting events. The opening celebration was spoiled when the promoter absconded with the money to pay the boat captains. Many attendees were stranded. (Courtesy of the SWHS.)

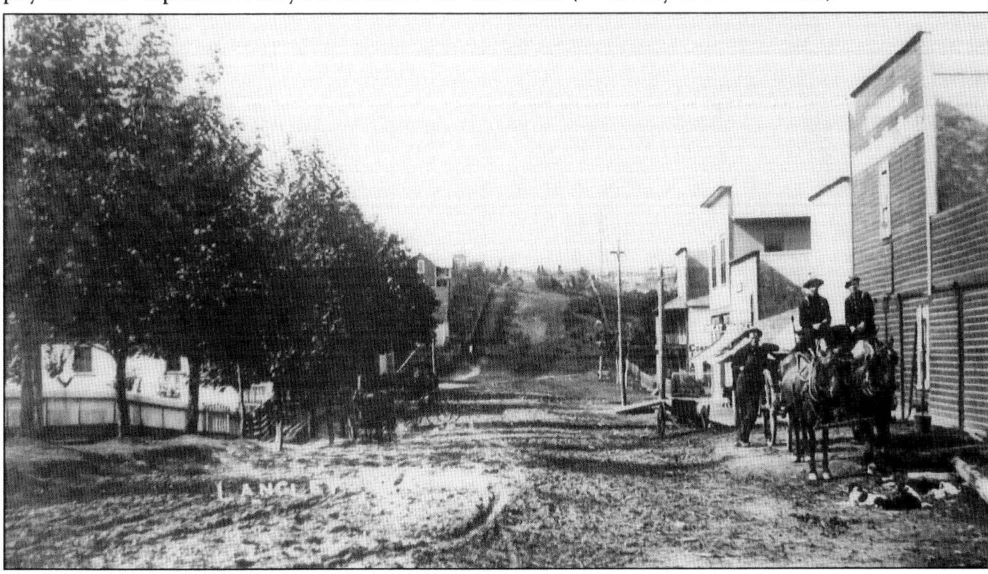

This photograph is looking west on First Street around 1908. Albert Melsen leans against the wagon in front of Brehm's Livery Stable, owned by William Howard. Sitting in the wagon are Martin Mortenson (left) and William Howard. Anthes's store (white building at left) can be seen through the trees. Melsen built the Olympic Club, among other businesses and homes. He also served several terms as Langley's mayor. (Courtesy of the SWHS.)

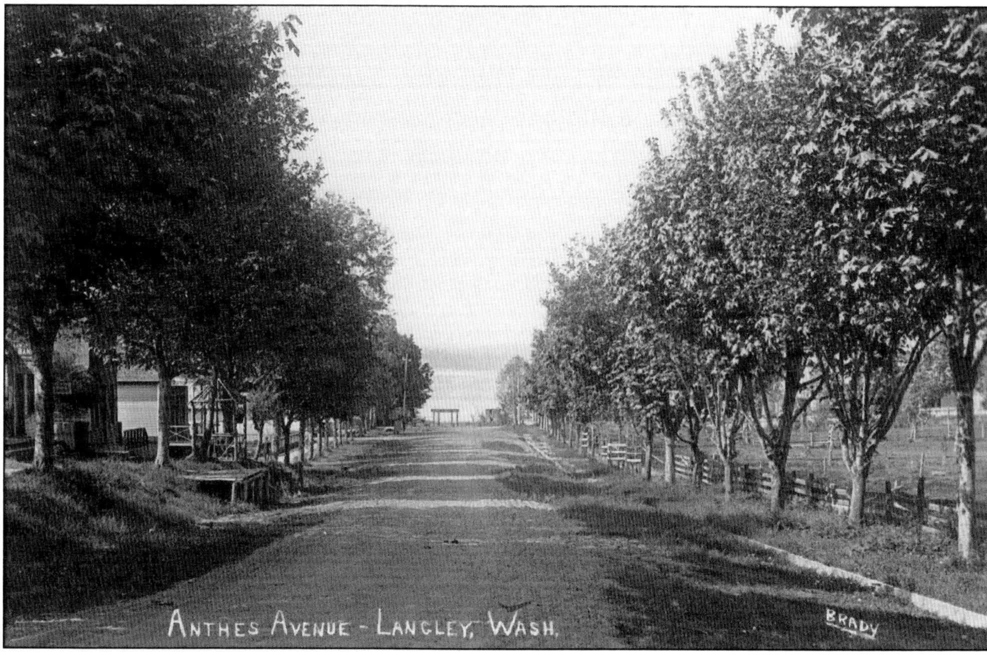

This photograph shows Anthes Avenue looking north toward Saratoga Passage. The sign at the end of the avenue says "Tourist Park." A town pump (left) in front of Hugh McLeod's justice of the peace office and living quarters was a popular place for residents and horses alike. (Photograph by Ferdinand Brady; courtesy of the ICHS.)

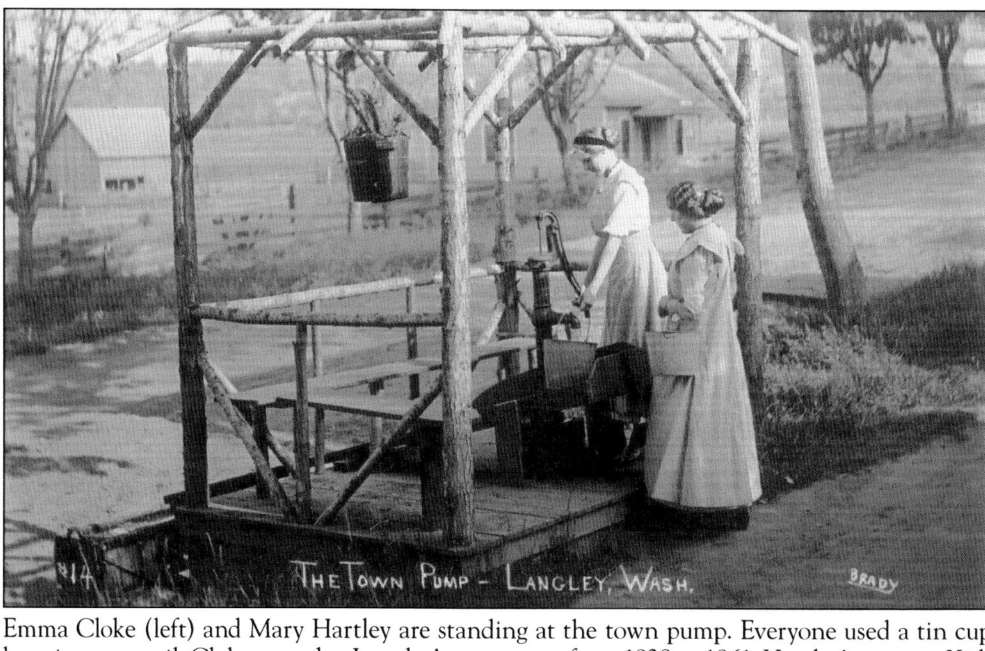

Emma Cloke (left) and Mary Hartley are standing at the town pump. Everyone used a tin cup hanging on a nail. Cloke served as Langley's postmaster from 1938 to 1961. Hartley's parents, Kirk and Minnie, lived on Sixth Street. The house across the street belonged to Herbert and Edith Hunziker. (Photograph by Ferdinand Brady; courtesy of Maureen Duryee.)

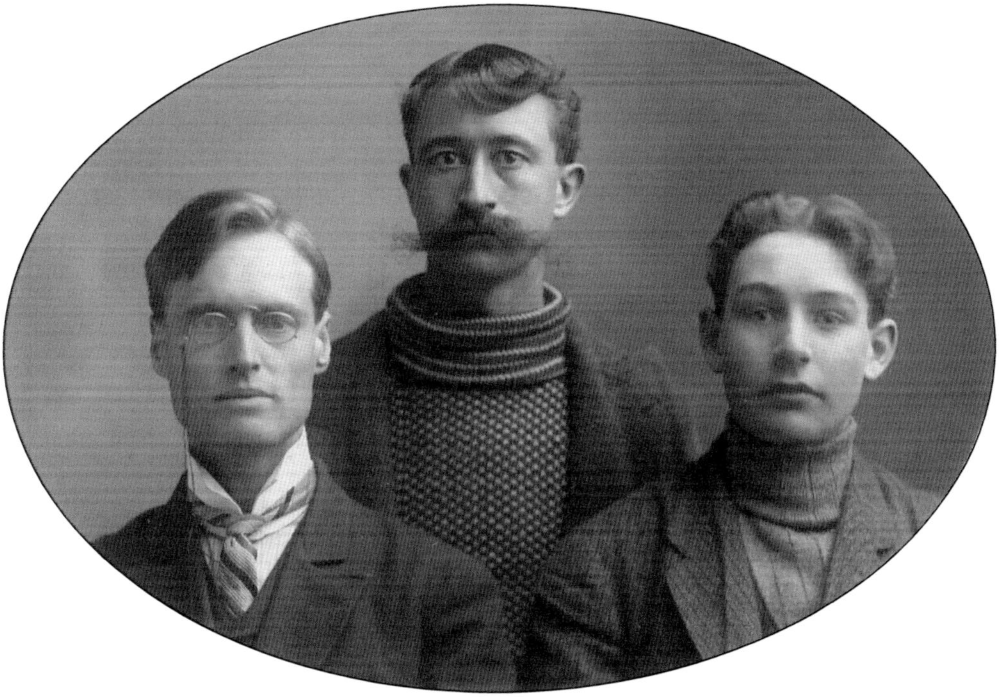

Three of the four McLeod brothers who came to Langley from Nebraska are shown here. They are, from left to right, Hugh, Angus, and Murdock. The fourth, Roderick, is not shown in this photograph taken in Nebraska. Hugh was the first to arrive, in 1902. A lawyer, he served as justice of the peace for many years, sold real estate, and participated in town affairs. (Courtesy of the SWHS.)

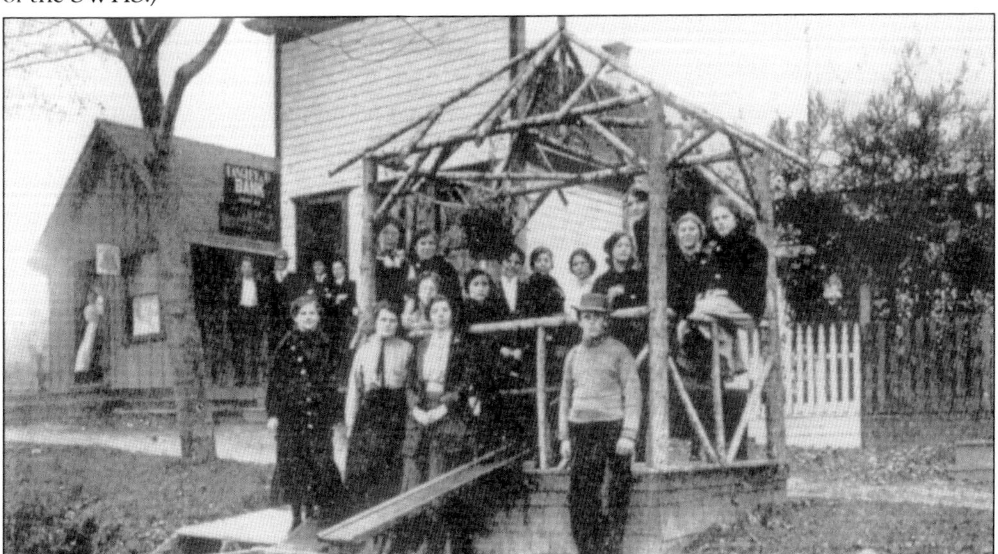

Hugh McLeod's office and living quarters are seen behind the town pump around 1908. In addition to his other activities, McLeod served as an early banker and was the first secretary of the Whidby Telephone Company, which was incorporated in 1908. He rented the small building (left) to house the telephone office for $8 per month. (Courtesy of the SWHS.)

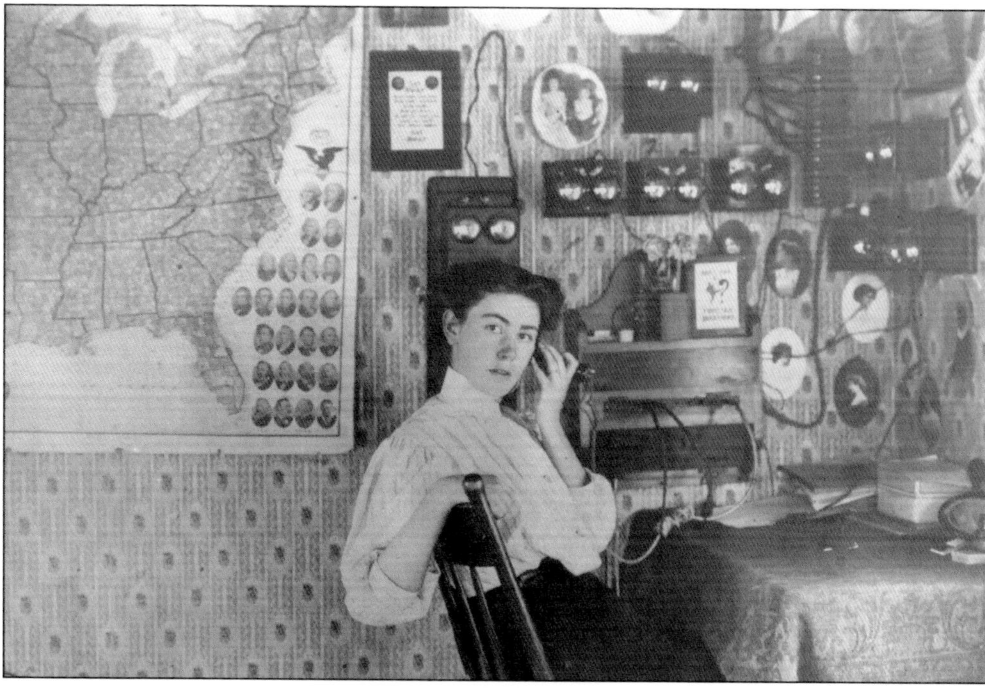

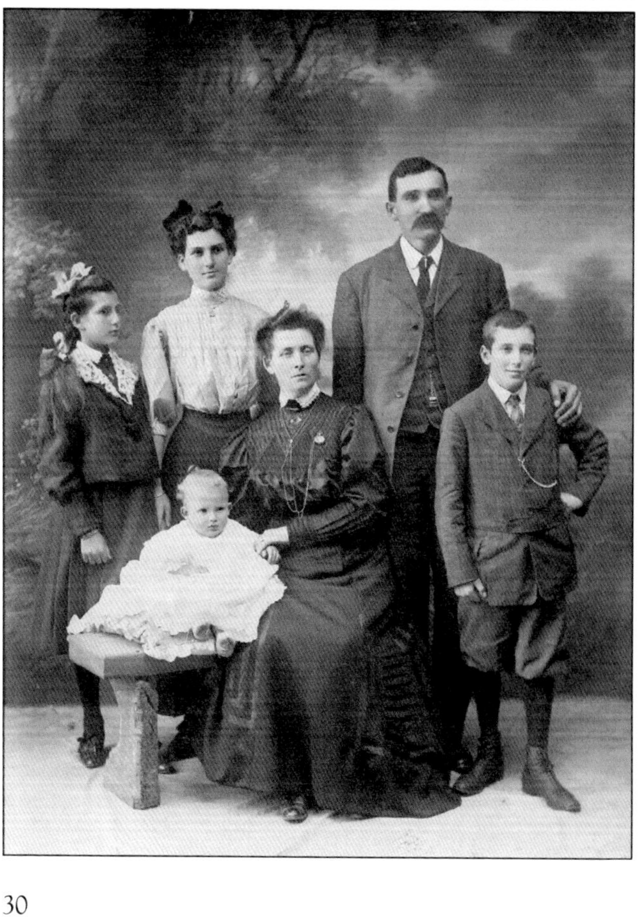

Roderick and Sarah McLeod's 16-year-old daughter, Vera, was one of the first telephone operators. By October 1908, there were 66 phones on seven party lines, and wire was strung to Brown's Point and Coupeville. Phone rates were 65¢ per month; businesses paid $1. Operators earned $13 a month and worked 13-hour days. (Courtesy of the SWHS.)

A major change for Langley occurred in 1908, when Jacob Anthes and his family moved to Everett after returning from a trip to Zurich, Switzerland, to bring his oldest daughter, Mabel, back from school there. He leased out his store and retained his land holdings and other businesses in Langley, but he remained in Everett until his death in 1939. (Courtesy of Helene Ryan.)

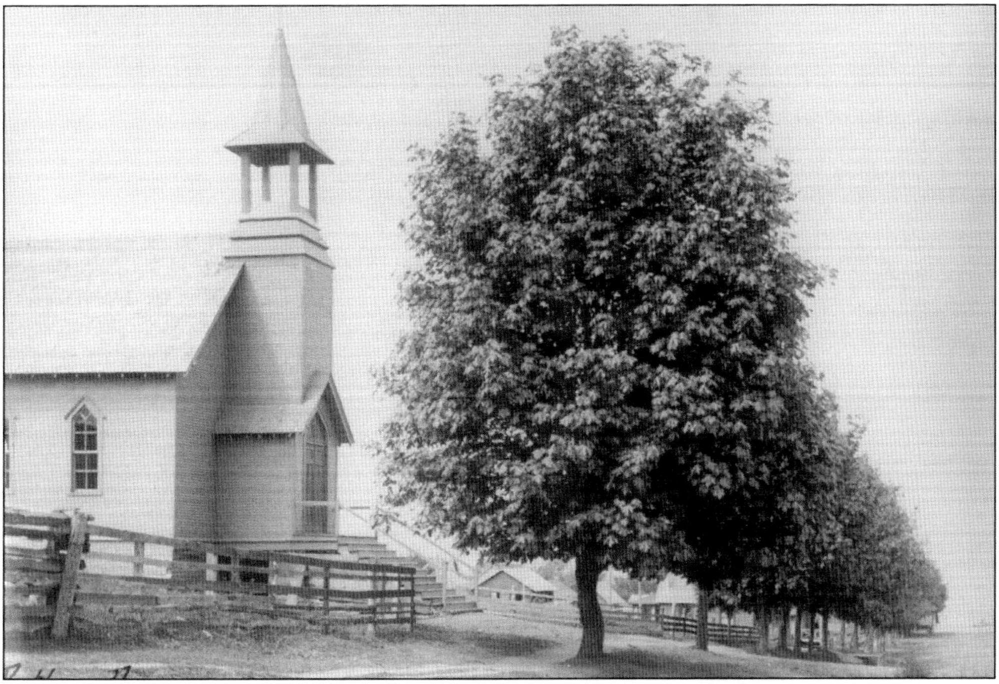

In 1901, a group that had been meeting in the Friends Community Church on First Street petitioned to become a Methodist church. Rev. Andrew McNamee arrived on April 1, 1909, and began fundraising. He purchased a lot at the corner of Third Street and Anthes Avenue from Anton Anderson and constructed a church that was dedicated in September 1909. A bell was installed in 1911. (Courtesy of the SWHS.)

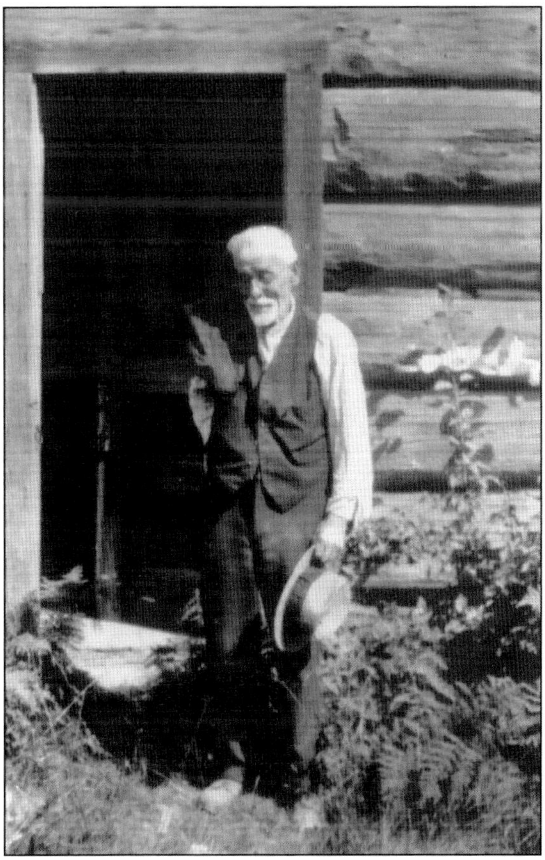

Rev. Andrew McNemee stands in front of his home on Edgecliff Drive. Arriving in Langley a sick man, he obtained funding and oversaw the building of the Methodist church. Albert Melsen was the contractor, and Edward Howard facilitated the purchase of lumber from Charles A. Blackman in Everett. The Langley church was the last church built by "Brother Mack" before he died in Langley in 1936. (Courtesy of the SWHS.)

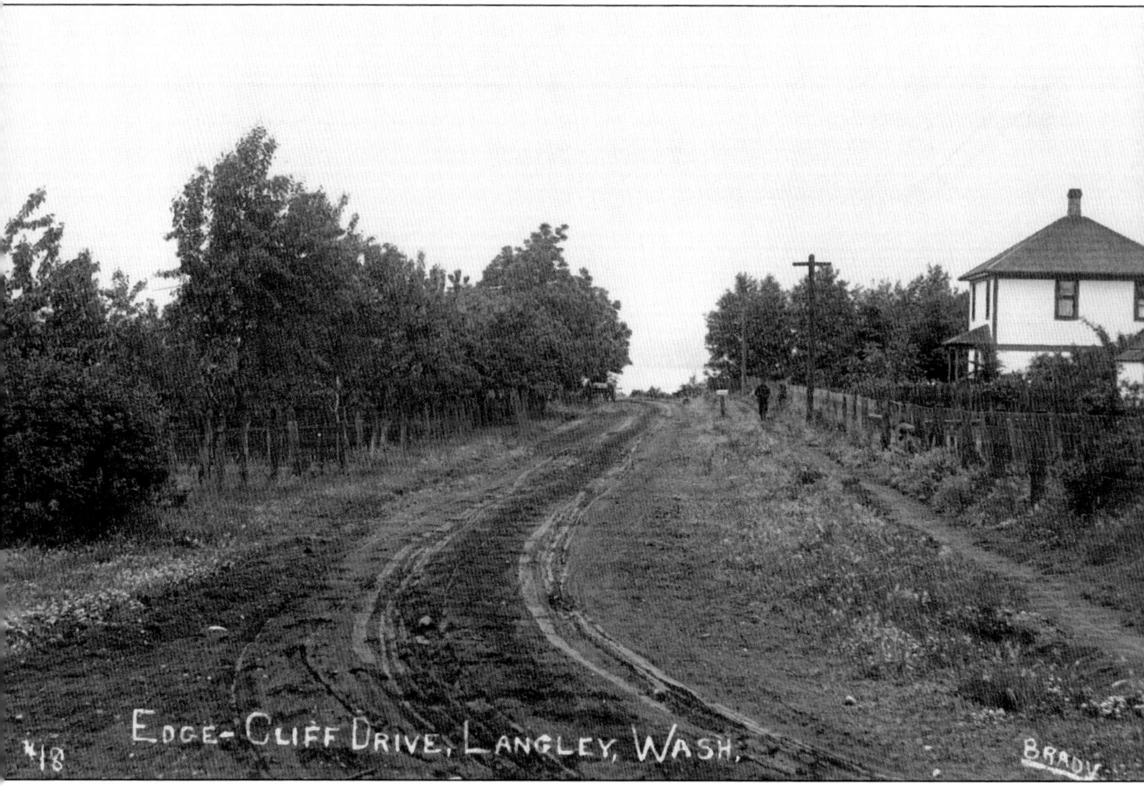

Homes and farms were scattered along the bluff east of town toward Brown's (Sandy) Point. In 1902, Zillah Skidmore, her bother Benjamin, and her foster son, Arthur Hoffman, shared this house on Cascade Avenue (labeled Edge-Cliff Drive by photographer Ferdinand Brady). Zillah Skidmore had 19 acres containing 15 varieties of apple trees. Further east were the Cattron, McGinnis, and Furman homes. (Courtesy of the ICHS.)

Three

FIRE AND TECHNOLOGY *1910–1920*

In these early days, nearly everyone and everything that came to Langley arrived by water. With the encouragement of Hans Peter Jenson and Phillip Simon, business around the new, U-shaped wharf grew to include a shingle mill, lumber mill, canning operation, wharfinger business, warehouses, a dance pavilion, and the Sea Breeze Confectionery.

Anthes's store burned down in 1910 under suspicious circumstances. Shortly after, Edward Howard's store went up in flames, also under suspicious circumstances. Howard relocated his store and post office to the Olympic Club building. Soon after, the area's first automobiles, owned by Edward Howard and Hans Jensen, putt-putted into town, and automobile service stations followed. First Street sprouted a number of new storefronts, and the town's commercial center began to shift uphill and away from the wharf. Fredrick Funk settled in with his family and established his general store on Anthes Avenue. Before long, Langley boasted three hotels, the beginnings of a library, a growing school system, two churches, and the Island County Fair.

The town incorporated in 1913 and elected Frank Furman as its first mayor. Members of the McGinnis, Bainter, and English families served on the first board of commissioners. That same year, on the site where Edward Howard's store had burned down, a bank was constructed, with James C. Langley, nephew of the town's namesake, installed as president. The Woodmen Cemetery, established up the hill south of town in 1902, was gifted to the city in 1913. The following year, an electrical powerhouse and a water system were installed. The telephone service was extended, and soon 100 miles of wire served South Whidbey and stretched to Coupeville. The town's weekly newspaper, the *Langley Islander*, began publication in 1910. Joseph Primavera arrived in 1917 and soon after established the Star Store.

Even in this relatively remote village, young men stepped forward to serve overseas in World War I, including members of the Jensen, Howard, and Wylie families. The flu epidemic that followed took its toll. As the town grew, saloons and pool halls offered gambling, boxing matches, and other boisterous activities, which prompted Langley's women to become more active in town politics.

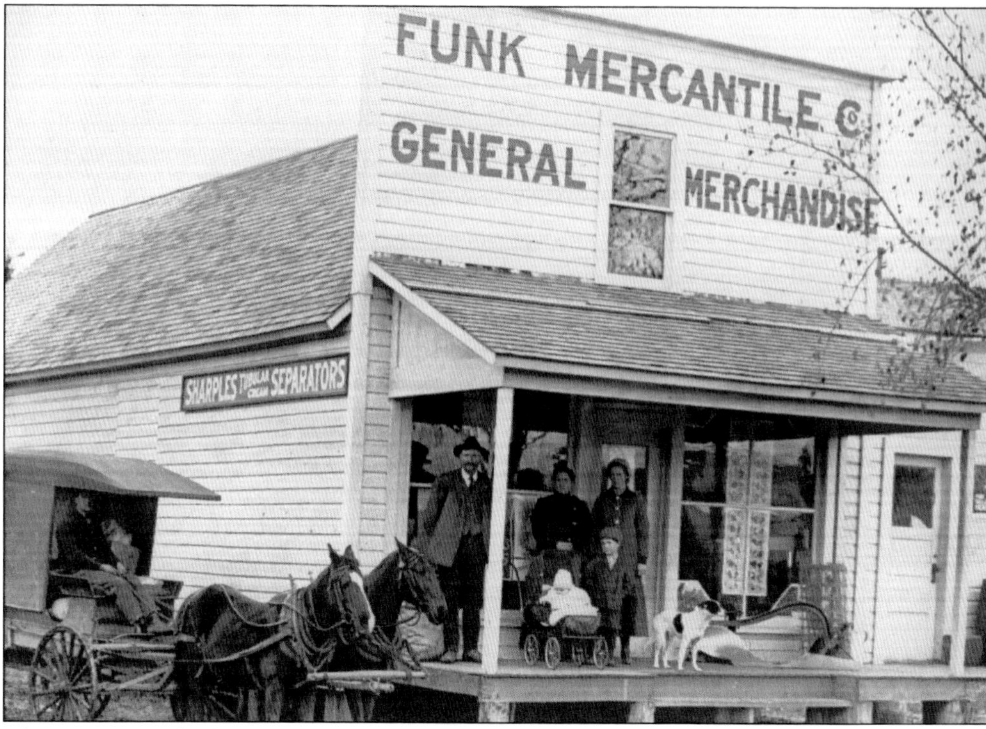

About 1910, Fredrick Funk, shown here on the porch with his wife, Mathilda, and several of their six children, came from Marysville to operate a mercantile on Anthes Avenue just south of the Howard store. Funk was active in community affairs and served as mayor from 1929 to 1932. His daughter Emma married Lloyd Cloke and was postmaster from 1938 to 1961. (Courtesy of the SWHS.)

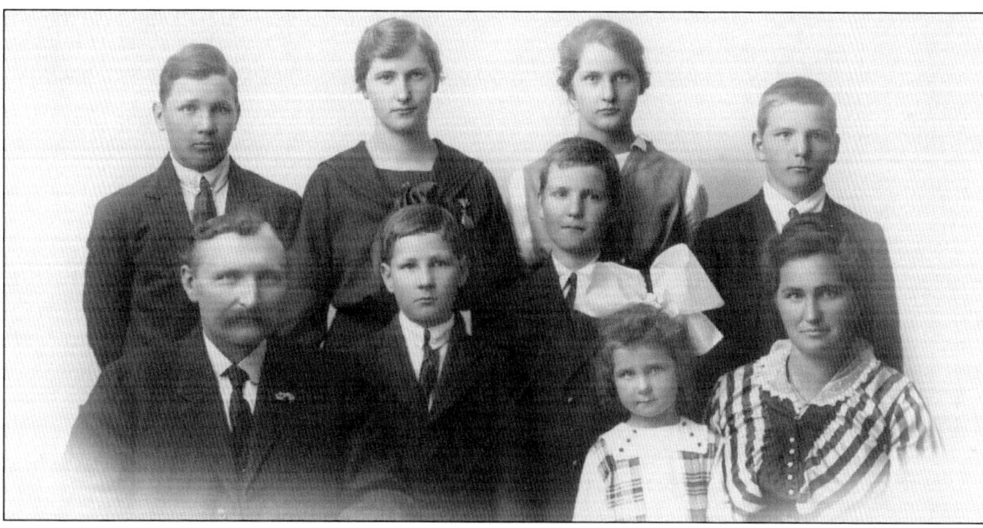

The Fredrick Funk family poses for a portrait in 1915. The family members are, from left to right, (first row) Fredrick, Howard, Alton, Delilah, and Mathilda; (second row) Fred Jr., Marina, Emma, and Phillip. In addition to the main store, Fredrick Funk built a number of smaller buildings along Anthes Avenue between First and Second Streets. Funk drove and organized wagons in the Morning Mine in Idaho before coming to Washington. (Courtesy of Hilma Brown.)

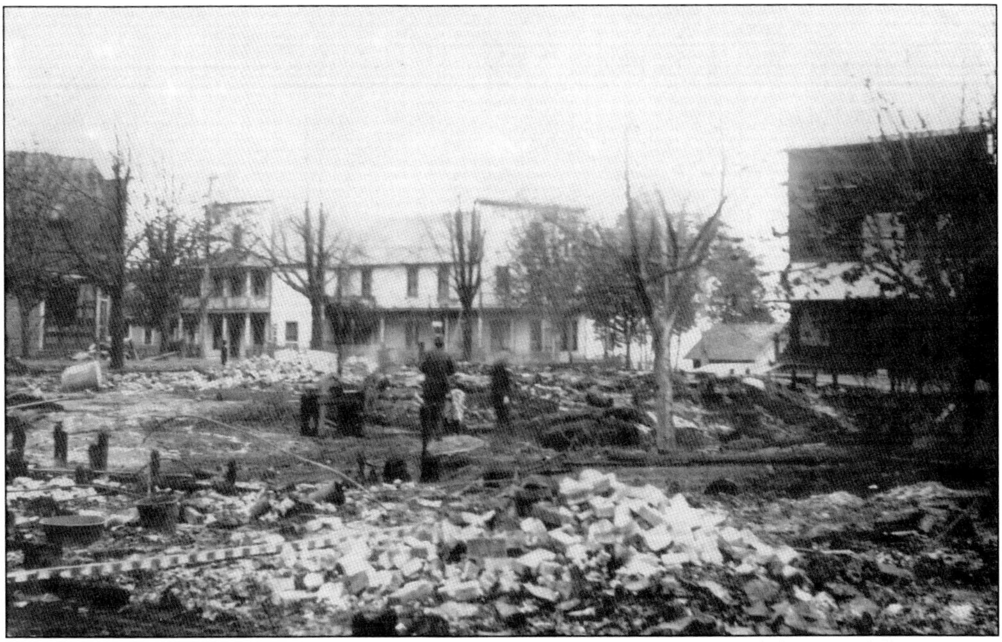

Jacob Anthes and others look at the site of his house and store that burned down under suspicious circumstances in October 1910. Howard's store (far left) burned down a short time later, also under suspicious circumstances. Edward Howard moved his store and family into the Olympic Club (right) and operated a mercantile and post office there until 1915. The store was managed by Walter and William Hunziker. (Courtesy of Helene Ryan.)

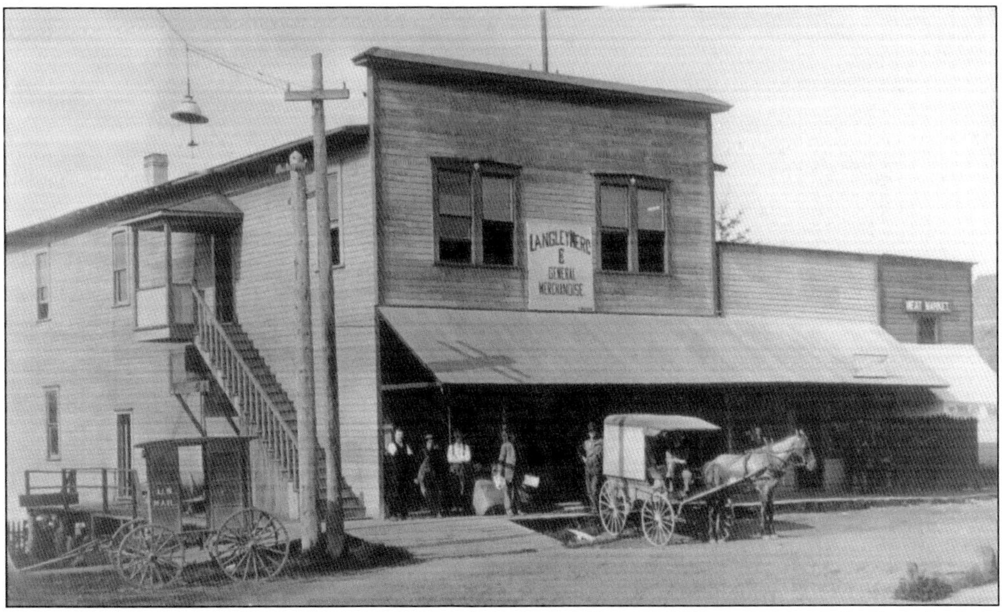

The Langley Mercantile and General Merchandise and post office occupied the first floor of the former Olympic Club from 1912 to 1915. There was a basketball court below and a stage and auditorium above. Edward Howard's son William assumed ownership of the Olympic Club building after the Hunziker brothers went out of business, and he turned it into a confectionery. (Photograph by Ferdinand Brady; courtesy of the SWHS.)

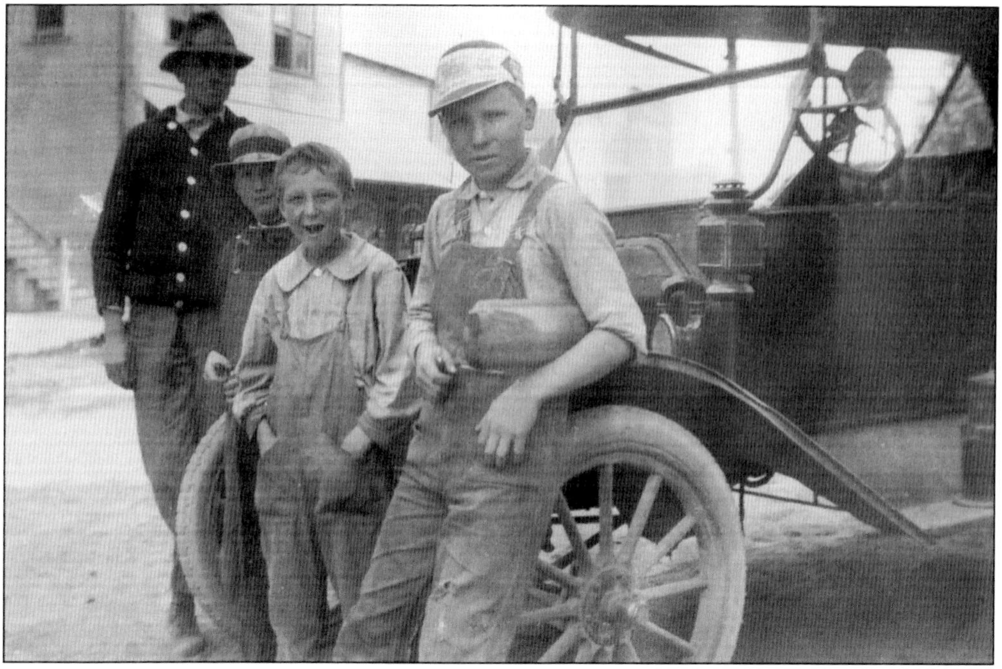

The first automobiles appeared in Langley about 1910. Hans Jensen was one of the first residents of Langley to own a car. He bought a Maxwell in Everett in 1917 and brought it to the island on the Deception Pass ferry. Edward Howard purchased a Ford Model T from the first dealer on South Whidbey, located in Glendale. (Courtesy of Karen Pauley.)

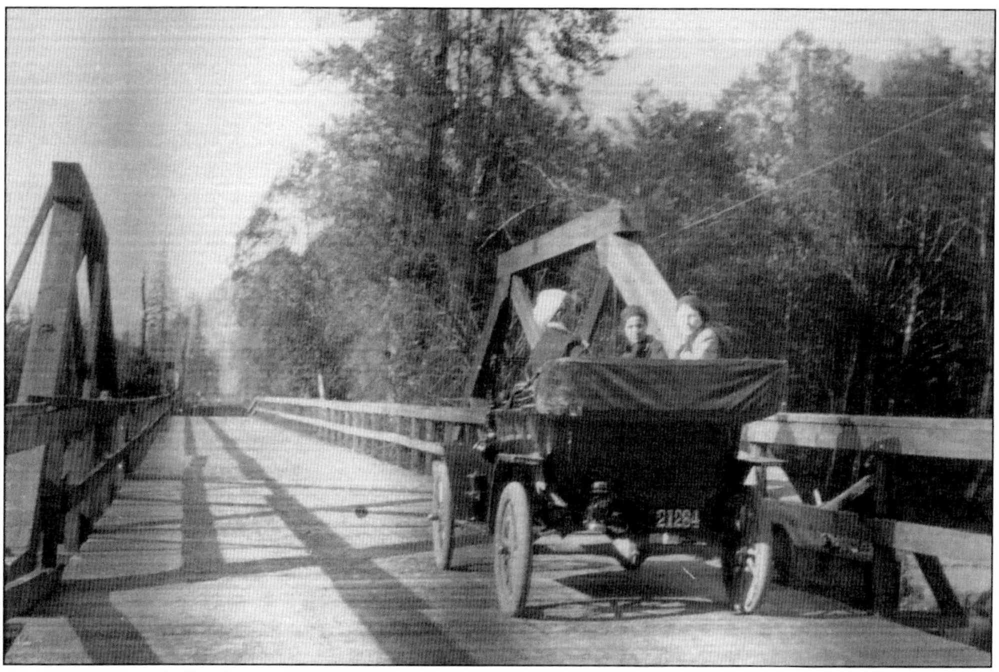

A wooden trestle bridge was constructed on Saratoga Road west of town, spanning the ravine over the Saratoga Creek. Prior to this, traffic into or out of town on Saratoga Road had to divert to Third Street to cross the creek before it entered the ravine. (Courtesy of the SWHS.)

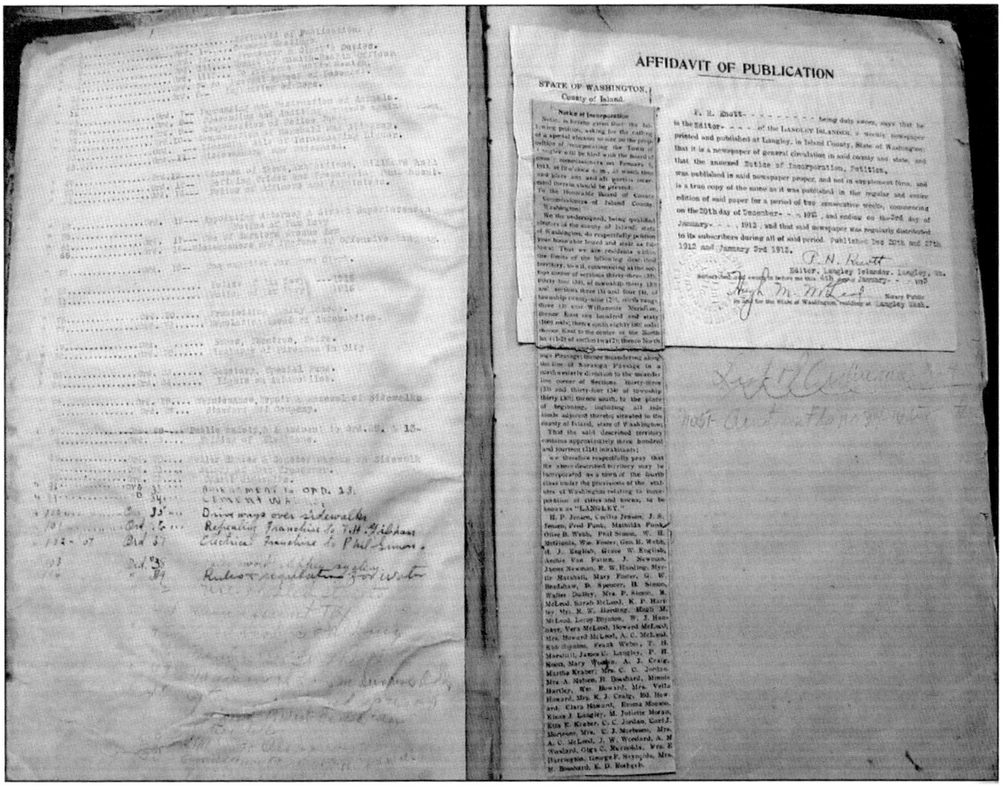

A petition for incorporation, photographed in the original ordinance book, was accepted by the Island County Commission. An election was held on January 28, 1913, and the votes were tallied on February 2. The town was incorporated by a vote of 64 to 57. The elected officers held their first town council meeting on March 4, 1913, with Mayor Frank Furman presiding. (Courtesy of the SWHS.)

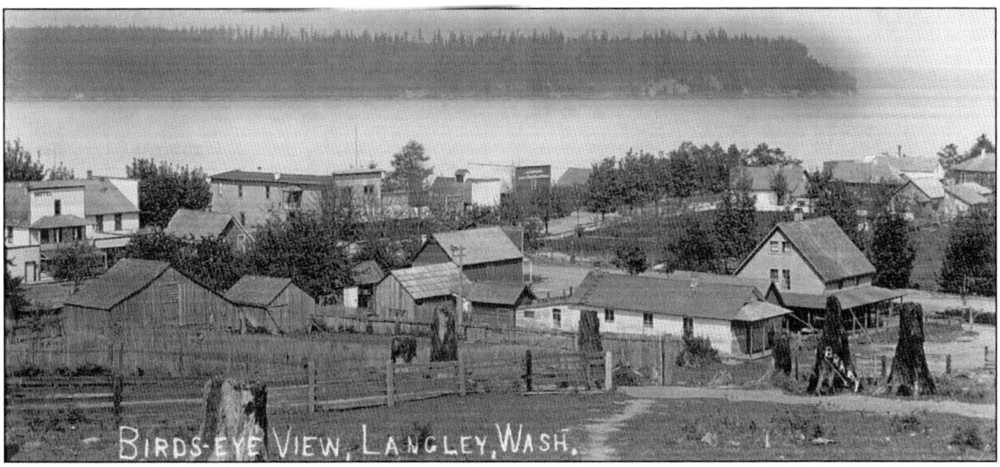

The Langley Hotel (left) was the largest of three hotels in town when this photograph of downtown Langley was taken around 1912. The long white building in the foreground was built by Jacob Anthes prior to 1900 as a bunkhouse for loggers. Blacksmith Anton Anderson purchased it in 1905. Anderson's daughter donated it to the South Whidbey Historical Society for a museum in 1989. (Courtesy of the SWHS.)

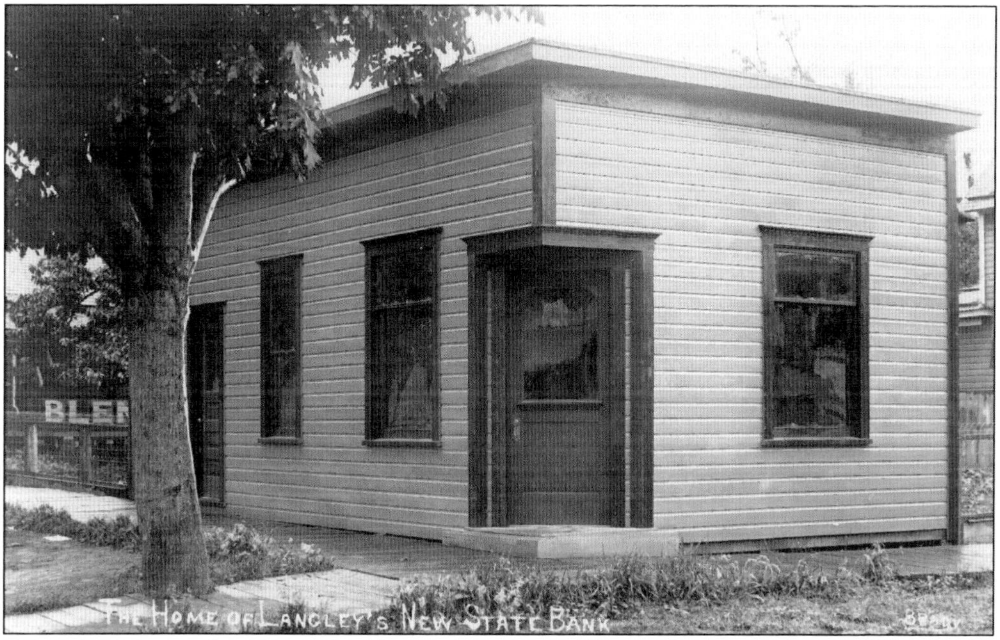

A wooden Langley State Bank building was constructed in 1913 on the site formerly occupied by Edward Howard's store. The bank president, James Curtis Langley, was a nephew of town namesake James Weston Langley. He had a farm on DeBruyn Avenue between First and Second Streets. He was also quite deaf. (Courtesy of the ICHS.)

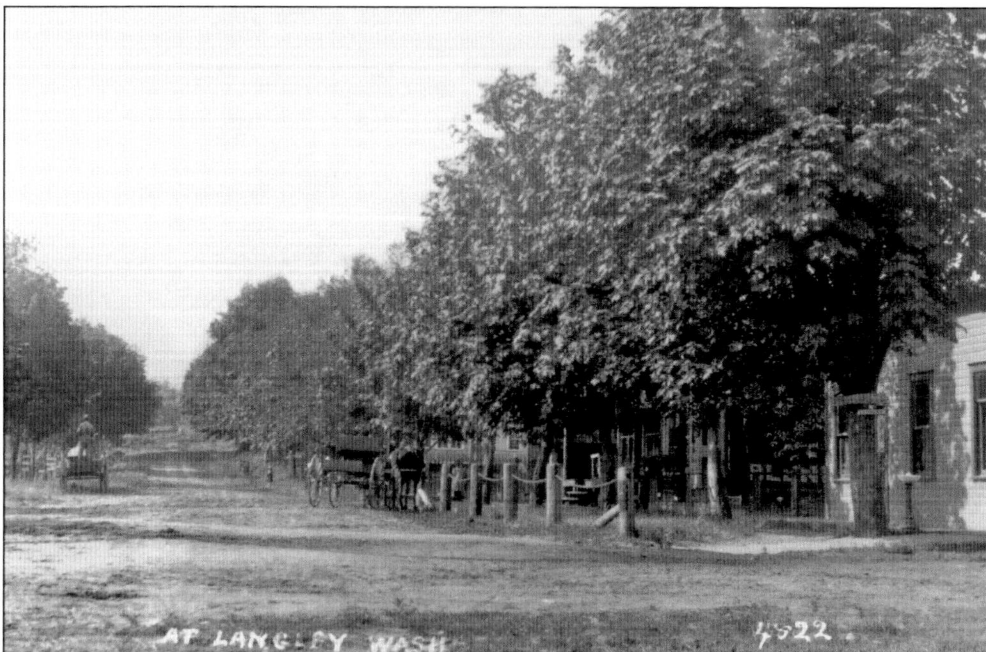

This c. 1915 photograph is looking south on Anthes Avenue from First Street. The maple trees planted by Jacob Anthes some 24 years before form a dominant feature of the avenue. A water fountain can be seen outside the Langley State Bank (right). The bank went into receivership in 1918. (Courtesy of the SWHS.)

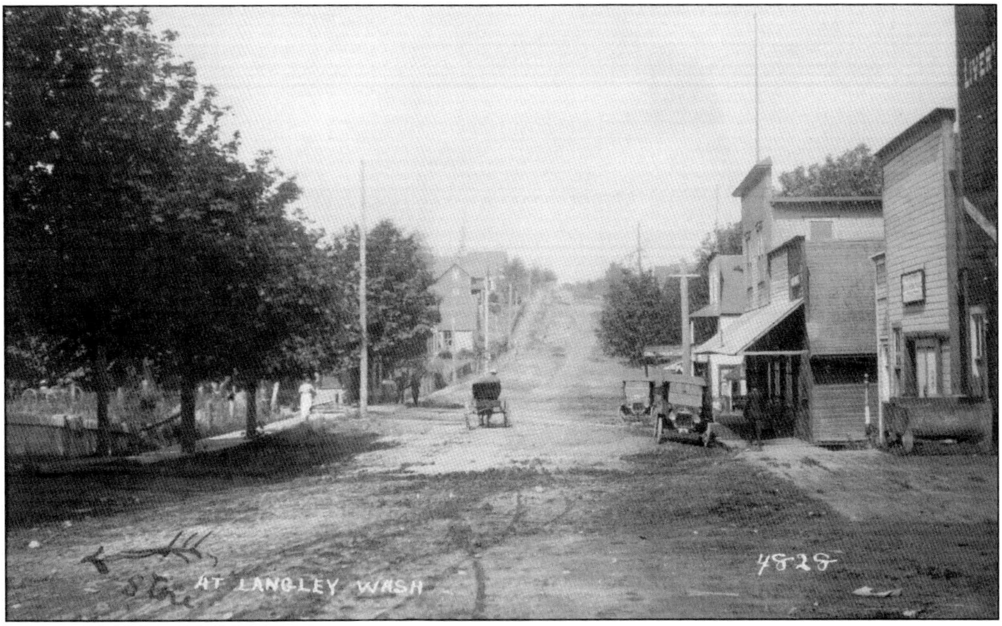

This view is looking west along First Street around 1915. Cars gradually became an important means of travel and commerce as roads connecting the growing number of Whidbey Island communities improved. The arrow indicates the store (out of frame to left) run by the Hunziker brothers in the two-story building constructed in 1914 by the Yeomen Brotherhood. (Courtesy of Bonnie Peters.)

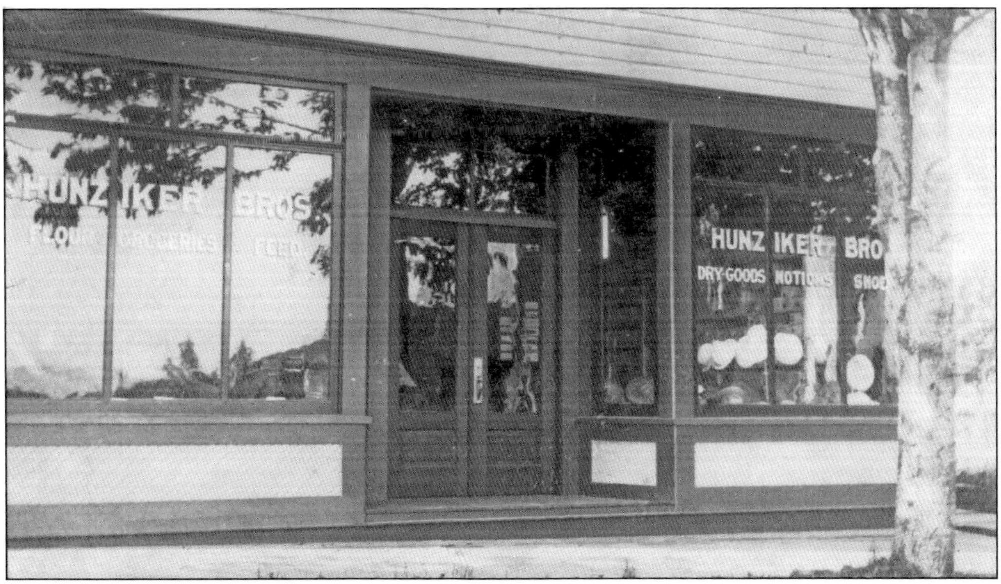

Walter and William Hunziker operated a store in the Yeomen Building from 1914 to 1915, when William decided to go to Alaska. According to Walter, smells included the oiled sweepings used to keep the dust down, dried prunes, sharp cheese, and pickles in a barrel. The brothers also ran the mercantile in the Olympic Club for Edward Howard and sold caskets during this time. (Courtesy of Bonnie Peters.)

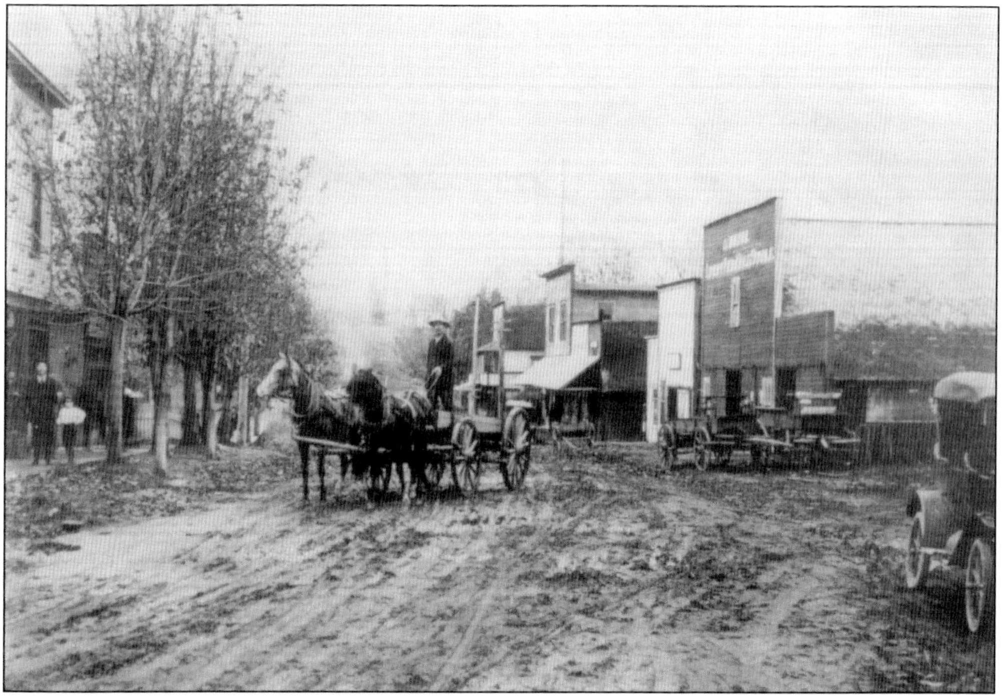

Jacob Brehm is standing in a wagon around 1914 in front of the livery stable that he built on First Street in 1904. His son Gus and grandson Vincent are in front of the Hunziker store (left). The livery stable changed owners several times. When the need for livery services diminished, owner Hans Jensen transformed the building into a mercantile operated by Arie Kuiper. (Courtesy of the SWHS.)

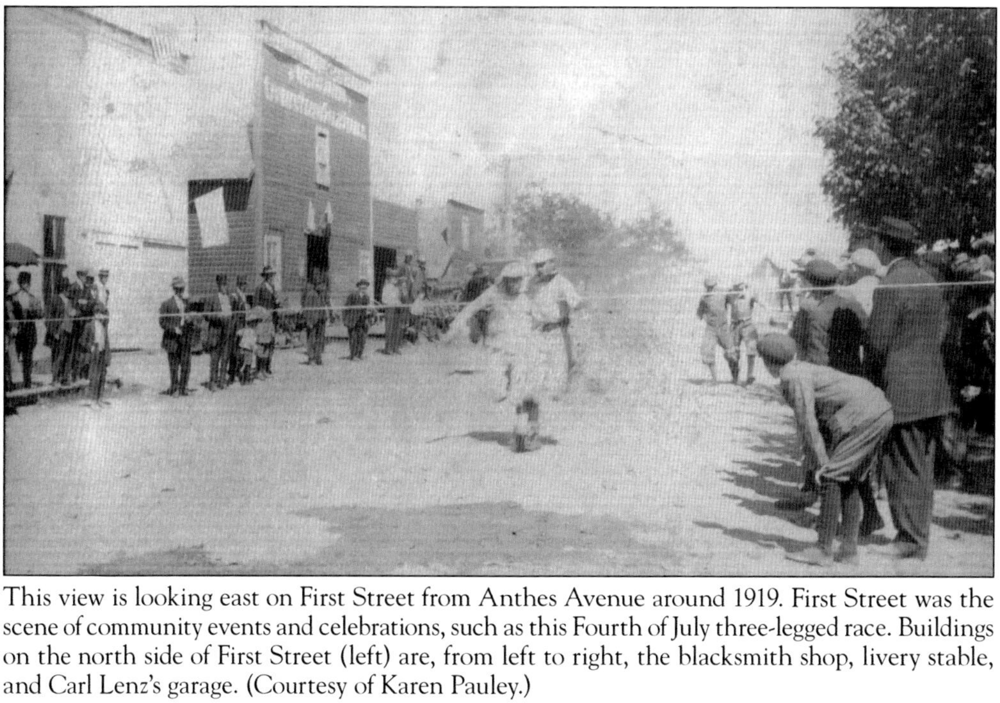

This view is looking east on First Street from Anthes Avenue around 1919. First Street was the scene of community events and celebrations, such as this Fourth of July three-legged race. Buildings on the north side of First Street (left) are, from left to right, the blacksmith shop, livery stable, and Carl Lenz's garage. (Courtesy of Karen Pauley.)

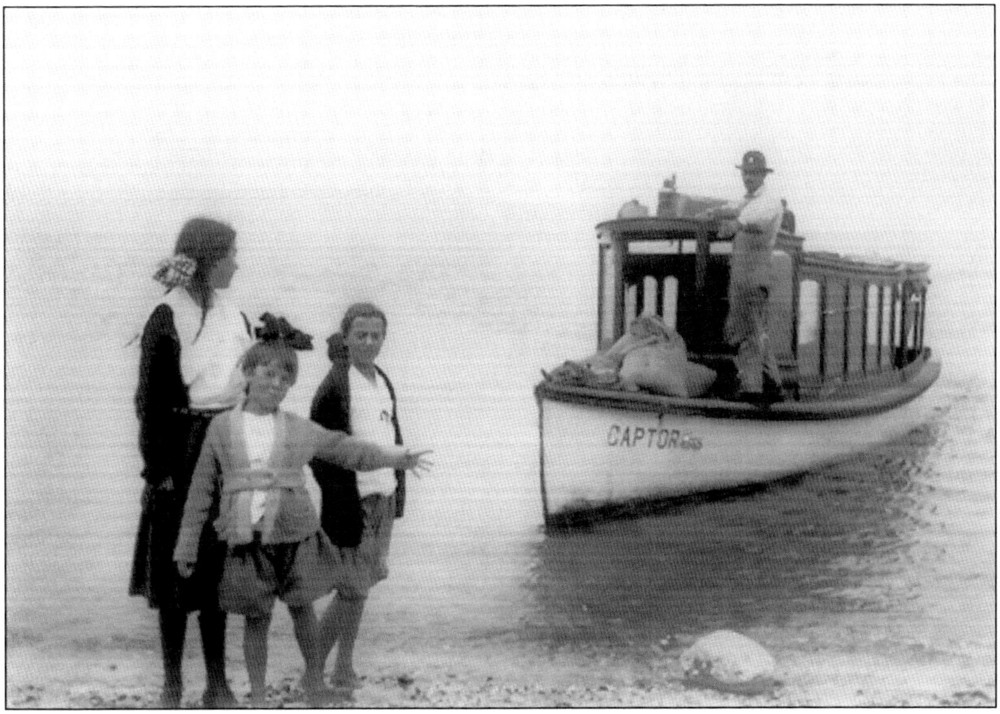

Phillip Simon on his boat *Captor* is approaching his wife, Anna, and daughters, Eleanor and Evelyn, around 1921. Phillip and Anna came to Langley in 1910 from Mukilteo as newlyweds and settled into the little house across the road from the Langley wharf. Their daughters and a son, Phillip Jr., were born there. (Courtesy of Phillip Simon.)

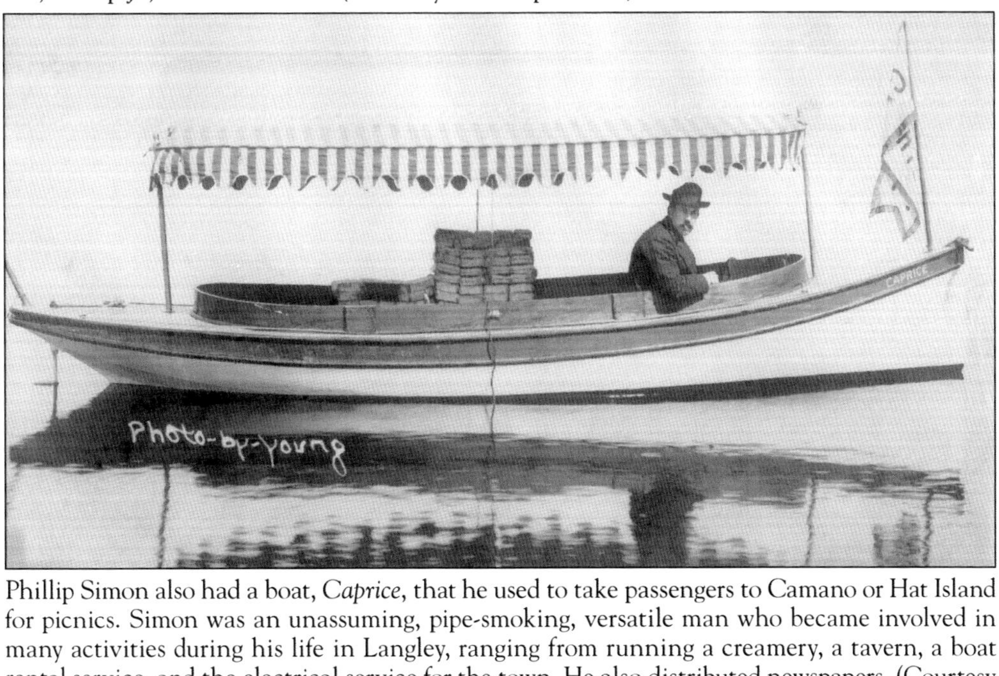

Phillip Simon also had a boat, *Caprice*, that he used to take passengers to Camano or Hat Island for picnics. Simon was an unassuming, pipe-smoking, versatile man who became involved in many activities during his life in Langley, ranging from running a creamery, a tavern, a boat rental service, and the electrical service for the town. He also distributed newspapers. (Courtesy of the SWHS.)

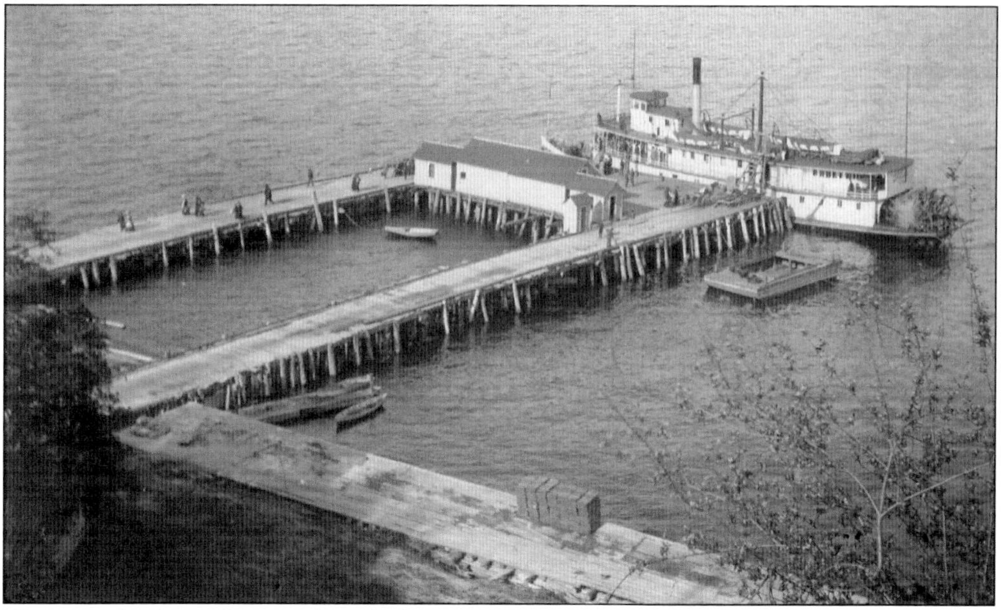

The sternwheeler *Fairhaven* is disembarking passengers in this c. 1910 photograph. The *Fairhaven* brought many early settlers to Langley. The small building hanging over the edge of the right leg of the wharf was a privy. Rowdy revelers were occasionally placed here until they could be dealt with properly. The barge was one of those used to transport brush to Everett and Seattle. (Photograph by Ferdinand Brady; courtesy of the SWHS.)

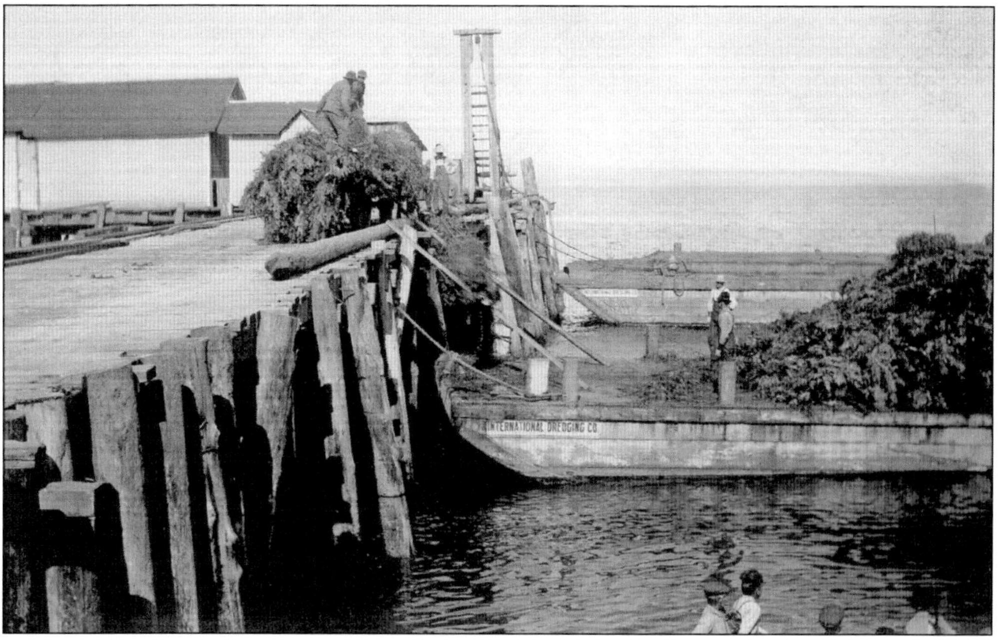

This photograph shows brush being loaded onto a barge around 1915. Jacob Anthes secured contracts for fill brush for the Seattle waterfront and started several brush camps here during the Yukon gold rush in 1897–1898. Construction of the Great Northern dock in Smith Cove north of Seattle from 1911 to 1916 called for even more brush, and Edward Howard secured contracts to supply it. (Courtesy of Helen Hulbert.)

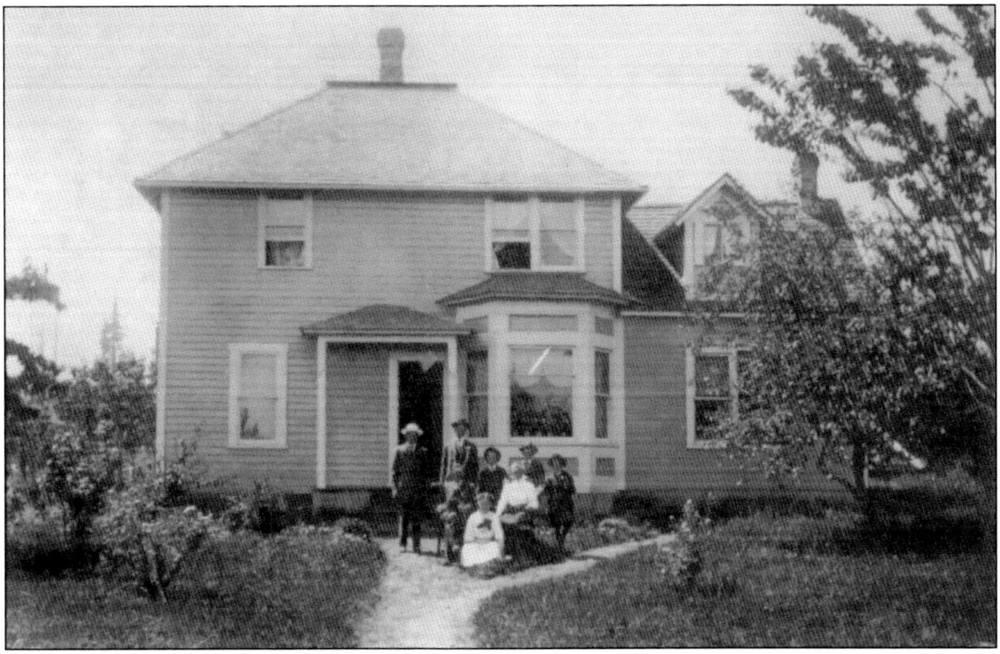

The Hans Peter Jensen family is posing in front of its home around 1912. Hans, his wife, Celia, and their six children came to Langley in 1910 and purchased this house and 100 acres at Sixth Street and Park Avenue from Henry Bosshard. Jensen became a well-known businessman in Langley, involved in or having ownership of the telephone company, a livery stable, and a bank. (Courtesy of the SWHS.)

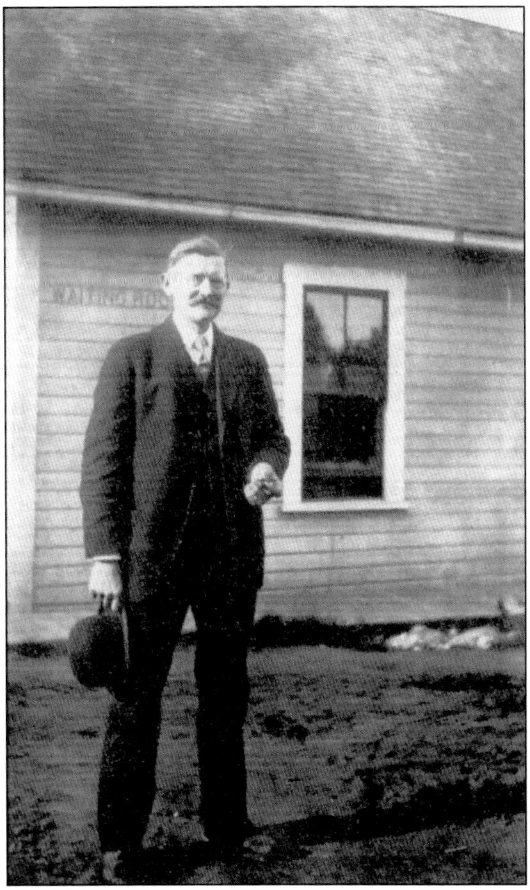

Hans Peter Jensen bought the wharf in 1912 and began making improvements. He had a large wheel on the side of a warehouse with letters that read: "Langley—The Hub of the Island." A map beside the wheel showed that Langley was halfway between Seattle and Oak Harbor. (Courtesy of the SWHS.)

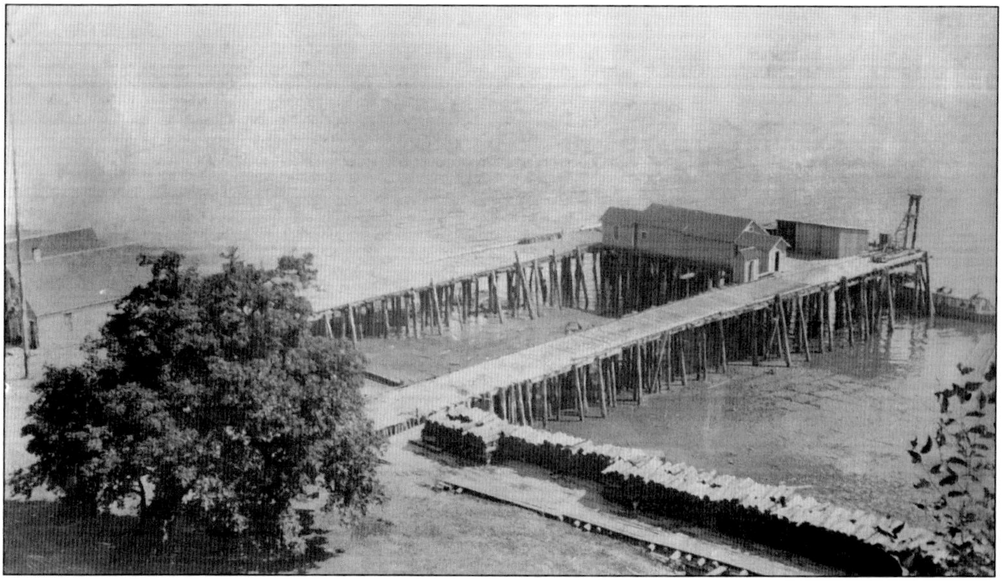

Prior to 1912, in addition to the privy, there were two small buildings at either side of two larger warehouses on the end of the wharf. Planking supported by piling along the water side of the shore (right) provided a surface for storing shingle bolts and shingles. (Courtesy of Karen Pauley.)

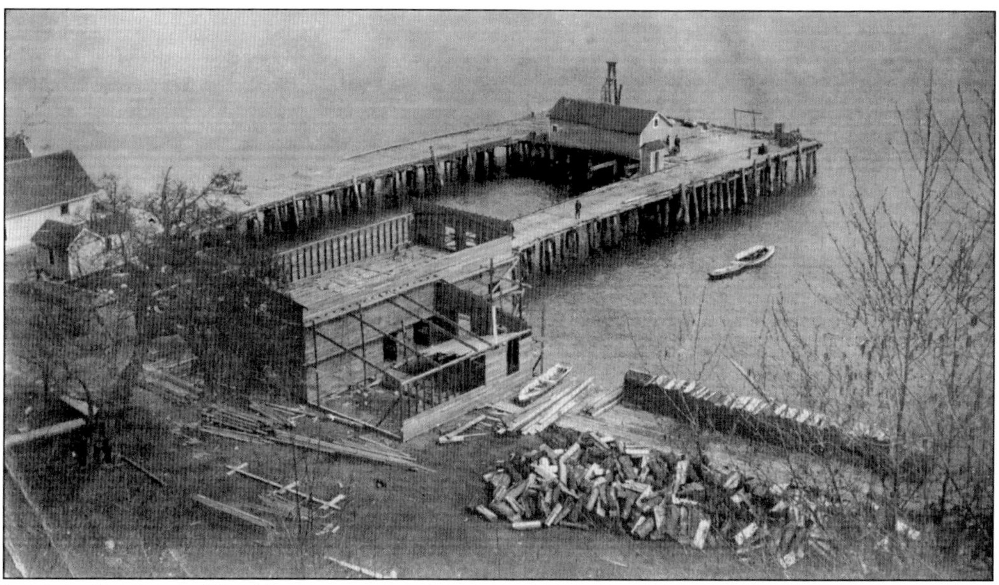

In 1912, the two small buildings were moved to the foot of the north leg of the wharf (left) and placed together to form the Sea Breeze Confectionery. A large cannery building and adjacent creamery were then constructed at the foot of the south leg of the wharf. (Courtesy of Karen Pauley.)

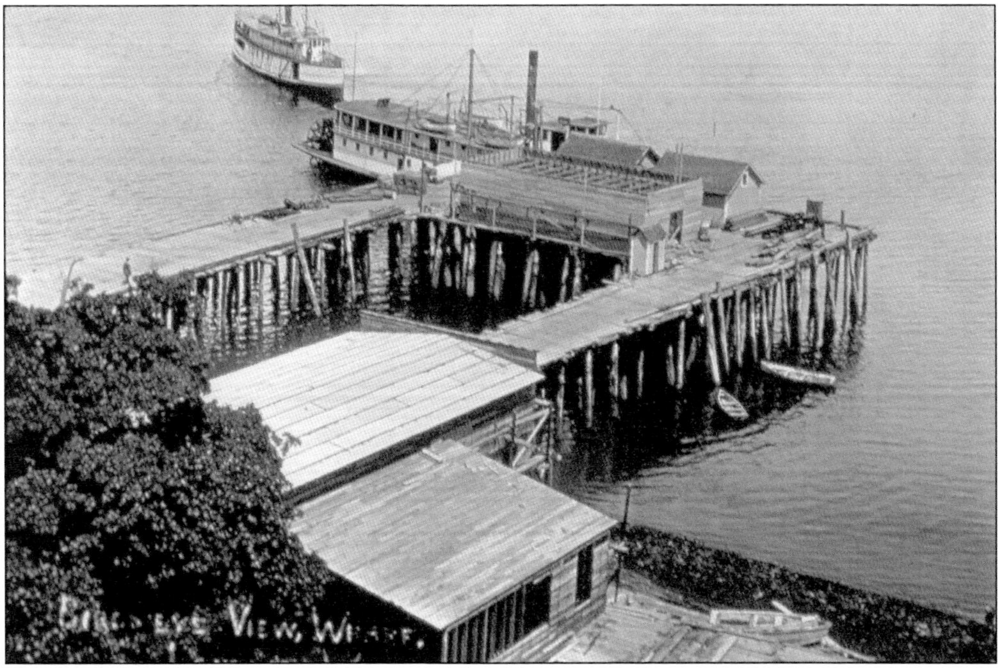

The cannery and adjacent creamery are nearing completion in this 1912 photograph. The two original warehouses at the end of the wharf have been moved to make room for construction of a larger single warehouse. The little privy remains. The sternwheeler *Fairhaven* is at the wharf, with the *Camano* waiting to dock. (Courtesy of the MOHI.)

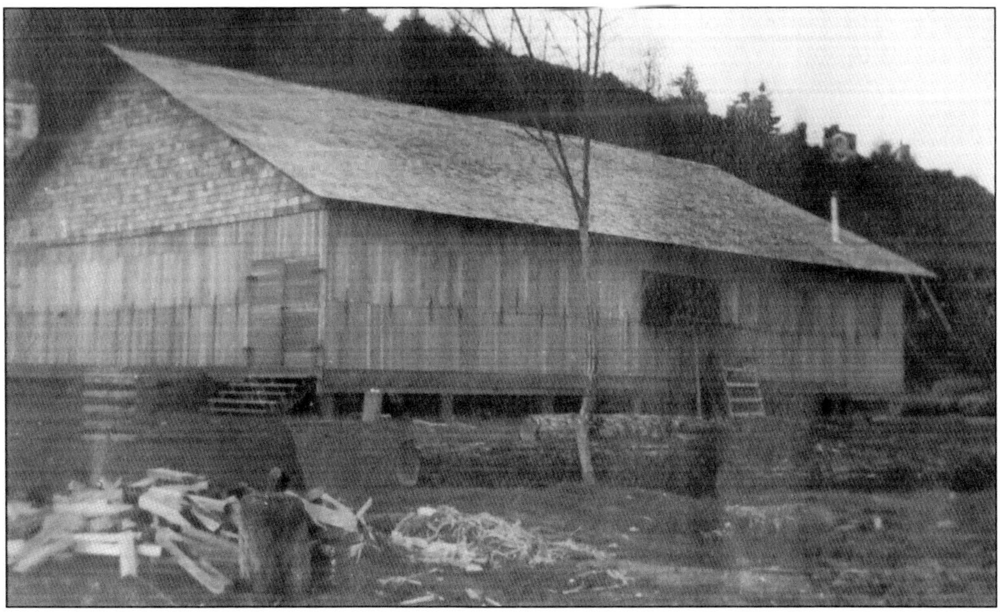

Hans Jensen built a dance pavilion with a large bandstand and hinged shutters along the sides just north of the warehouses in 1914. Because the street leading down the hill was either dusty or muddy, girls carried their shoes and walked barefoot until they reached the pavilion. Mothers often accompanied the girls. During World War I, soldiers from Fort Casey came by boat from Coupeville to attend dances. (Courtesy of Karen Pauley.)

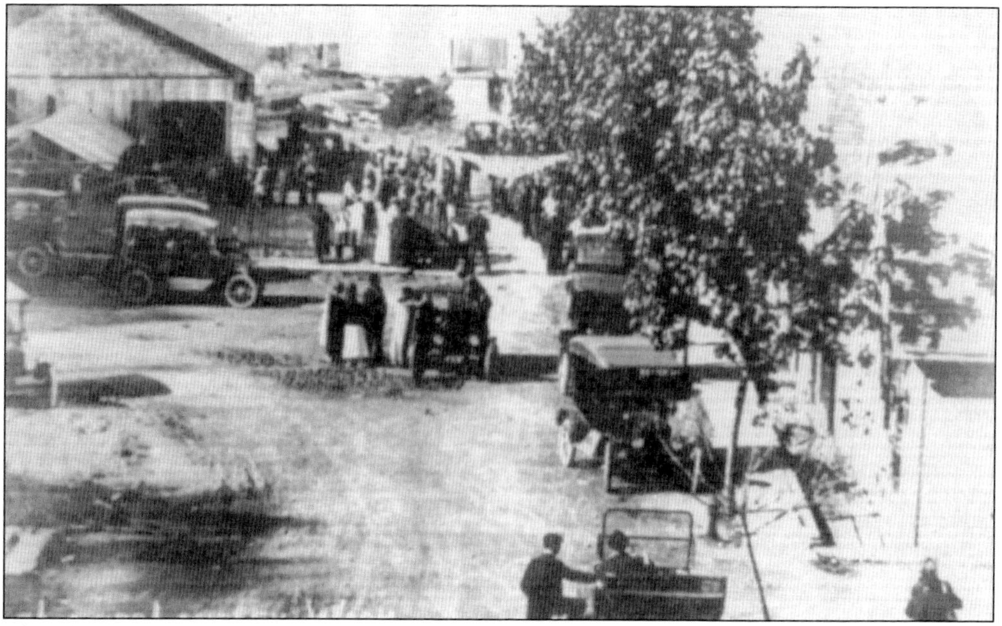

The Island County Fair (Langley Community Fair) was held at the Langley marina from 1917 to 1920. Exhibits were housed in the dance pavilion (left). Hans Jensen won first place in 1917 with his Wolf River apple, early cabbage, and Himalaya blackberries. He also won five gallons of Standard Oil gas for "auto servicing." (Photograph by Ferdinand Brady; courtesy of the SWHS.)

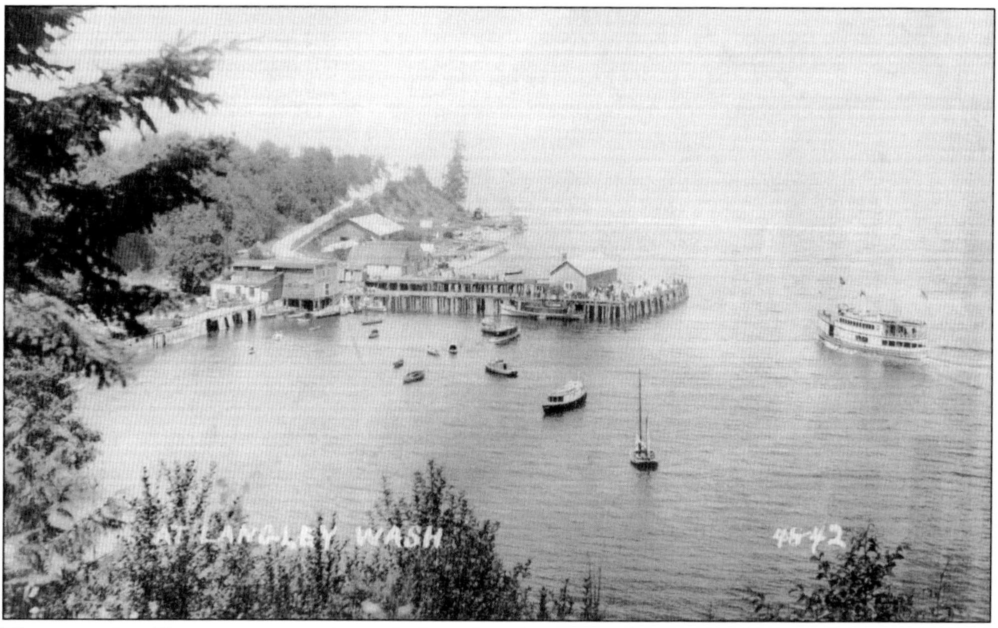

The steamship *Clatawa* is approaching the Langley wharf around 1918. The marina was experiencing its peak of commercial and community activity. Numerous ships made frequent stops. The cannery was in operation during canning season, and the creamery was in business. Philip Simon had taken over the electric system in 1916 and set up a generating plant using the cannery boiler until a diesel engine was installed. (Courtesy of Douglas McLeod.)

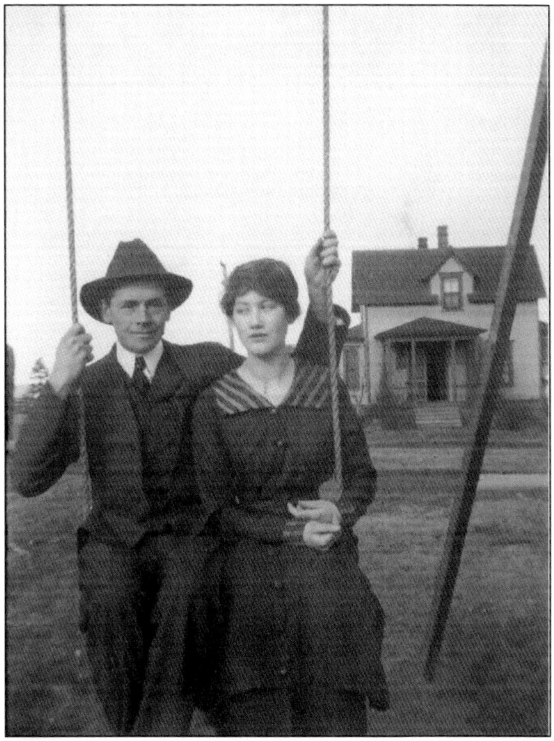

In 1919, Hans Jensen sold the wharf property to his sons Jacob (right, on schoolyard swing with Florence Monson) and Neils Frederick "Fred" (below) on their return from World War I. Jacob was in charge and moved into a small cabin some 300 feet south of the wharf. He had served in France and nearly died from pneumonia. Neils was awaiting deployment when the Armistice was signed. They were two of several young men from Langley who entered the service. The brothers maintained the wharfinger business. (Right, courtesy of Karen Pauley; below, courtesy of the Fossek family.)

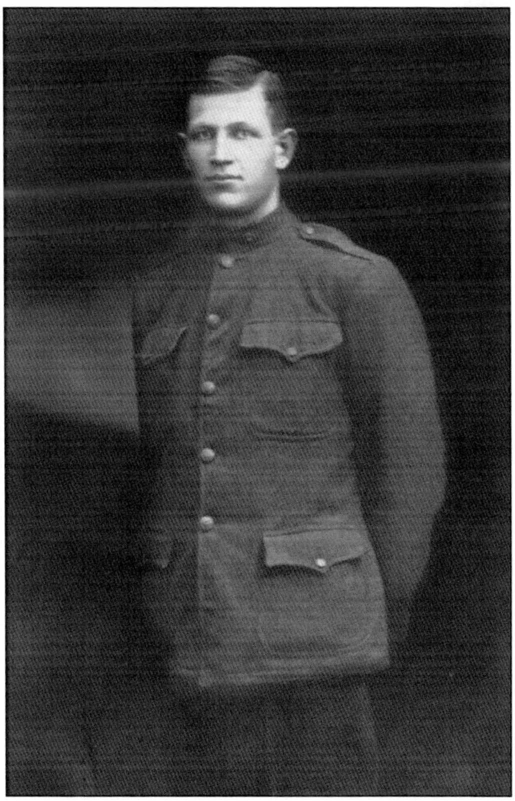

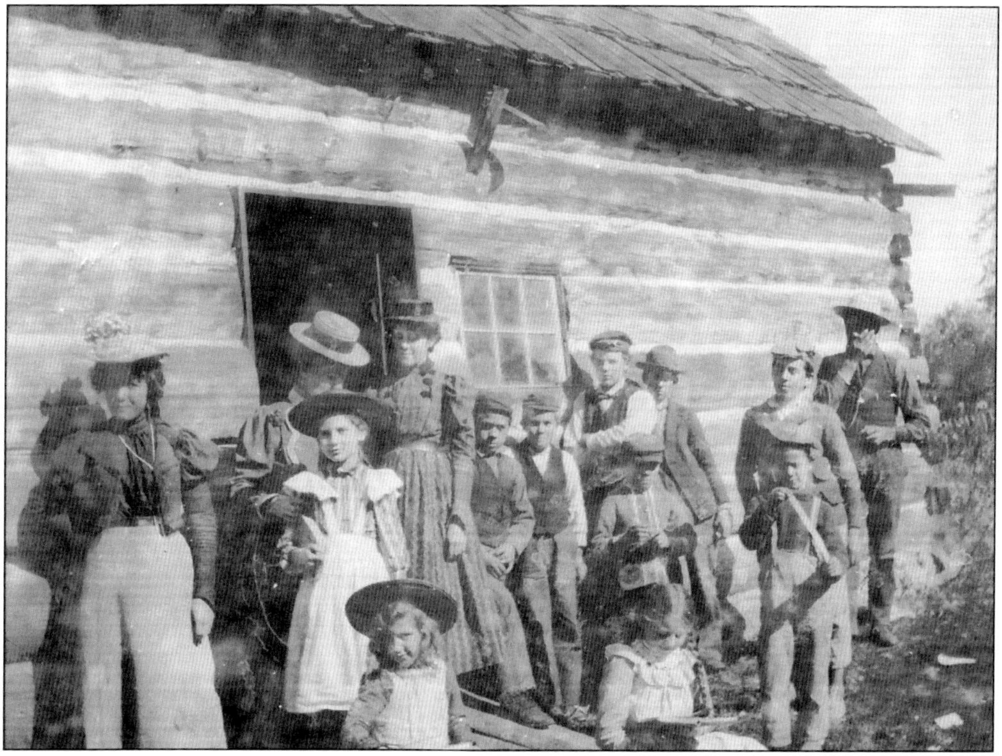

A school district was organized in 1898 and a schoolhouse built in the woods between Langley and Brown's Point. The log schoolhouse shown here was subsequently built on the bluff above the marina. The teacher was paid $2.50 for each pupil. According to Jacob Anthes, this was enough to keep the children out of mischief. (Courtesy of William Hunziker.)

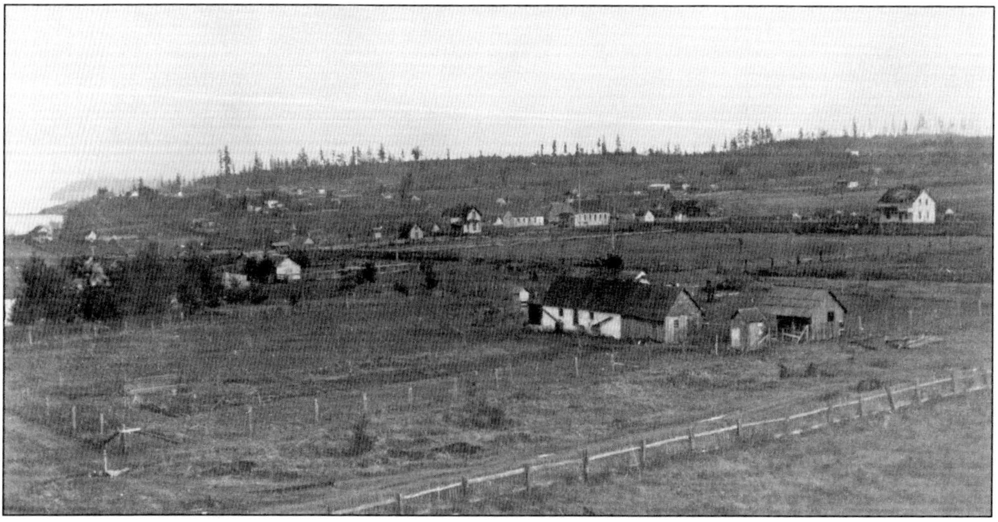

This view is looking east from a water tower at First Street and DeBruyn Avenue in 1915. The downtown is off to the left. Two white school buildings (center) occupy the southeast corner of Third Street and Park Avenue. The larger building with a bell tower was built in 1900. The smaller one, built in 1907, accommodated the younger grades. (Photograph by William Oscar Hunziker; courtesy of Douglas McLeod.)

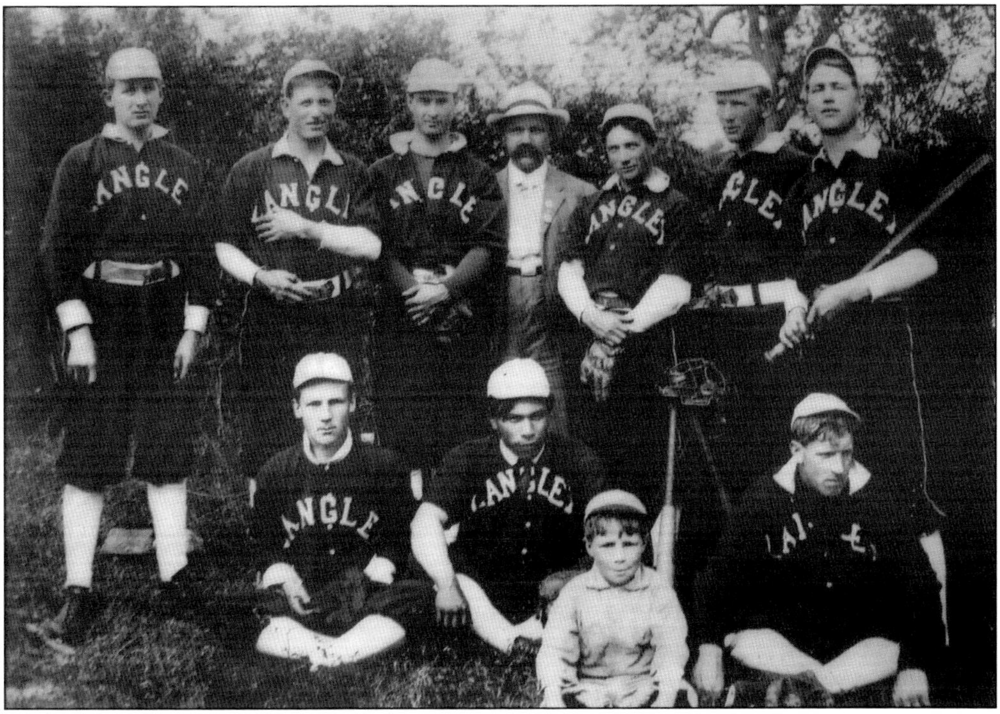

The 1911 Langley High School baseball team poses for a photograph. Shown here are, from left to right, (first row) Fredrick Howard, Charles Alex, Ray Howard, and Walter Stoddard; (second row) Leon Hurley, Elmer Rothgeb, Edward Boynton, Edward Howard (manager), Carl Gillespie, Harry Kraber, and William Howard. Baseball was a favorite pastime, and rivalry between surrounding towns was fierce. (Courtesy of Helen Hulbert.)

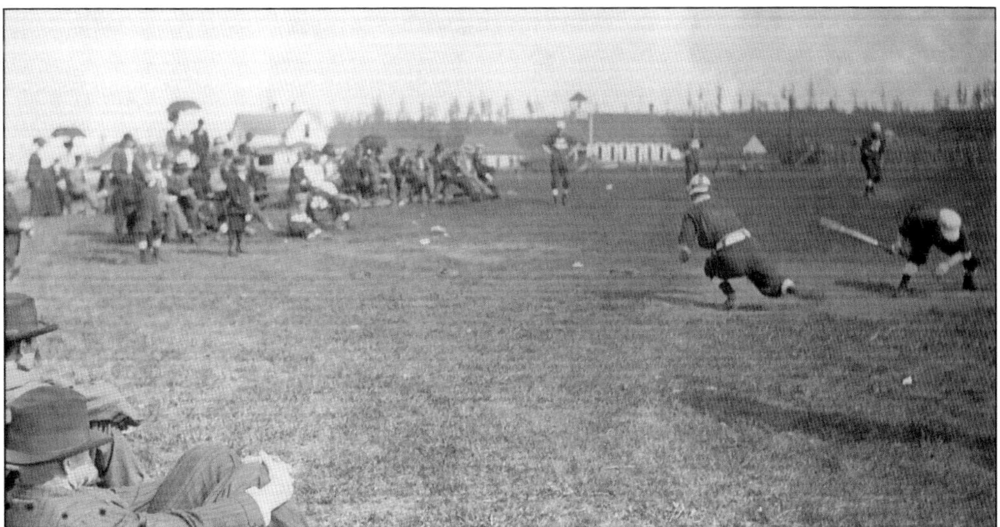

The field across the street from the schools served as the baseball field. A basket social helped purchase a bell for the first one-room building. The basket bringing the highest bid belonged to Eleanor Maud Hunziker, who was a very popular clerk in the Anthes store. The two-story house (left of the school buildings) was the home of the Monson family. (Courtesy of Karen Pauley.)

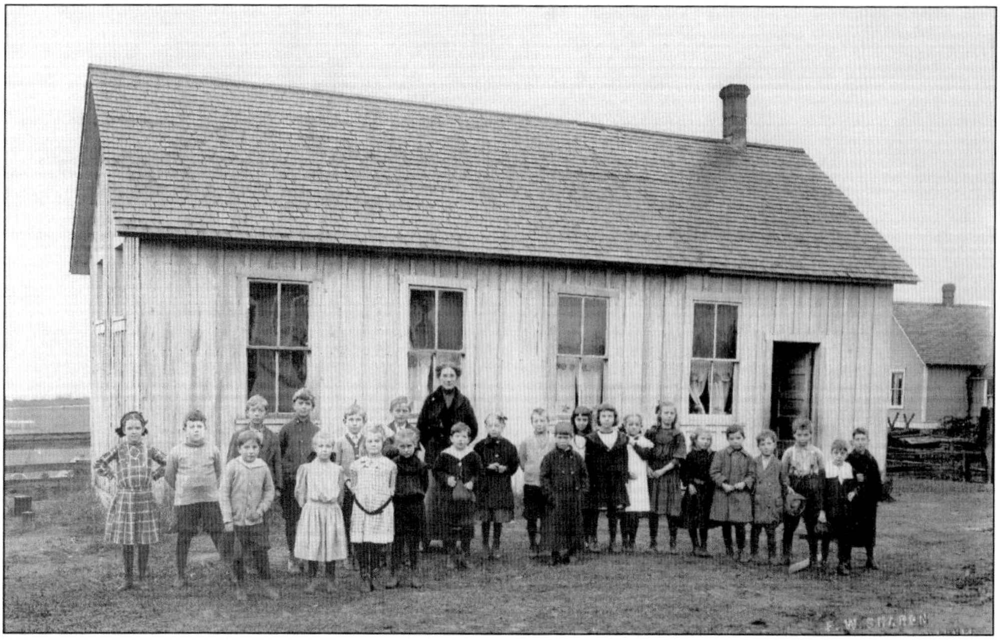

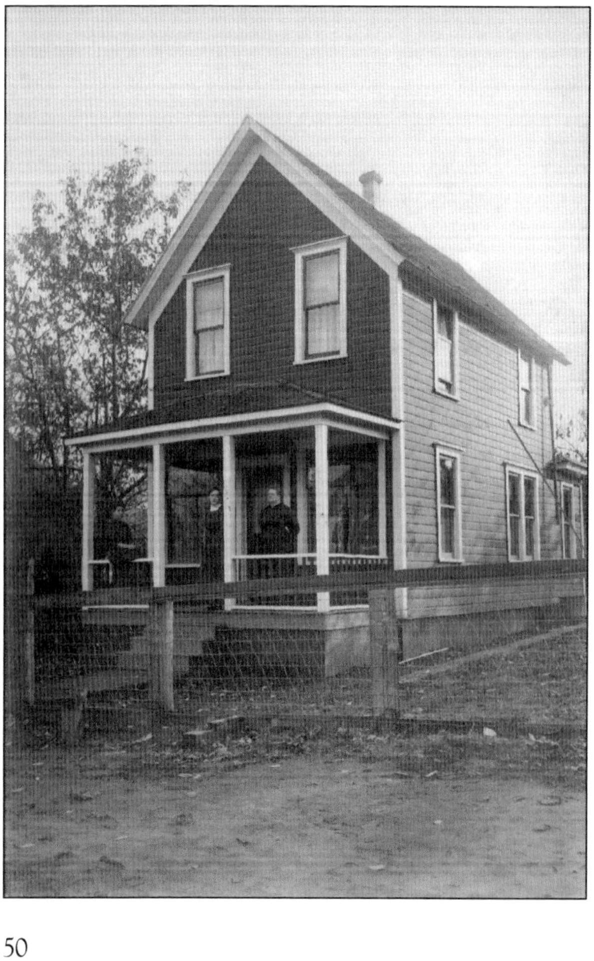

Here is the 1908 class picture in front of the small school building at the southeast corner of Third Street and Park Avenue. The teacher, Henrietta Kraber (center), came to Whidbey Island from Seattle in 1907 after graduating from high school to teach in Clinton, riding her pony to school every day. She then taught in Langley from 1908 to 1912. (Courtesy of the SWHS.)

In 1913, Henrietta Kraber (on the porch, center) married Martin Mortenson in this home owned by her parents, William and Martha Kraber. The house was located on First Street next to Howard's store. Henrietta worked as a telephone operator and Martin ran a hardware store on First Street in the 1940s. He later was part-owner of the Langley Garage with his son-in-law, Edward Christoe. (Courtesy of Sue McQueen.)

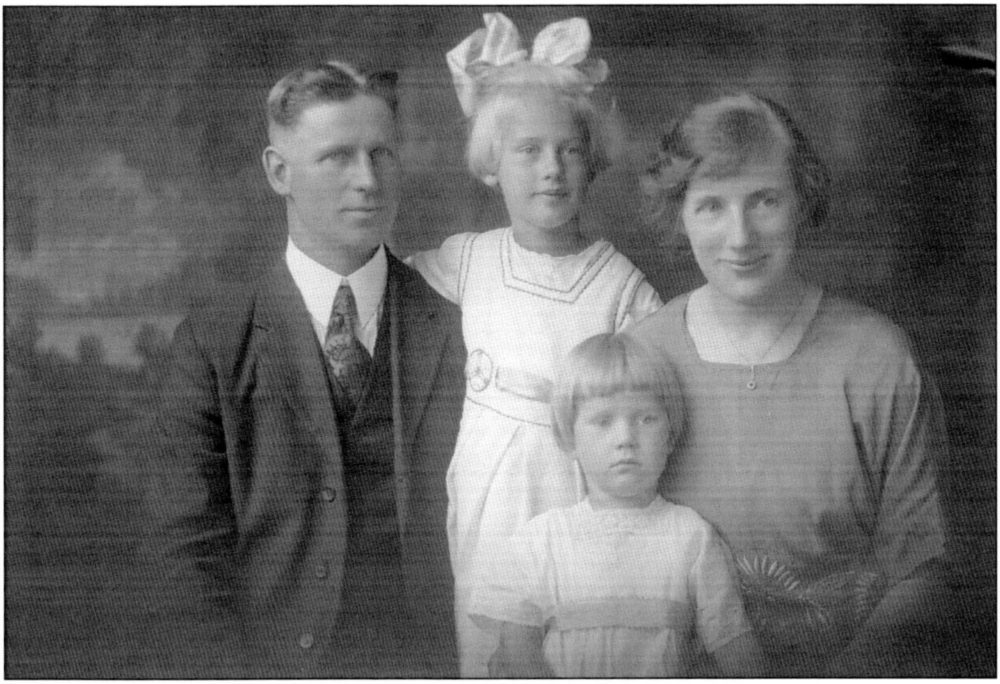

The Mortenson family is, from left to right, Martin, Kathryn, Dorothy, and Henrietta. Martin Simon Mortenson came to Whidbey Island in 1907 to visit his half-sister, Anna Simonson, who was married to Henrietta's brother Harry. Mortenson met Henrietta at the Kraber home in 1911. They were married in the house on November 24, 1913. Following the death of Henrietta's parents, they moved into the house. (Courtesy of Sue McQueen.)

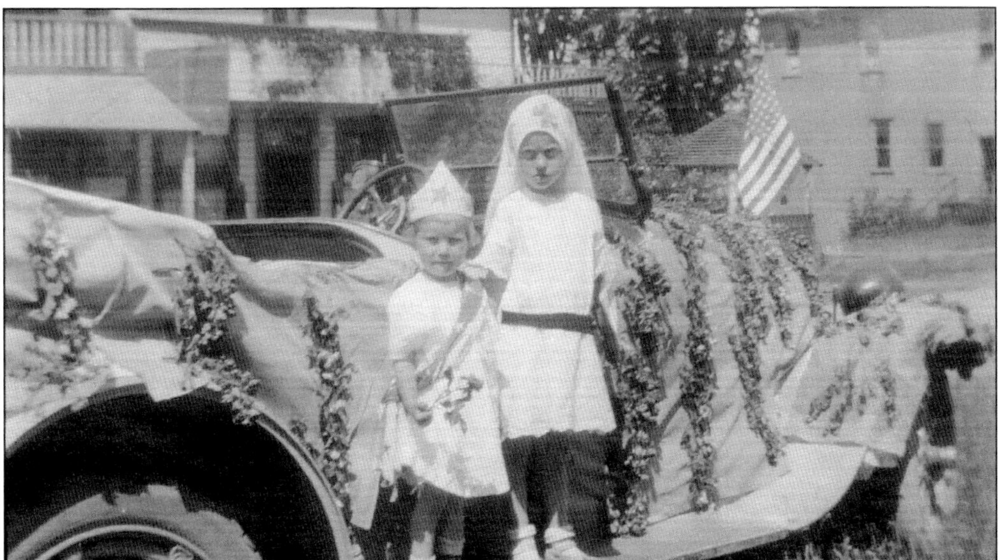

Dorothy (left), born December 5, 1916, and Kathryn Mortenson, born September 14, 1914, are standing on the running board of their father's car dressed for a Fourth of July parade. The car is parked in the front yard of the Mortenson home, across First Street from the hotel. The side of the old Olympic Club is seen at the right. (Courtesy of Sue McQueen.)

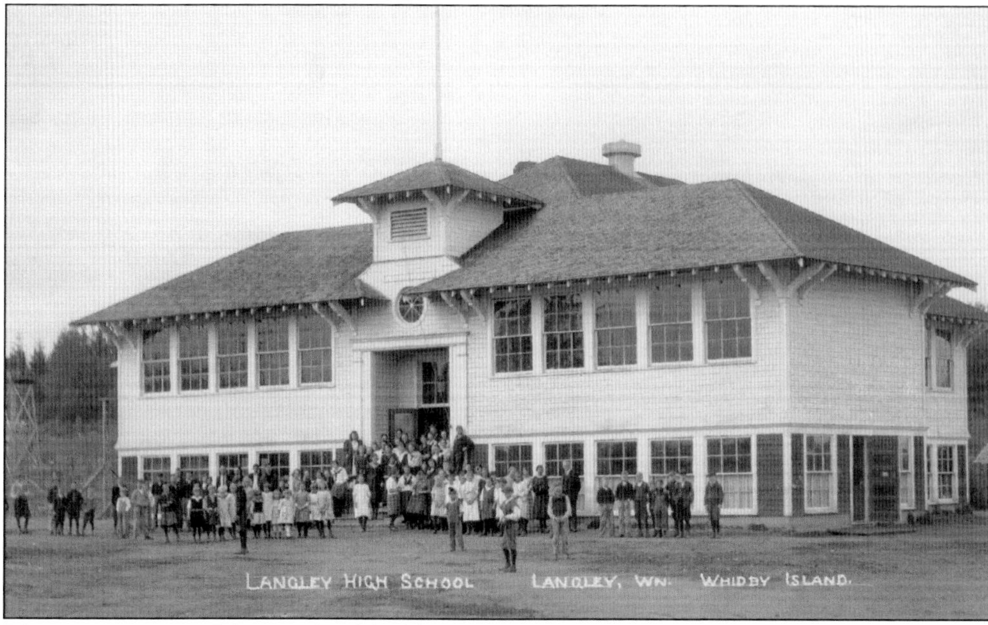

This two-story, wood-frame school building was constructed in 1915–1916 on Camano Avenue near the south end of town. The high school occupied the second floor, and the lower grades met on the first floor. The first high school graduation was in May 1920, with one graduate, William McGinnis. The graduation exercises were held in the old Friends Community Church on First Street. (Courtesy of the SWHS.)

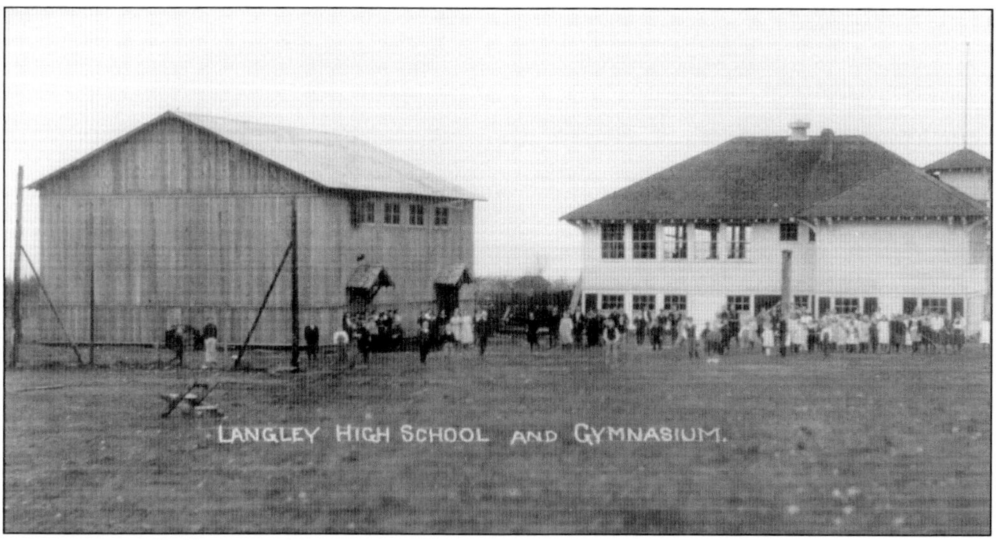

A gymnasium (left) was built behind the school in 1920. Exhibits were housed in the gymnasium when the Island County Fair moved up from the marina to the area due south of the school in 1922. The gymnasium burned down in 1943 when a group of soldiers who were studying radar and using the gymnasium in the evening let an oil stove overheat. (Courtesy of the SWHS.)

Four

All-Woman Town Administration *1920–1922*

Many of Langley's women were active in the Langley Civic Club, trying to clean up the town, but their patience waned at the slow pace with which Langley was rising to their standards of decorum. Among other things, they wanted the muddy streets improved and a curfew imposed on the hours the saloons were open.

Just months after the US Congress passed the 19th Amendment giving women the right to vote and sent it to the states for ratification, Langley elected an all-woman town council and a female mayor in 1919. (Washington State had granted suffrage in 1910.) Rumors have persisted that Langley was the first incorporated town in the United States to have an all-woman ruling body, but Kanab, Utah, had obtained that distinction nine years earlier.

On December 2, 1919, Langley elected Helen Coe, Grace English, Lillian Wylie, and Emma Monson to join two men serving unexpired terms, along with Mayor George Woodruff. At the January 13, 1920, council meeting the men resigned, Margaret McLeod was added to the council, and Helen Coe was sworn in as mayor. A few months later, Clara Brown joined them. This all-woman council faced a town without funds and with difficult problems. Still, they set to work. They limited gambling and punchboards, closed pool halls on Sundays, and looked into ways of improving the muddy streets.

Helen Coe resigned as mayor in March 1922 to establish the town's first library. She was instrumental in bringing the Camffermans to Langley, who established an art colony at the west edge of town. After Coe resigned, Margaret McLeod took over as mayor. McLeod, along with several other Langleyites, was aboard the *Calista* when a Japanese freighter struck it. All survived. Lillian Wylie, a self-educated nurse, set up a practice in her Edgecliff home, working with doctors to provide reliable local medical services. Well-educated and musical, Emma Monson opened her home up as a cultural oasis. Both Grace English and her husband, Henry, were leaders in Langley's civic affairs. Langley has had female mayors and council members since this time but no other administration composed solely of women.

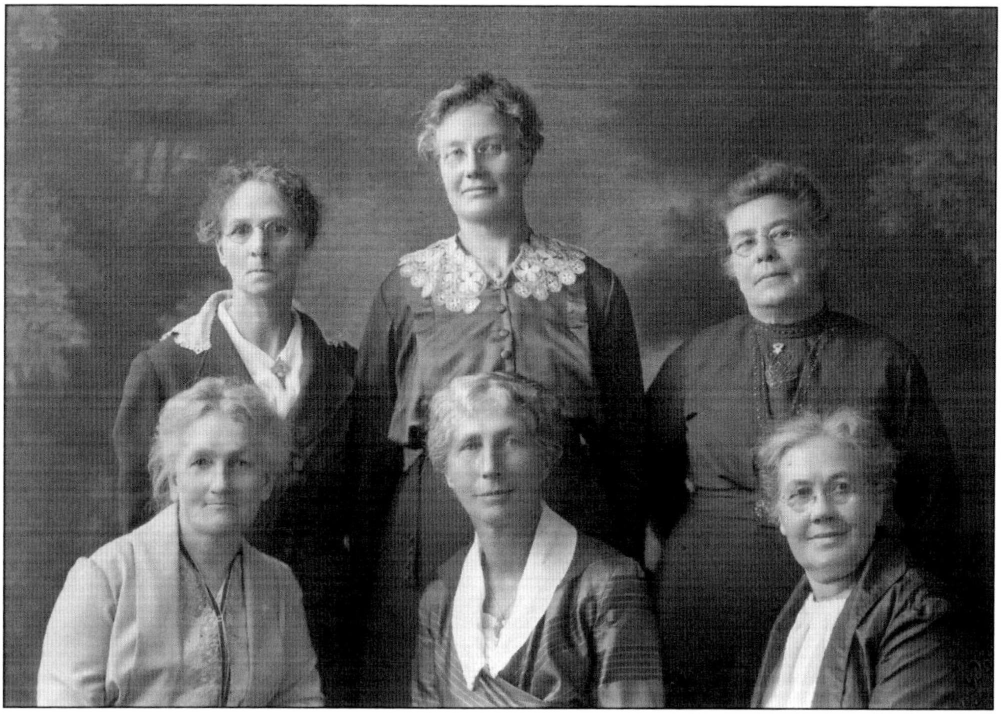

A female mayor and three female councilors were elected in December 1919. After swearing in the new councilwomen in January 1920, the sitting mayor and remaining male councilman resigned. Two additional women were appointed, leaving Langley in the hands of an all-woman administration. Shown here are, from left to right, (first row) Grace English, Helen Coe (mayor), and Emma Monson; (second row) Clara Brown, Lillian Wylie, and Margaret McLeod. (Courtesy of Karen Pauley.)

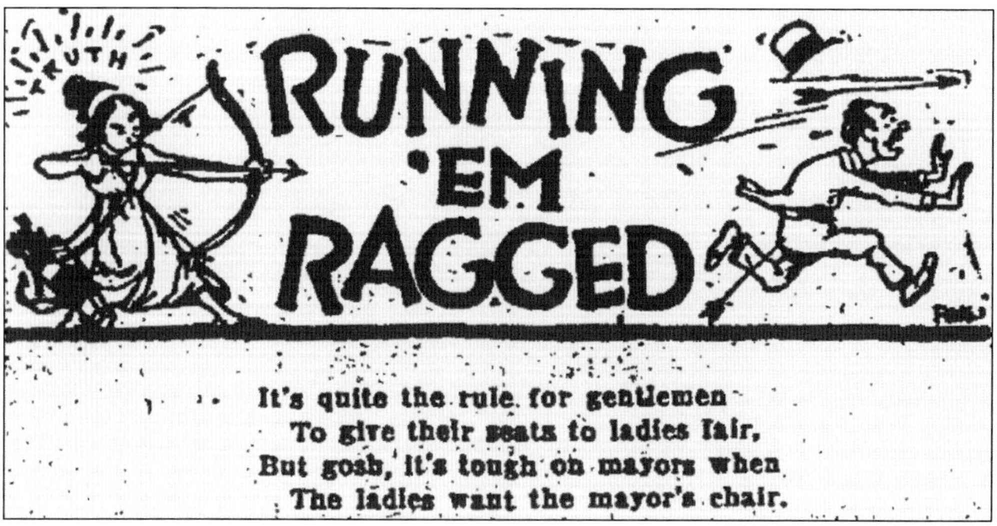

This cartoon from the Langley newspaper was pasted into the town council minutes. Diana as "Truth" is shooting arrows at perhaps a fleeing mayor. When the women began enforcing the town ordinances, the result was a rapid turnover of town marshals, who were called on to collect fines and impound stray animals roaming the streets. (Courtesy of the City of Langley.)

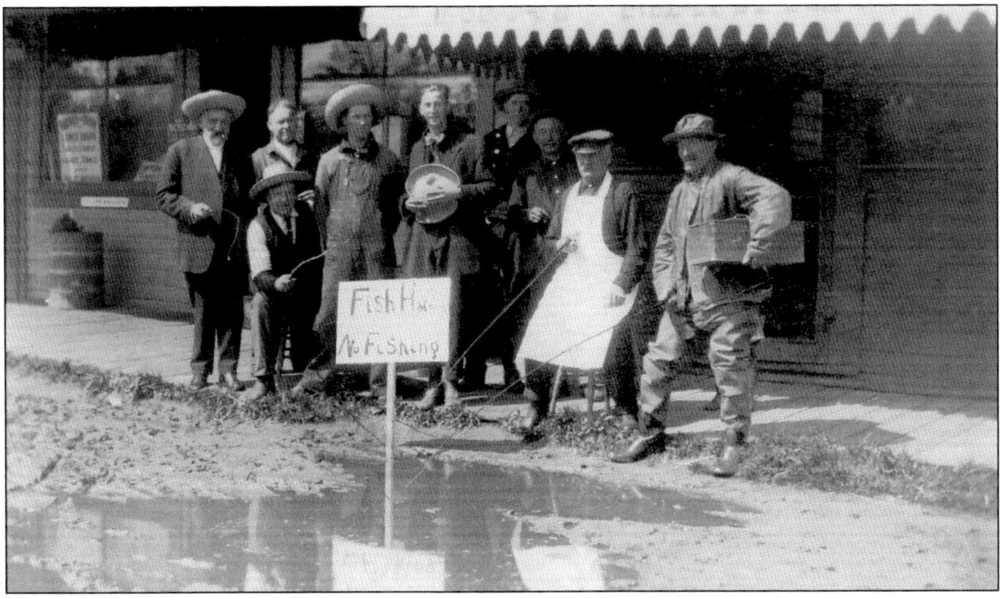

Following election of the all-woman town administration in 1920, some of the male citizens posed for this satirical photograph in front of the meat market on First Street. The men are, from left to right, Joseph Hess, a Mr. Rhodie, Walter Hunziker Sr., Axel Anderson, Fredrick Jensen, two unidentified men, Henry Weber, and Anton Anderson (blacksmith). The sign says, "Fish Hatchery. No Fishing." (Courtesy of the SWHS.)

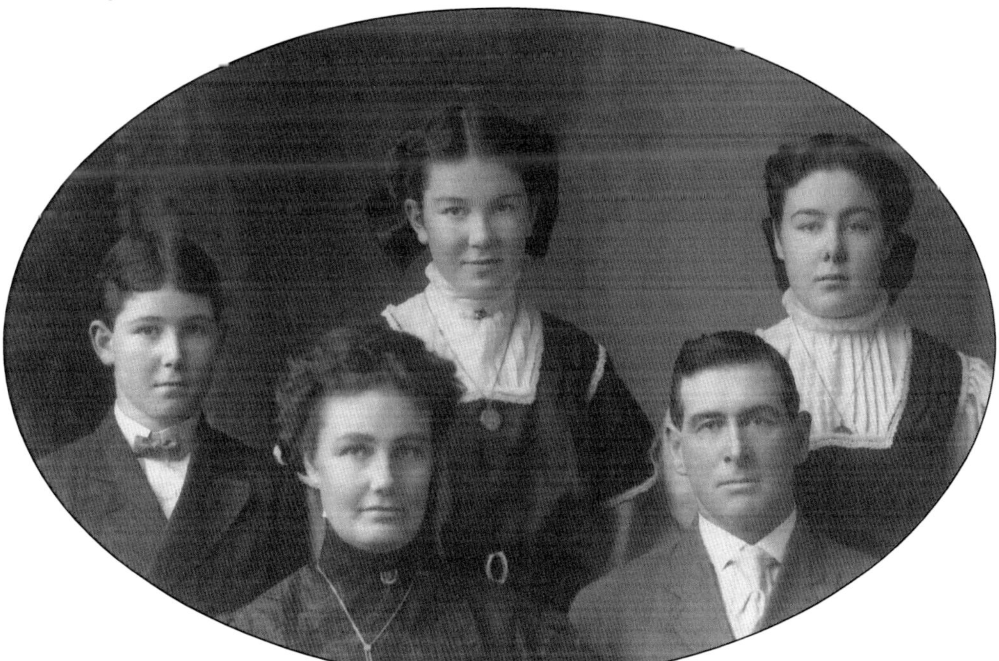

The Wylie family around 1910 is, from left to right, Chester, Lillian, Ruby, Francis, and Myrtle. Lillian Wylie served in the all-woman administration despite personal hardship. The Wylies came to Langley from Everett in 1913. Francis, a real estate agent, returned to Everett, leaving Lillian to support her children. They later divorced. (Courtesy of Connie and Seth Mackie.)

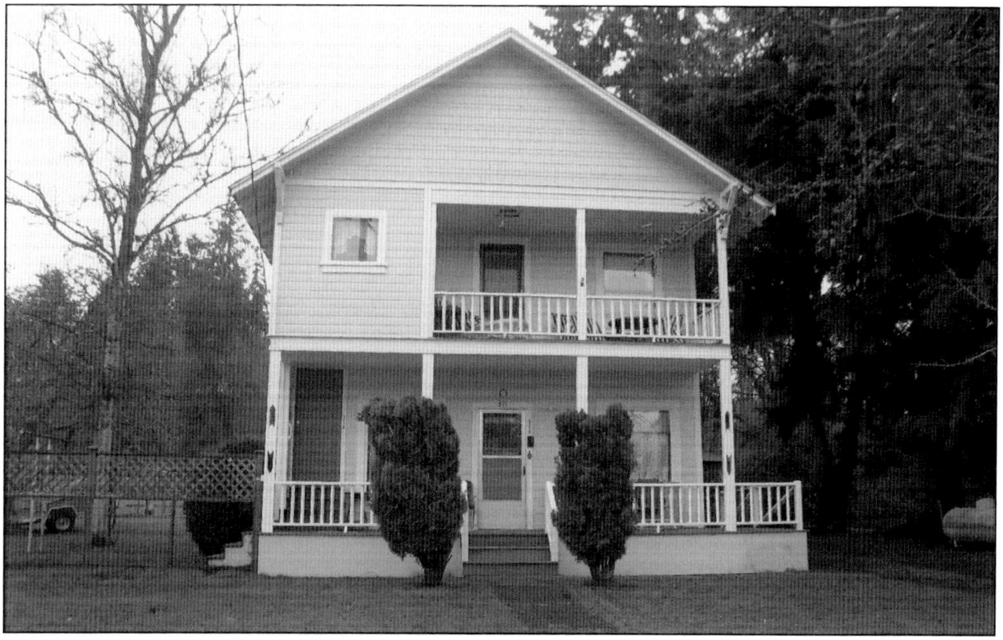

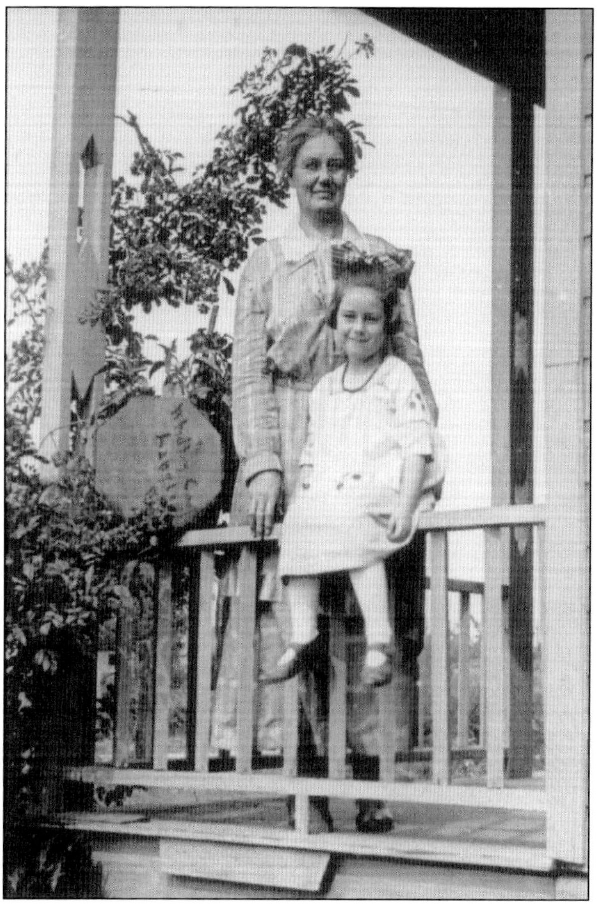

This photograph shows the Wylie house on Edgecliff Drive in 2010. Lillian's husband obtained the unfinished house in 1910. He completed construction, and the family occupied it in 1913. Lillian took a variety of jobs to make ends meet after Francis left her. Impounded animals were kept in her barn. A caring person, she served as a midwife, and her home became a hospital and birthing house. (Courtesy of Robert Waterman.)

Lillian and her granddaughter Enid are shown on the front porch of the Wylie home. Enid's mother, Ruby Wylie, married George McGinnis from across the street. They left the island but returned when Ruby became ill and lived on Decker Avenue. When Ruby began labor with her son, George tied a dishtowel to the clothesline (as a signal) and Lillian went to help with the delivery. (Courtesy of Connie and Seth Mackie.)

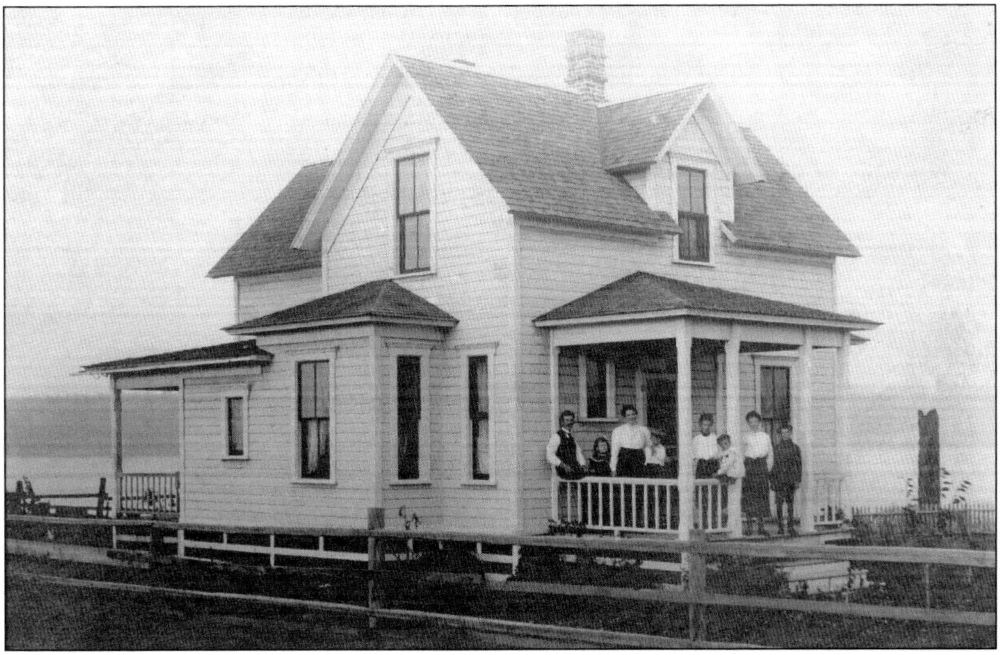

Another councilwoman, Emma Monson, came to Langley about 1903 with her husband, Leander, and their six living children. They built this two-story home at the northeast corner of Third Street and Park Avenue. They are, from left to right, Leander, Florence, Emma, Carl, Esther, Arthur, Elvira, and Ernest. Leander owned most of the land between Second and Third Streets between Park and Anthes Avenues. (Courtesy of Karen Pauley.)

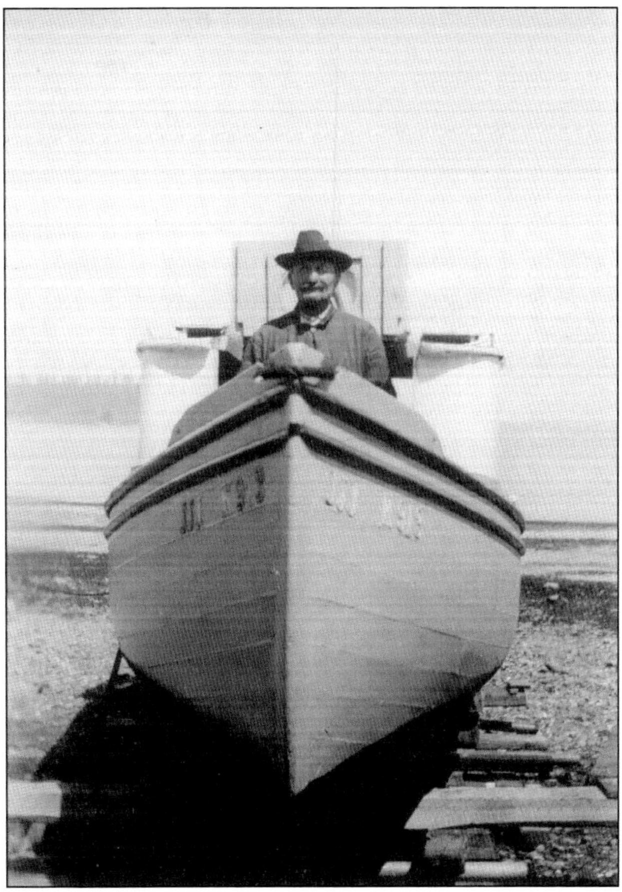

Anton Anderson, a blacksmith, seen here in his boat in 1921, came to Langley in 1904 with his wife, Josephine, and their children, Alma and Otto. He rented a building at Third Street and Anthes Avenue from Leander Monson for his shop. He soon built a blacksmith shop on First Street and moved his family into the old Anthes bunkhouse on Second Street. (Courtesy of the SWHS.)

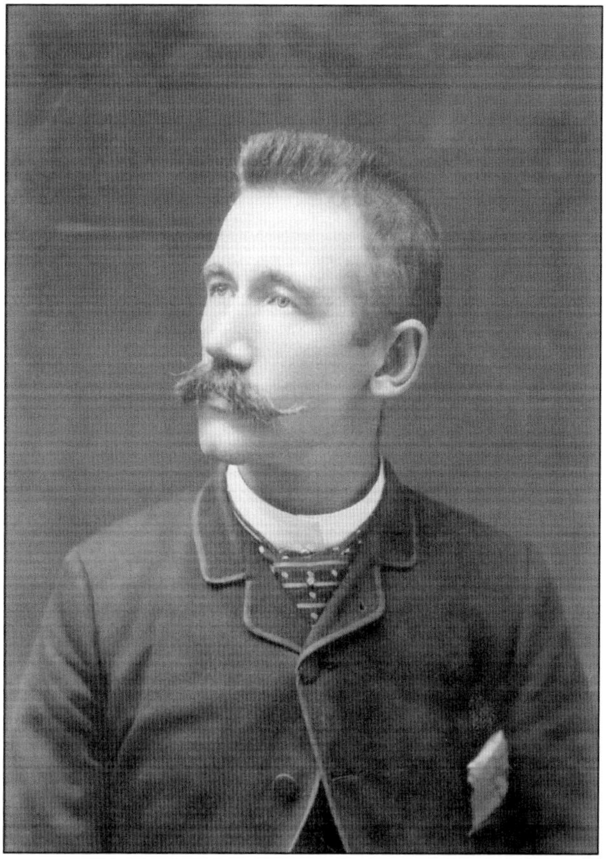

When Leander Monson drank, his family would occasionally leave the house. On December 16, 1906, thinking Anton Anderson had kidnapped his family, he fired a shot into the bunkhouse, scaring Josephine Anderson and the children. Monson was charged with attempted murder and sent to the county jail to await trial. Two years later, on March 18, 1908, Leander committed suicide by slitting his throat in his home. (Courtesy of Karen Pauley.)

Emma Monson suffered another loss when her oldest son, Ernest (right), accidentally shot himself in the thigh while getting out of a boat on February 8, 1910. He was brought to the Howard Hotel, then transferred to the Everett hospital. He initially fared well but developed gangrene and died a week later with his mother and sisters in attendance. Pictured at left is Arthur Monson. (Courtesy of Karen Pauley.)

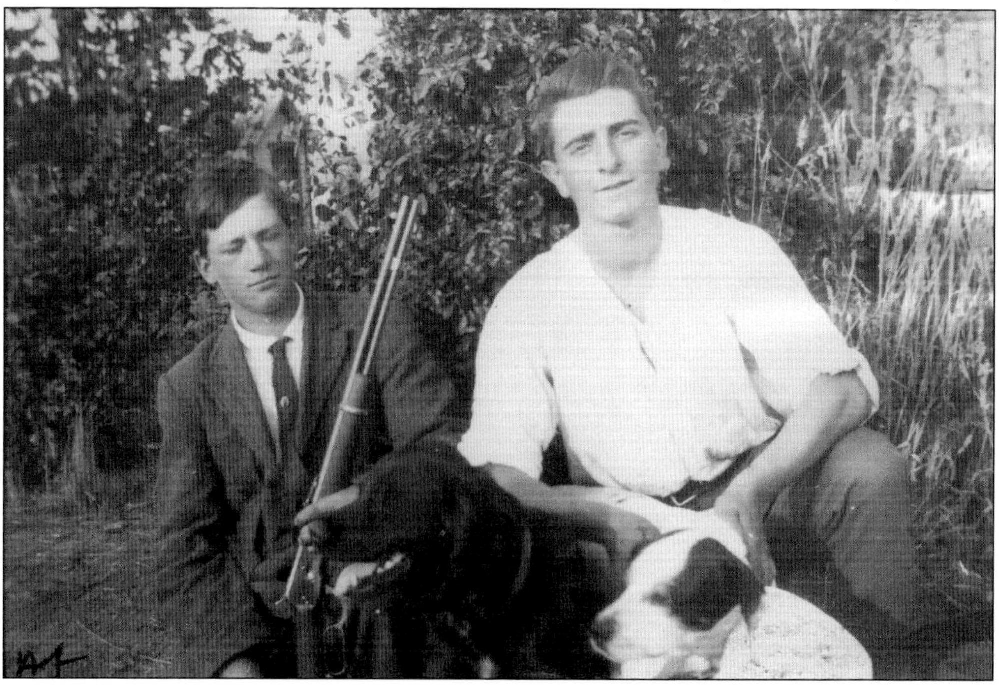

Esther Monson worked as a telephone operator for several years and was appointed the town clerk in 1920, joining her mother in the female town administration. Her sister Elvira was also a telephone operator and served as clerk of the first town council from 1914 to 1916. Elvira later served as Island County auditor for 24 years. (Courtesy of Karen Pauley.)

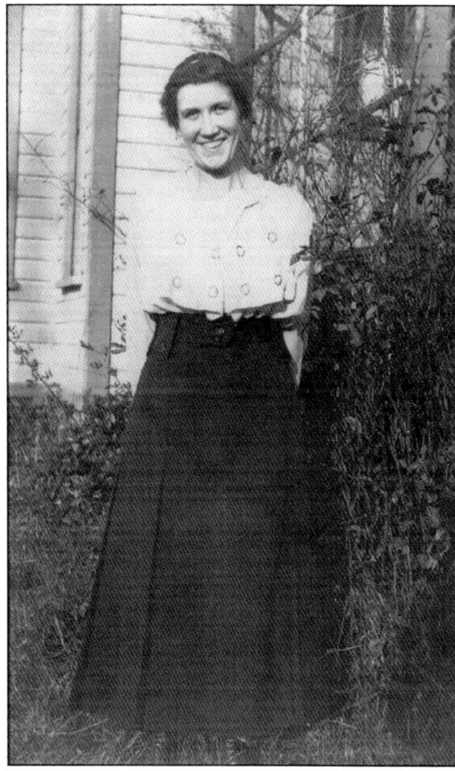

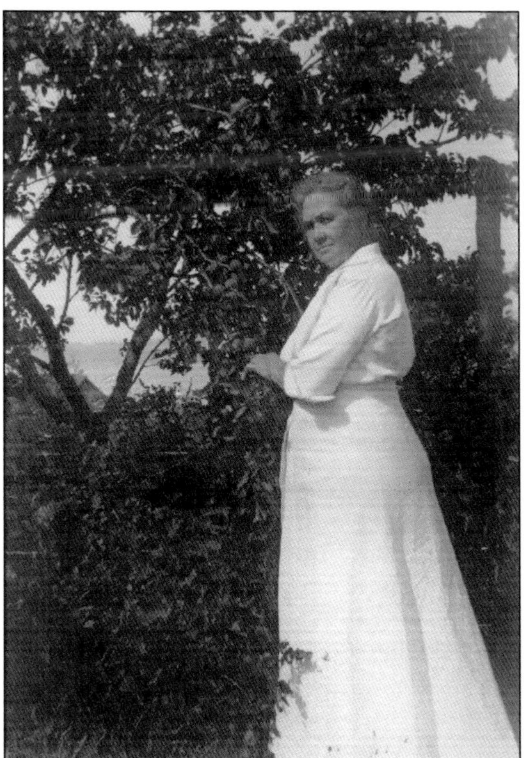

In spite of the loss of her husband and son, Emma Monson continued to play an active role in the Langley community. She served one year on the town council and was replaced by Mary Kohlwes. Emma took in boarders and helped at the Howard Hotel. She died in 1934 and was buried in the Langley Woodmen Cemetery. (Courtesy of Karen Pauley.)

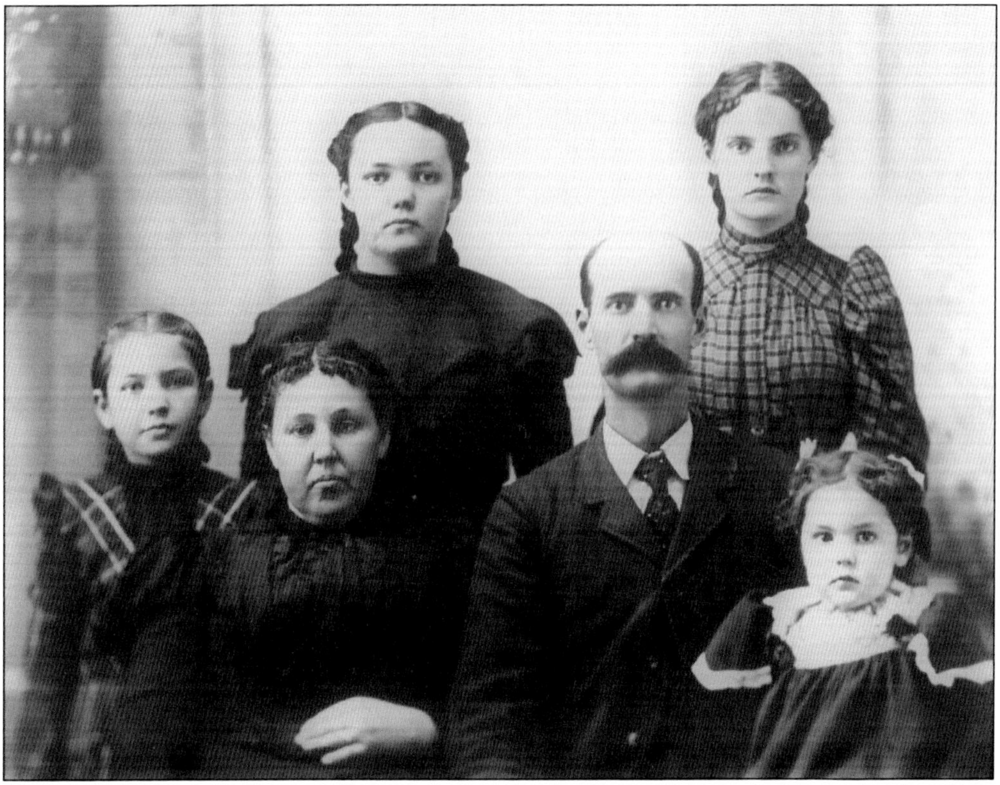

Councilwoman Margaret McLeod was the second wife of Angus McLeod. Angus was the oldest of the four McLeod brothers who came to Langley from Nebraska. The McLeod family is, from left to right, Jessie, Minnie, Edith, Angus, Stella, and Gertrude. Minnie died shortly after arriving in 1908 and was the first woman buried in the Langley Cemetery. Angus married Margaret, a widow, in 1909. (Courtesy of the SWHS.)

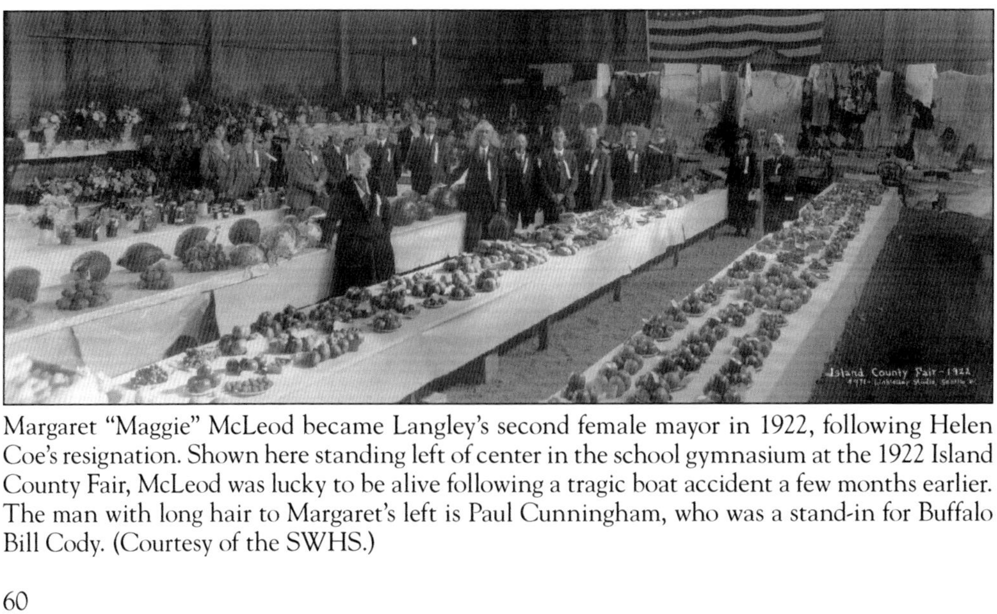

Margaret "Maggie" McLeod became Langley's second female mayor in 1922, following Helen Coe's resignation. Shown here standing left of center in the school gymnasium at the 1922 Island County Fair, McLeod was lucky to be alive following a tragic boat accident a few months earlier. The man with long hair to Margaret's left is Paul Cunningham, who was a stand-in for Buffalo Bill Cody. (Courtesy of the SWHS.)

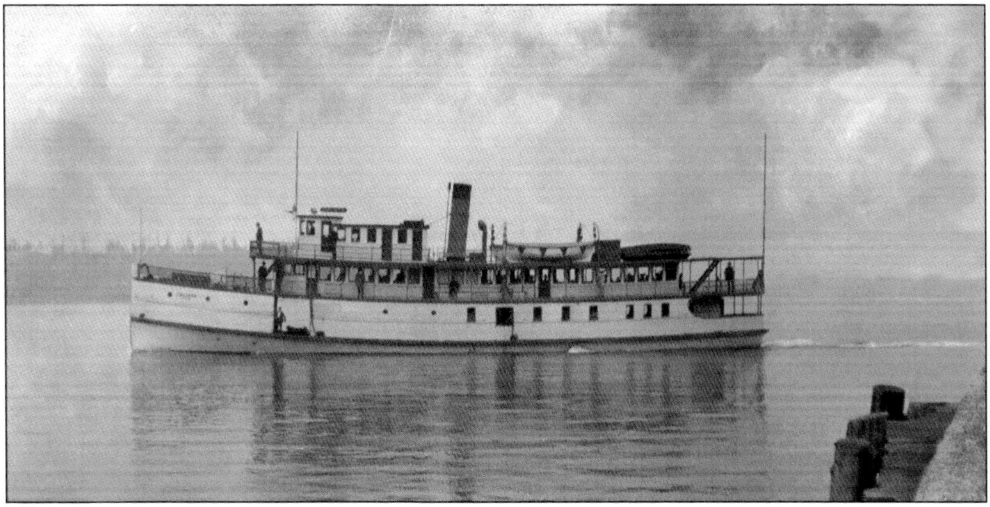

Margaret McLeod, her niece Ruth, and nephew David were among those who boarded the *Calista* on the morning of July 27, 1922, on their way to Seattle. Capt. Bartlett Lovejoy was in command as they left the Langley wharf. After transferring passengers bound for Everett to the smaller *Clatawa*, the *Calista* stopped at Clinton and Glendale before starting the two-hour run to Seattle. (Courtesy of Karen Pauley.)

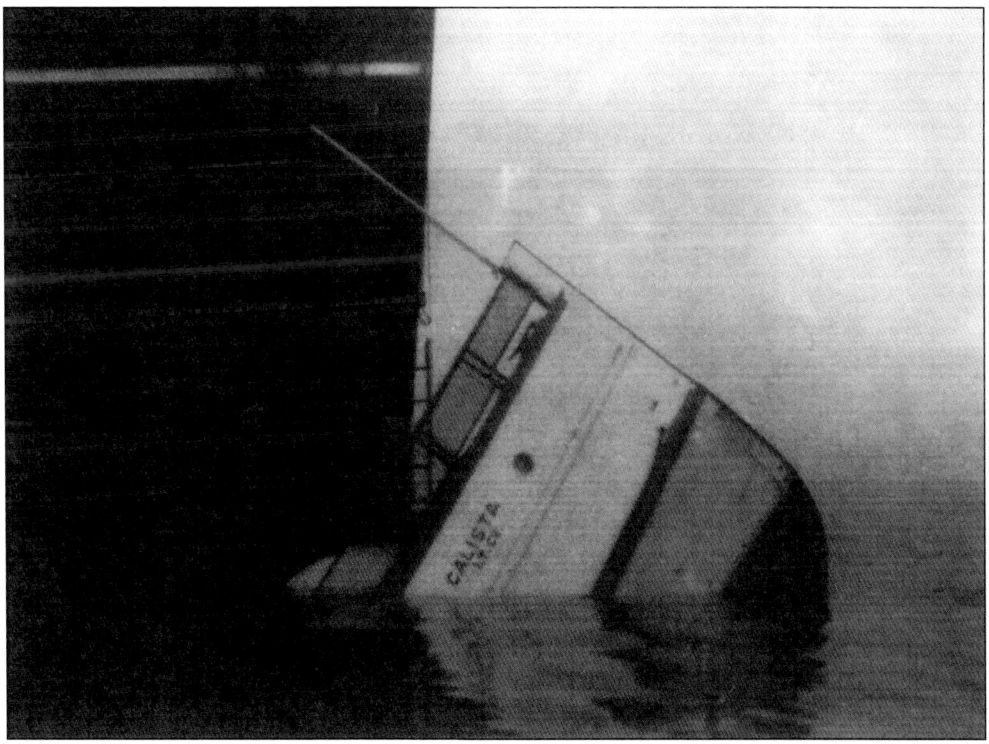

Encountering dense fog as the ship neared Elliot Bay, Capt. Bartlett Lovejoy stopped the engine to listen for approaching traffic. Suddenly, the bow of the freighter *Hawaii Maru* appeared and struck the *Calista* amidships. It sank in 28 minutes, but all aboard were rescued. Newly appointed mayor McLeod was one of the last to leave the sinking ship and was taken to Seattle aboard a tug. (Courtesy of the PSMHS.)

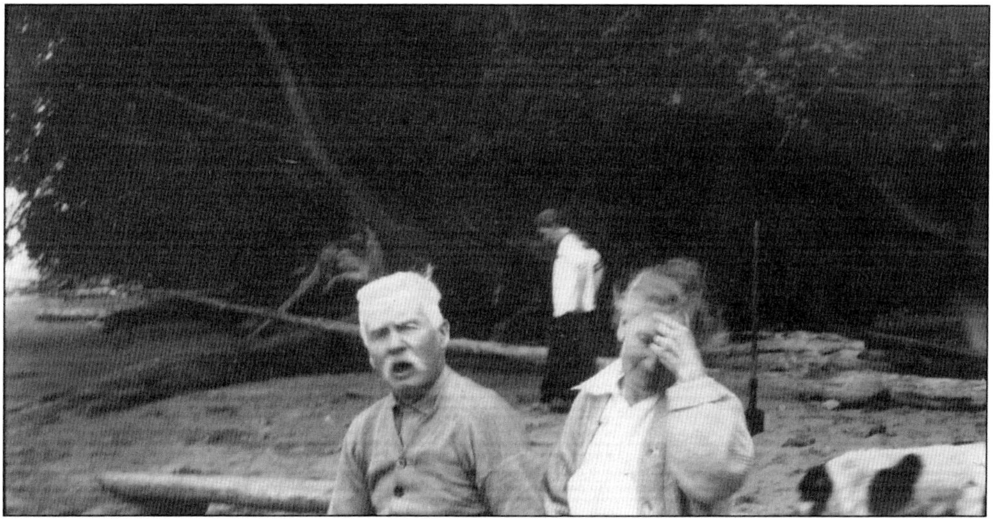

Councilwoman Grace English (right) did not suffer great hardship but did have to deal with her husband's pranks. Henry English (left) became Langley's second mayor when Frank Furman resigned in 1915 to become postmaster. Henry would release Grace's pet pig as she walked to a council meeting. It ran after her and sat outside and squealed during the meeting. (Courtesy of Helen Hulbert.)

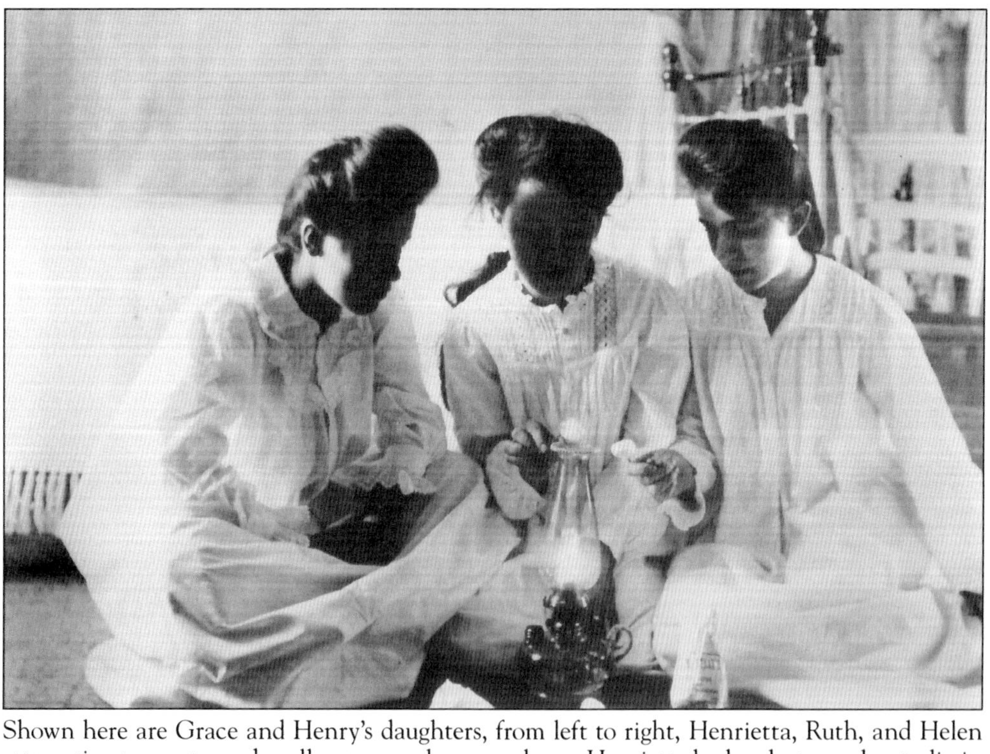

Shown here are Grace and Henry's daughters, from left to right, Henrietta, Ruth, and Helen attempting to roast marshmallows over a kerosene lamp. Henrietta had a photography studio in Langley and specialized in portraits and school graduation pictures. Ruth helped her sister and worked for the telephone company before going to Alaska in 1916 and marrying Leon Hartley, whose parents, Kirk and Minnie, lived on Sixth Street. (Courtesy of Helen Hulbert.)

Five

HELEN COE AND THE CAMFFERMANS *1915–1960*

Helen Coe, a young, single, and wealthy woman, arrived prior to 1900. She purchased land with a beautiful water view located across the ravine west of town. Once established in town, she taught Sunday school and was active in the Women's Civic Club. Coe enjoyed the theater arts and participated in a production of Shakespeare's *As You Like It* in the woods on her property. She attracted many visitors to the town, most significantly her niece Margaret Gove. In 1915, Margaret married a young artist, Peter Camfferman, whom she had met at the Minneapolis School of Fine Arts. Peter and Margaret studied art in Paris and were among the earliest modernist painters in the Northwest. They both taught painting and became active members of Seattle's "Group of Twelve," which included Mark Tobey, Kenneth Callahan, and Morris Graves. Both Camffermans were highly regarded within the regional art community. Margaret had a solo show of her paintings at the Seattle Art Museum and exhibited widely, including shows in New York and San Francisco.

The pair purchased land from Margaret's aunt Helen and built a large home and an extensive garden. They decided to establish an art colony, and Peter built several small cottages nestled in the park-like setting of their property to house visiting artists. Inspired by a glen of bracken fern, they named their compound Brackenwood. Artists came from the mainland to attend classes and paint in the fresh air at this idyllic spot. Margaret Camfferman's sister, Helen Gove, also frequently visited Brackenwood. Helen, who often traveled to teach in India, settled permanently into one of the cottages when she retired.

The artist colony survived the Depression of 1929 and remained active until around 1940, when Peter's health began to fail. After he died in 1957, Margaret became a recluse. However, the Camffermans' legacy in Langley remains manifest in the many artists who live here and the numerous galleries that now grace the town.

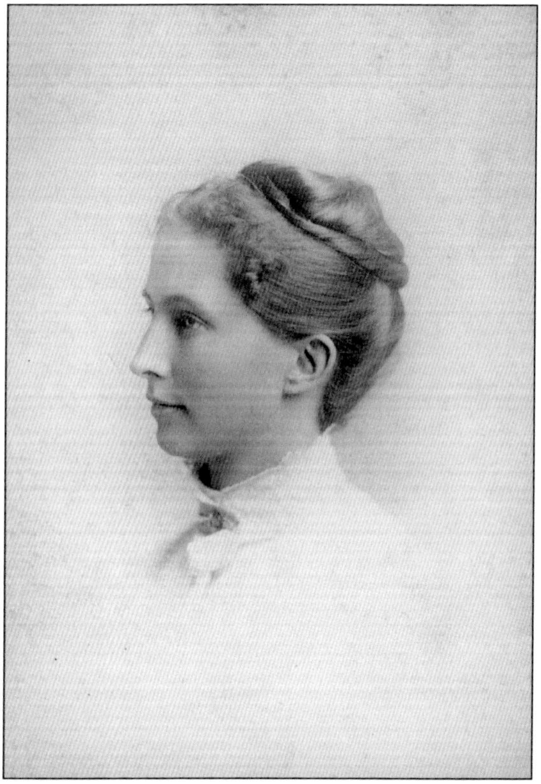

Helen Burwell Coe, the first female mayor of Langley, was born in 1858 in Winnebago, Minnesota, and attended the State Normal School in Oswego, New York. She inherited considerable money and never married. She visited Whidbey Island with family members in 1896–1897 and liked the area around Langley. She bought 10 acres with a small house on the bluff overlooking Saratoga Passage west of Saratoga Creek. (Courtesy of Maureen Duryee.)

Helen Coe was an educated and refined person. She loved children and wrote a small children's book, *Nature Tales*. She also taught Sunday school at her home for several years. Helen was very interested in improving the town. She joined the Ladies' Civic Improvement Club, formed in 1916, and worked toward creation of a public library. (Courtesy of Maureen Duryee.)

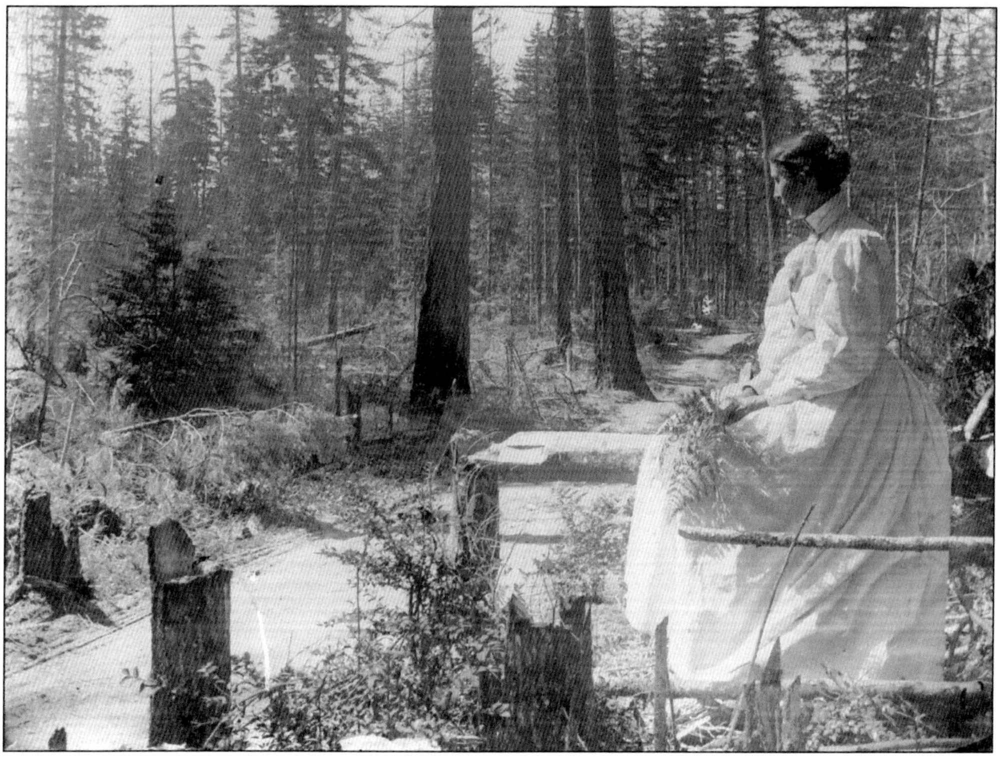

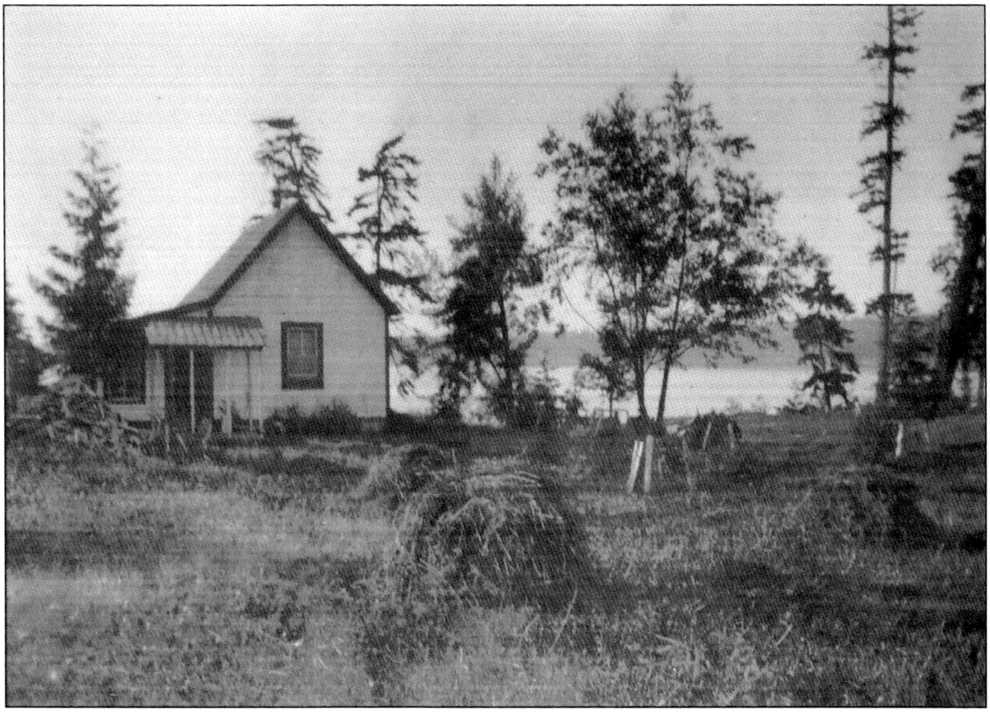

This is Helen Coe's first house, located on the bluff overlooking Saratoga Passage. With the help of her uncle, Archibald Gove, a Tacoma architect, Coe enlarged the house in stages over the next 20 years, adding a fireplace and chimney, a porch on the north side, and a sunny room on the southeast corner. (Courtesy of Maureen Duryee.)

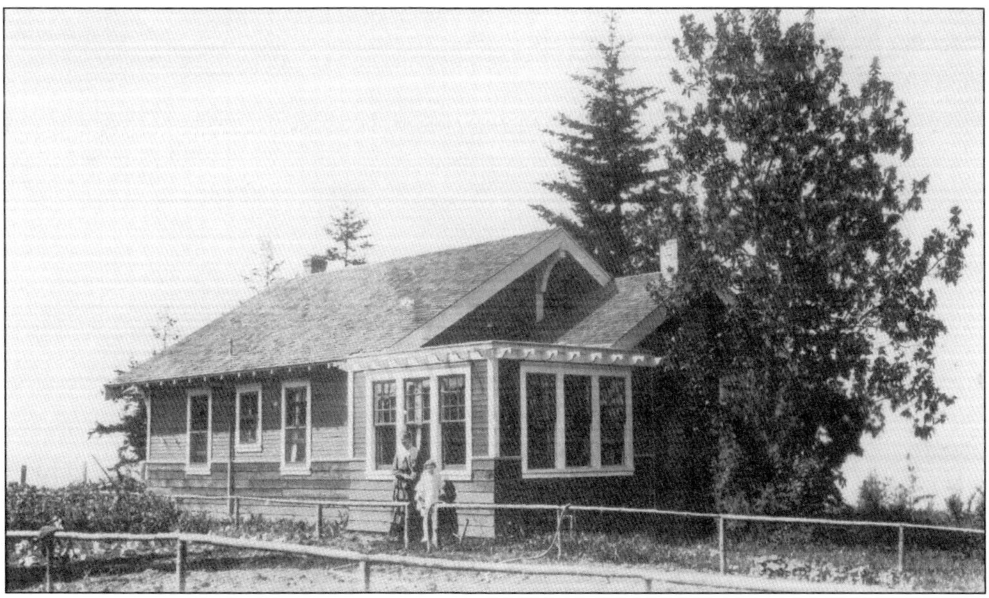

Helen Coe's house, shown here in 1916, was remembered by visitors to be an elegant place, with fine china and tablecloths used at tea and dinner parties alike. Several friends and family members stayed with her at various times, including her cousin, Alice Rollitt Coe, a poet who published a book of poems titled *Lyrics of Fir and Foam* in 1908. (Courtesy of Maureen Duryee.)

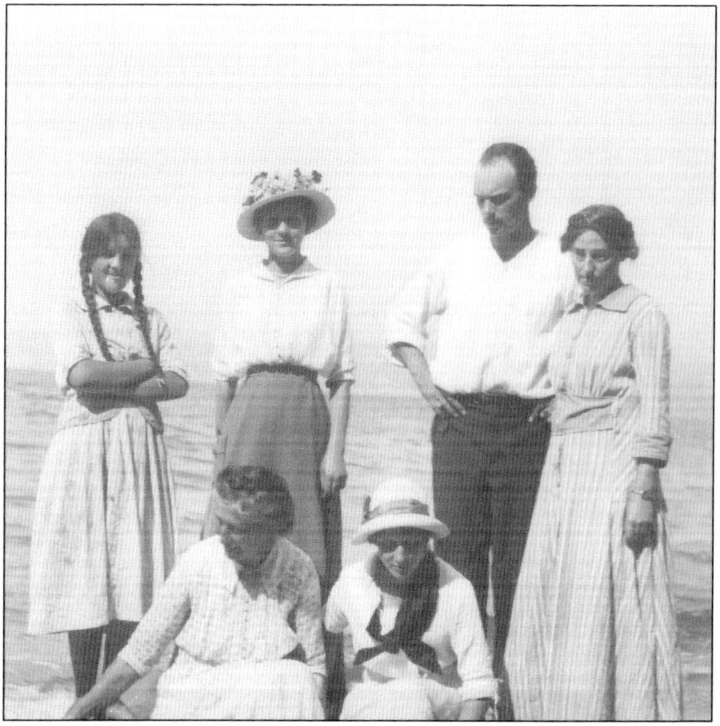

In 1915, Helen Coe's niece, Margaret Gove (right), married a young artist from the Netherlands, Peter Camfferman. The newlyweds visited Helen Coe in Langley and called the site Brackenwood. Seen here on the beach below Helen Coe's house are, from left to right, (seated) Helen Coe and Cora Anthes; (standing) Katchen Anthes, Mabel Anthes, Peter Camfferman, and Margaret Camfferman. (Courtesy of Maureen Duryee.)

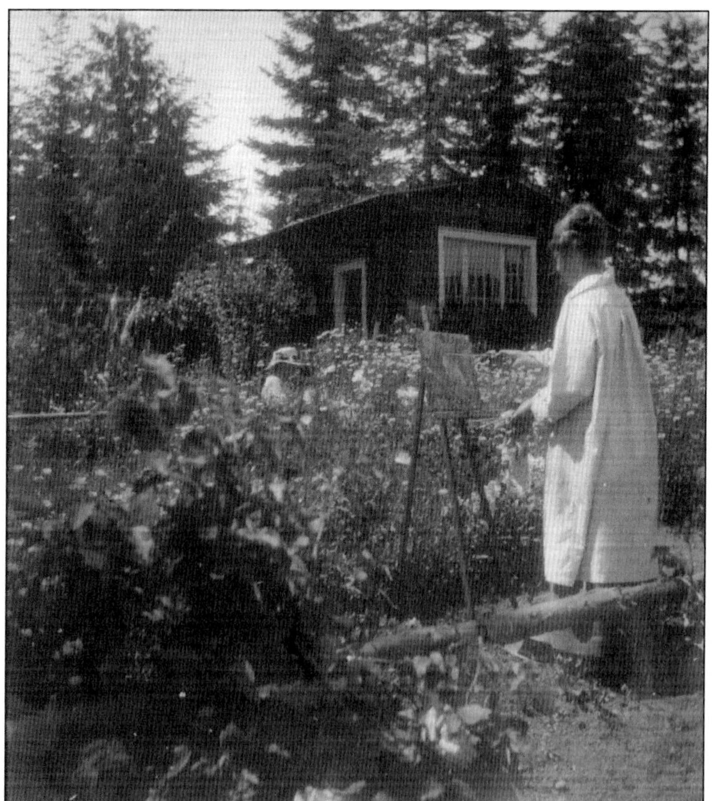

Margaret Camfferman is painting in front of the small cottage Peter built in 1915 a short distance from Helen Coe's house. He and Margaret stayed there when they visited. Margaret and Peter met at the art school in Minneapolis, Minnesota. She was a pianist as well as an artist. He played the violin. (Courtesy of Maureen Duryee.)

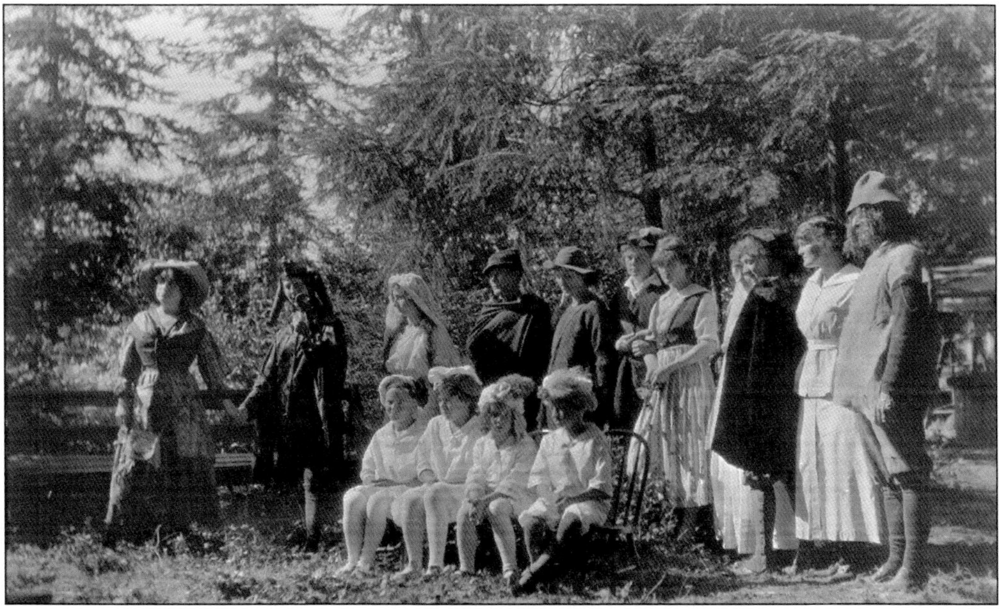

Here are cast members of *As You Like It*. The play was a function of the Yggdrasil Club organized by Jeanett Peck. Actors included Edith McKenzie as Rosalind, Ethel Manly as Orlando, Ruth English as Celia, Frederick Carrington as the melancholy Jacques, Gertrude Carrington as Audrey, and Helen Coe (second from left) as Touchstone. (Courtesy of Maureen Duryee.)

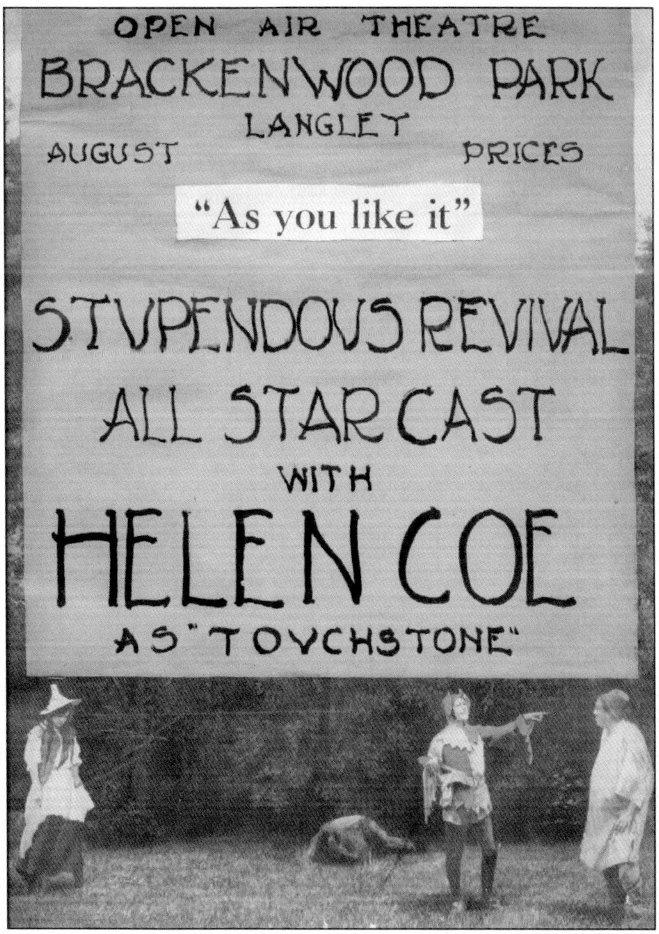

This poster promoted the Shakespeare play presented at Brackenwood in July 1916. Peter Camfferman attended to the lighting. A globe was attached to the inside of a five-gallon oilcan, which made a good reflector on the stage. The audience sat on church pews in the darkness. (Courtesy of Maureen Duryee.)

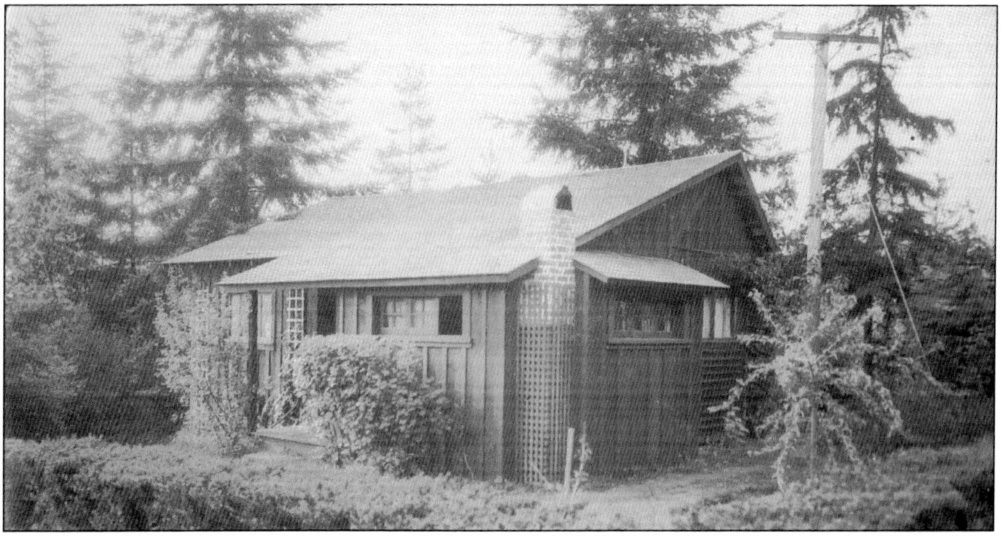

The Camffermans decided to make Whidbey Island their permanent home. Peter bought a portion of Helen Coe's property in 1917 and began constructing a home there in 1918. He steadily added to the original house, shown here in 1923, and later added a second story. Peter did most of the construction himself and also planted fruit trees, flowering bushes, and a garden. (Courtesy of Maureen Duryee.)

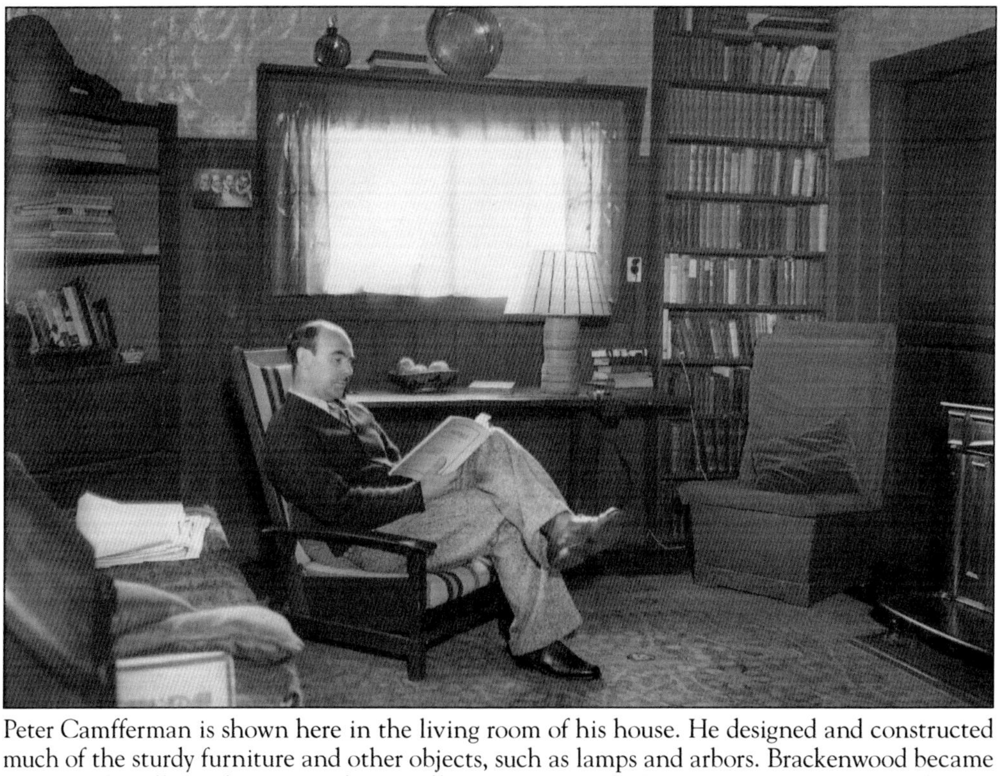

Peter Camfferman is shown here in the living room of his house. He designed and constructed much of the sturdy furniture and other objects, such as lamps and arbors. Brackenwood became an oasis of intellectual activity. The Camffermans participated in community affairs in addition to painting, and Peter painted backdrops for several local theatrical productions. (Courtesy of Maureen Duryee.)

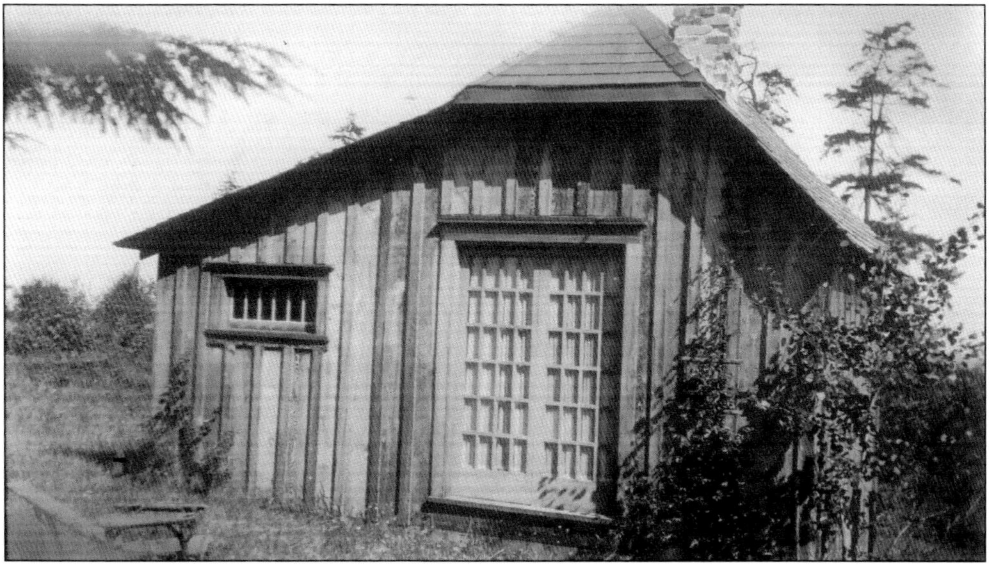

In addition to working on their house, Peter Camfferman also built several small cottages on the grounds to be used by students attending summer art classes. These had a stove for heat and room for a bed. A larger studio with windows facing north was built near the bluff to house larger groups and events. (Courtesy of Maureen Duryee.)

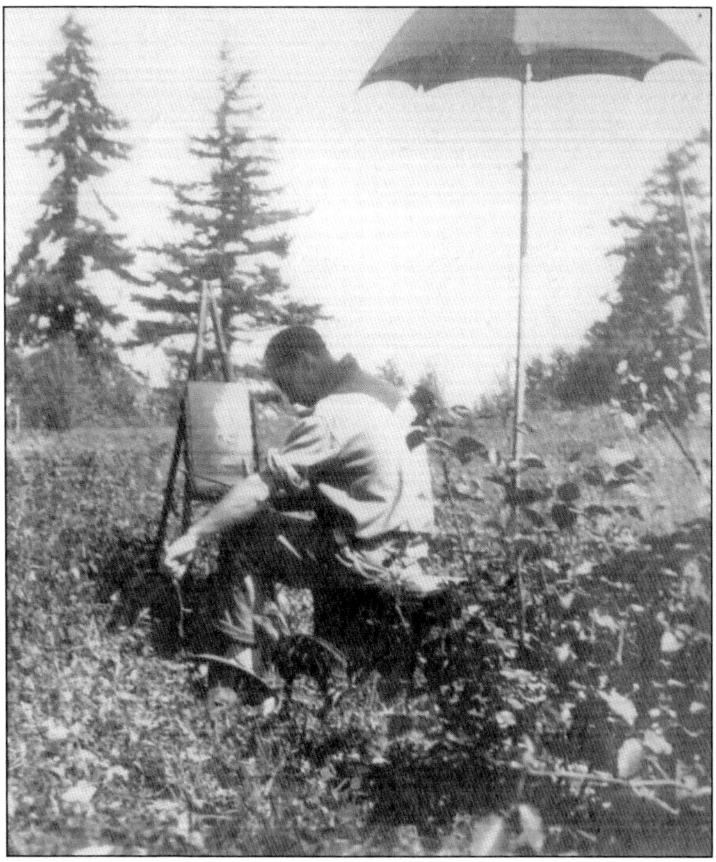

Peter Camfferman is shown here painting at Brackenwood. Peter and Margaret taught art in local schools as well as summer classes at Brackenwood. Except for a stint in New York in 1925–1926, the Camffermans lived the remainder of their lives at Brackenwood, with occasional trips to the East Coast, Mexico, and Europe, sometimes accompanied by Helen Coe. (Courtesy of Maureen Duryee.)

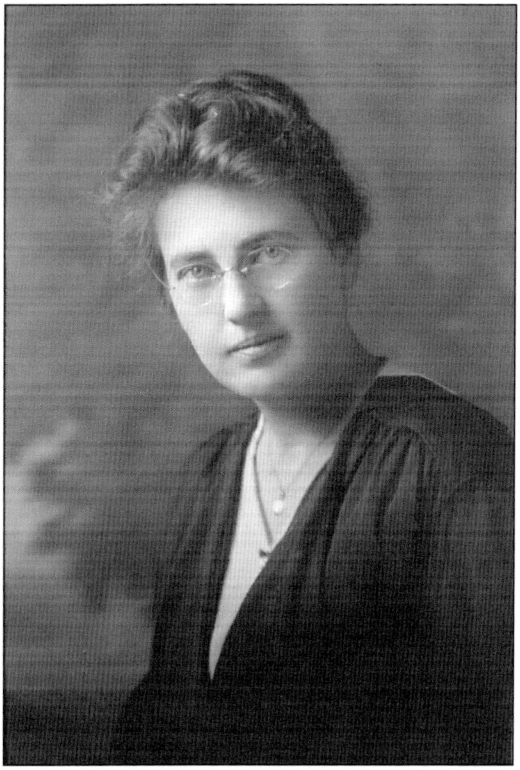

Margaret Camfferman's sister, Helen Gove, was a graduate of the University of Minnesota and taught for many years at the Isabella Thoburn College for Women in Lucknow, India. She was a frequent visitor to the Brackenwood compound. She eventually settled into the original summer cottage built by Peter when she retired and lived there until her death in 1956. (Courtesy of Maureen Duryee.)

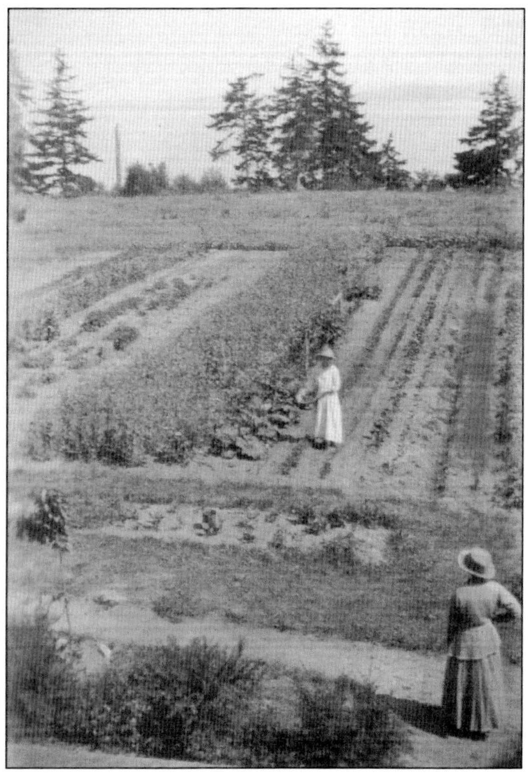

A large garden was created on the land between the houses at Brackenwood, as shown in this photograph taken from the roof of the original cottage on June 5, 1919. The Camffermans and art students alike spent many hours painting the flowers here. Brackenwood became an oasis of intellectual life; dinner parties and outdoor picnics for friends and visitors were remembered fondly years later. (Courtesy of Maureen Duryee.)

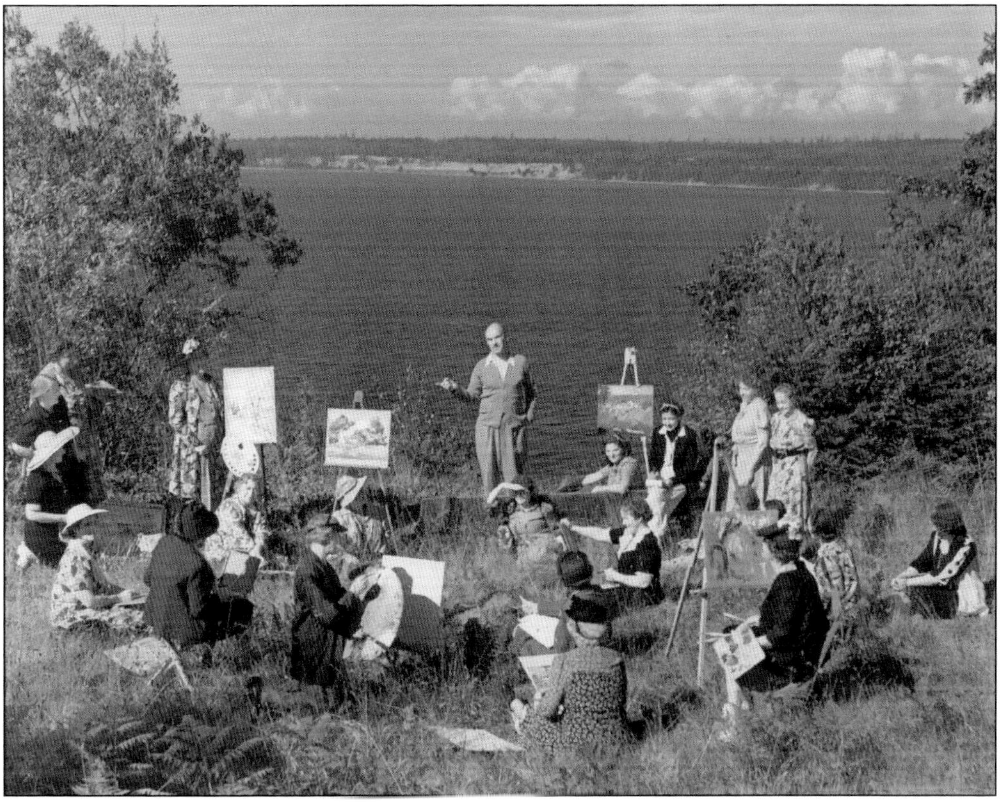

Peter Camfferman (center) and Margaret (standing in a white dress to Peter's left) are leading a class for the Women Painters of Washington in front of the main studio at Brackenwood in 1941. The Camffermans were some of the earliest modernist painters in the Northwest and were part of Seattle's "Group of Twelve," which included Mark Tobey, Kenneth Callahan, Viola Patterson, and Morris Graves. (Courtesy of Maureen Duryee.)

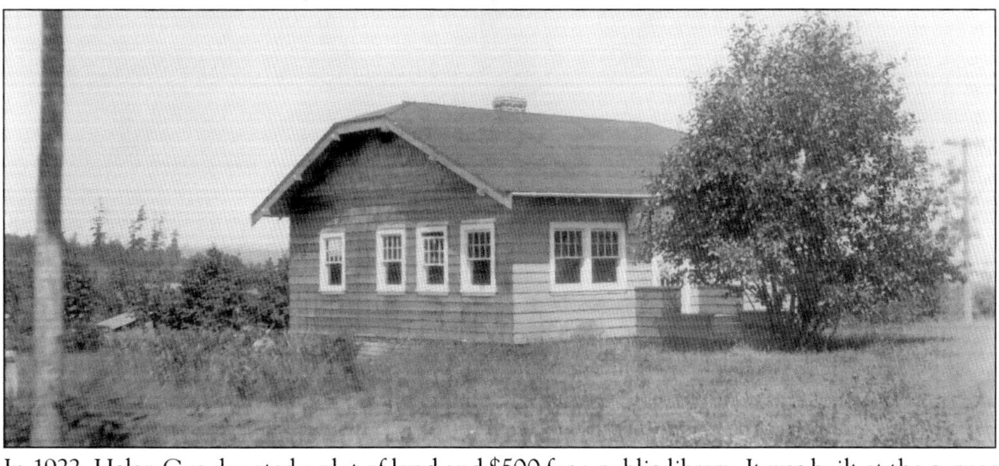

In 1922, Helen Coe donated a plot of land and $500 for a public library. It was built at the corner of First and Second Streets and based on a set of purchased plans. The library was dedicated in 1923 to the young men who served in "the war." Elected mayor in 1919 and reelected in 1920, Helen resigned in 1922 to become Langley's first librarian. She died in 1940. (Courtesy of the SWHS.)

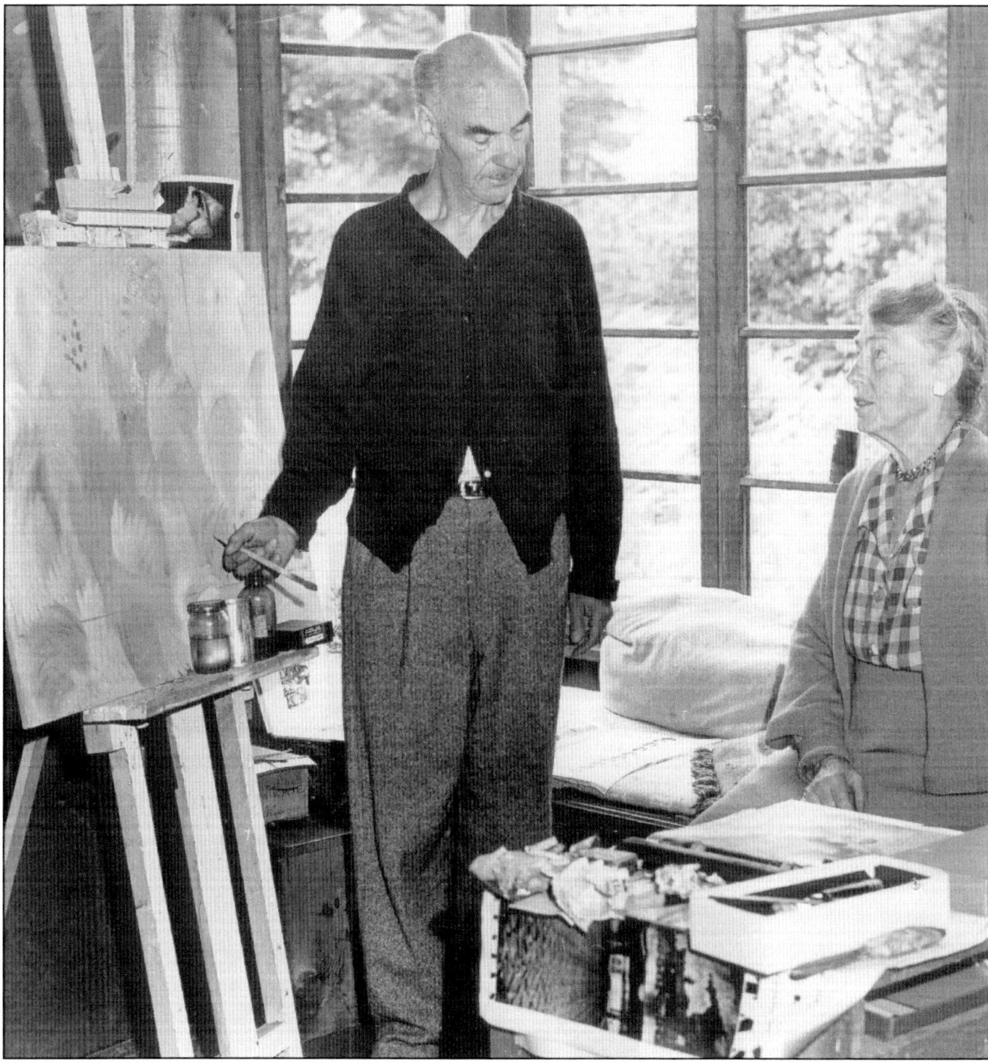

This shows Peter and Margaret Camfferman in the main studio in their later years. The Brackenwood art colony flourished from the 1920s until 1957, when Peter died. Margaret continued living in the house until her death in 1964. Although their work received wide acclaim and influenced a generation of young artists, they are relatively unknown by present-day curators. (Courtesy of Maureen Duryee.)

Six

A Commercial Hub
1920–1930

In Langley, as in the rest of the country, the 1920s began with businesses growing and ended with an economic slowdown. In 1922, Joseph Primavera purchased a building on First Street and established a leather goods store. He named it the Star Store, after a famous brand of shoes. Following the fashion of the day, the Star Store sported a large brick facade, giving the impression of a much larger establishment. Also about that time, a new bank building replaced the old wooden one, and Ernest Noble Sr. was soon hired to manage the newly formed bank. Further, in 1922, the Island County Fair moved to the present-day fairgrounds just south of the high school, and movies began to be shown at the Olympic Club.

Norman and Hazel Clyde arrived from Texas in 1927 to console his father, William, after the death of William's wife and sister. William was teaching eighth grade in the Langley schools. Norman and his wife stayed on and built a small garage in 1928. Norman coached the town's first high school football team and eventually became town marshal.

Trucks began replacing horses and oxen for transporting downed timber, and cars were becoming a popular form of personal transportation. Following this trend, the Standard Oil Company purchased property near the wharf and constructed storage tanks that replaced the dance pavilion. Although a car ferry ran from Clinton to Everett beginning in 1919, it wasn't until 1923 that Langley became part of that run with the building of the *Whidby II*. However, the euphoria was short-lived when the ferries gave up the Langley stop six years later due to changes of ferry ownership. A group of local businesspeople formed the Langley Dock Company and maintained the wharf for passenger and freight traffic, but the die was cast. With no car ferry service, the town now found itself off the main road.

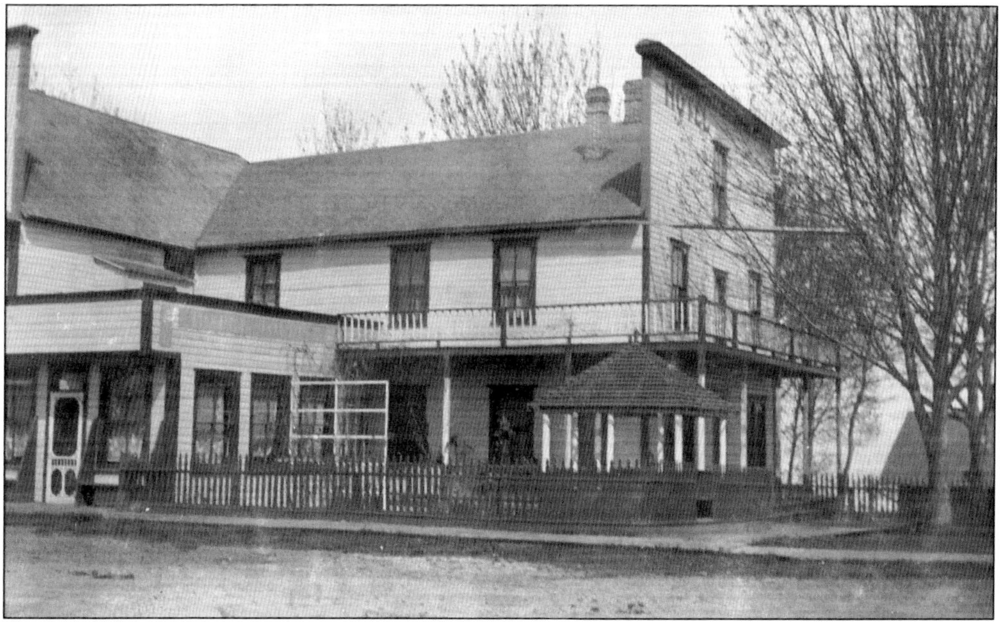

The hotel on First Street burned down on April 24, 1921. The fire started in a chimney at the back of the Pioneer Store. Bernice Hartley, Nellie Harmon, and Esther Anderson waded into the water and passed buckets to a line onshore. The kitchen boiler exploded, but no one was injured. The bank and telephone office across the street were saved by residents pouring water on the roofs. The windows of the Mortenson house across First Street blew out with the heat. Only the little cottage on the northeast side of the hotel and the little pergola next to the hotel were spared. The owner of the hotel, Arie Kuiper, moved goods rescued from the Pioneer Store to his other store in the old livery stable up First Street. (Both, courtesy of the SWHS.)

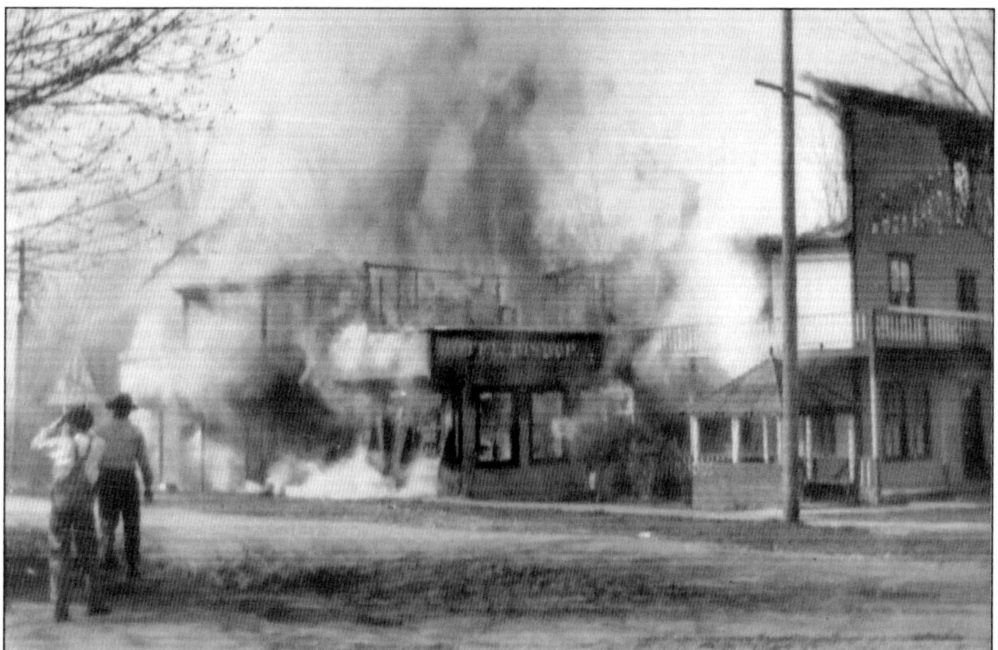

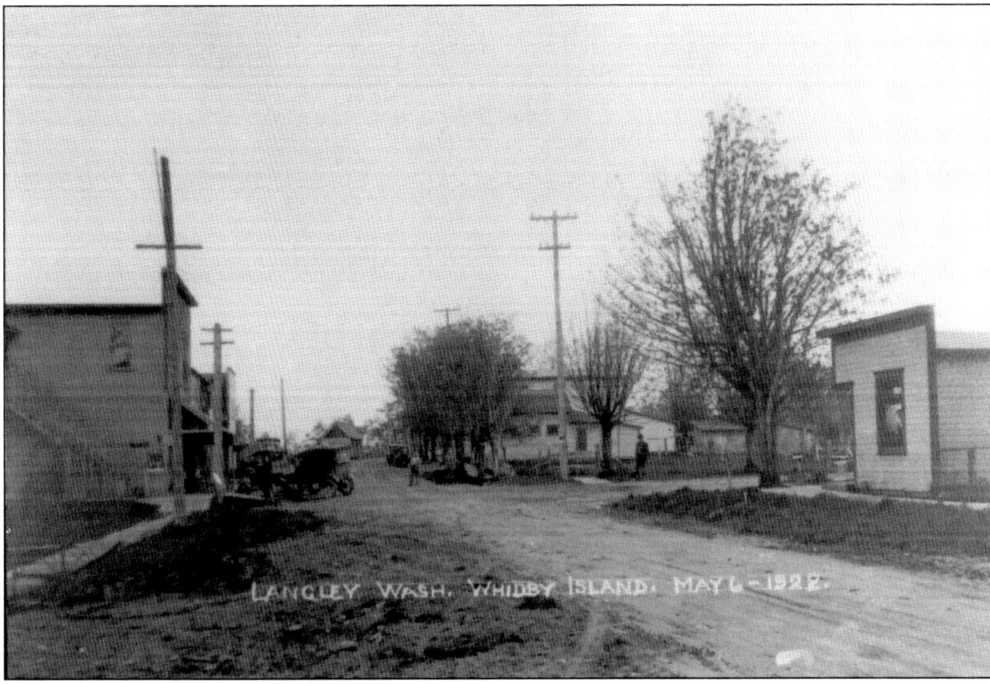

The vacant lot (left) off First Street, shown here in 1922, is the site of the hotel that burned down. The vacant lot across Anthes Avenue from the Langley State Bank (right) is where Jacob Anthes's store burned down in 1910. The next buildings on that side of First Street are the post office and the building constructed by the Brotherhood of Yeomen in 1914. (Courtesy of Paul Sarkis.)

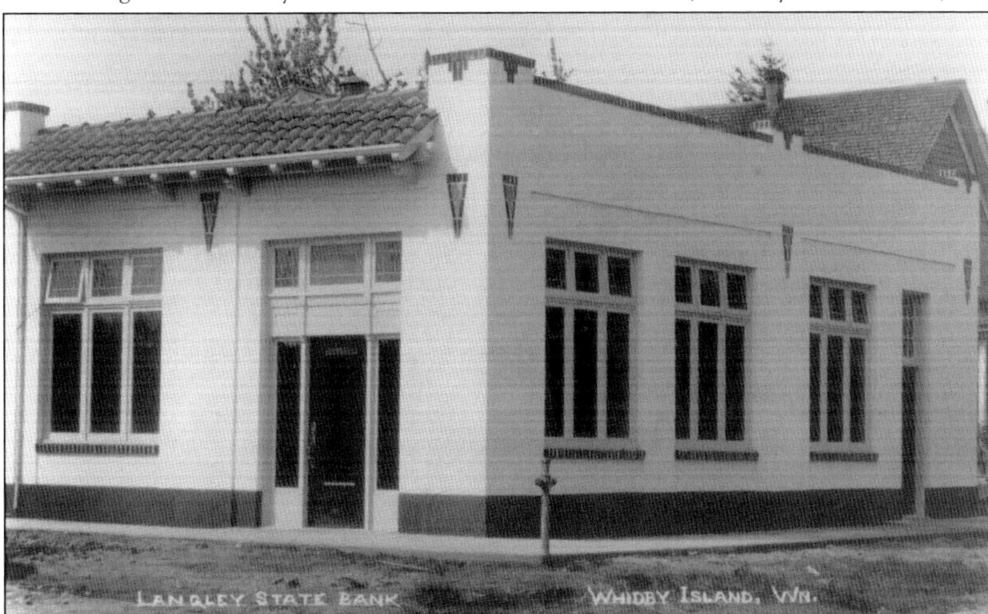

A new bank replaced the wooden bank in 1922–1923. The wooden bank building was moved a short distance south on Anthes Avenue to serve as the Whidby Telephone Company office. The maple trees that lined the avenue were cut down to make room for the town's first concrete sidewalk. (Courtesy of the SWHS.)

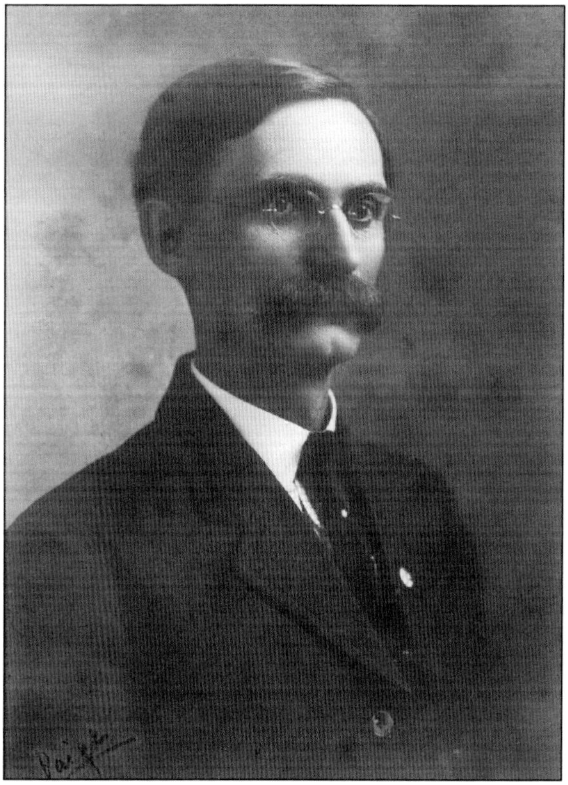

In 1924, Ernest Noble Sr. came to Langley to run the bank. He arrived from Canada with his wife, Bessie, and their children, Helen, Ralph, Ernest Jr., Betty, and Claude. He performed the job successfully until 1929, when he became ill with cancer. His son Ernest Jr. came home from the university to help and became bank president when his father died in 1934. His brother Ralph joined him. (Courtesy of Robert Noble.)

William Hunziker and his father, Stanley, are standing in the front yard of the home of Stanley's father-in-law, William Wolfe, on Easter, April 4, 1926. Across First Street is the Howard Hotel (left) and the Roderick McLeod house, purchased by Ernest Noble Sr. in 1925. His son Ernest Jr. lived in the house after his father's death. In 1942, he sold the house to the Livingstons. (Courtesy of William Hunziker.)

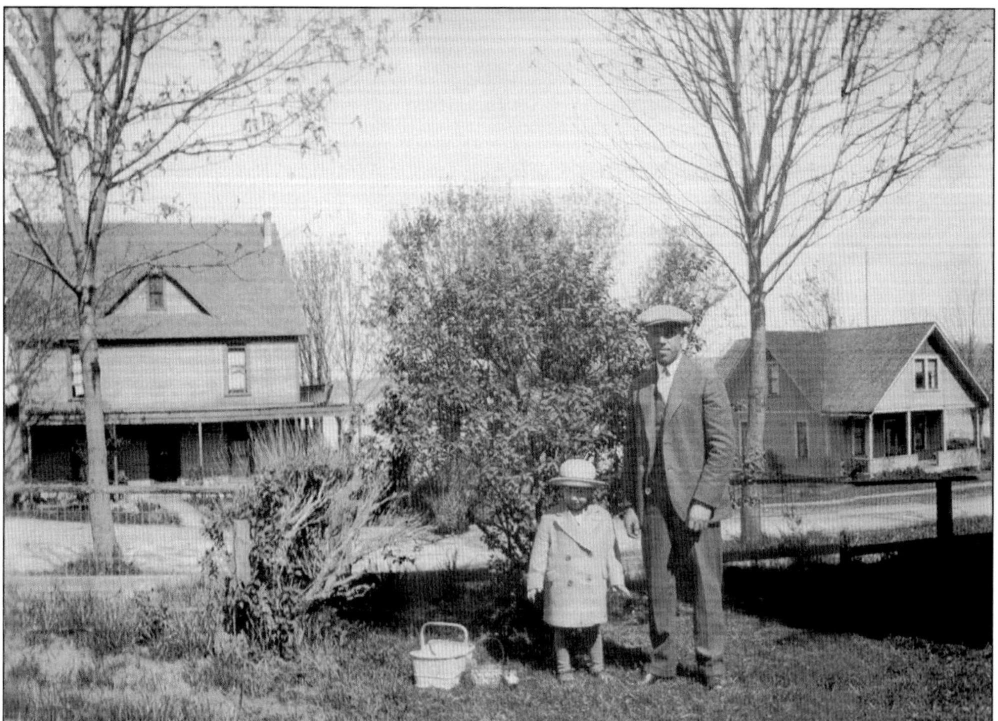

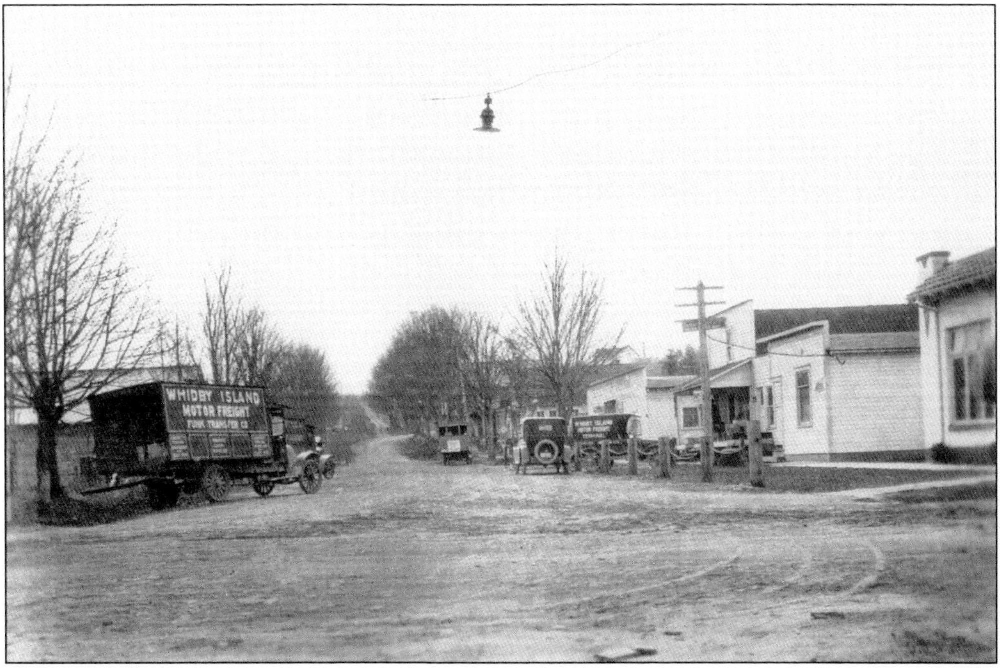

This view is looking south on Anthes Avenue around 1926. The old bank building was moved a short distance south of the new Langley State Bank (right) and housed the Whidby Telephone Company office. Trucks of Funk's transfer company are parked along the street. The sign on the front of the old Funk Mercantile next to the telephone office reads "United States Tires, Sales and Service." (Courtesy of the SWHS.)

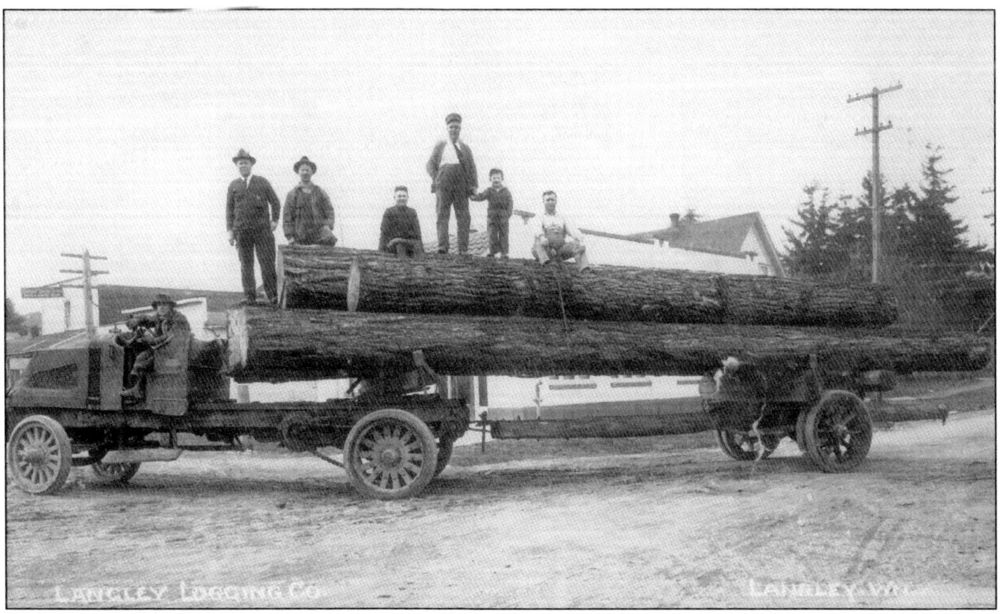

Logging trucks began replacing horses and oxen as a means of transport. Raymond Howard was the driver of this logging truck, parked in front of the Langley State Bank around 1926. Atop the logs (from left to right) are William Howard, Martin Mortenson, Ernest Noble, Edward Howard, Jack Peters, and Joseph Hess. (Courtesy of the SWHS.)

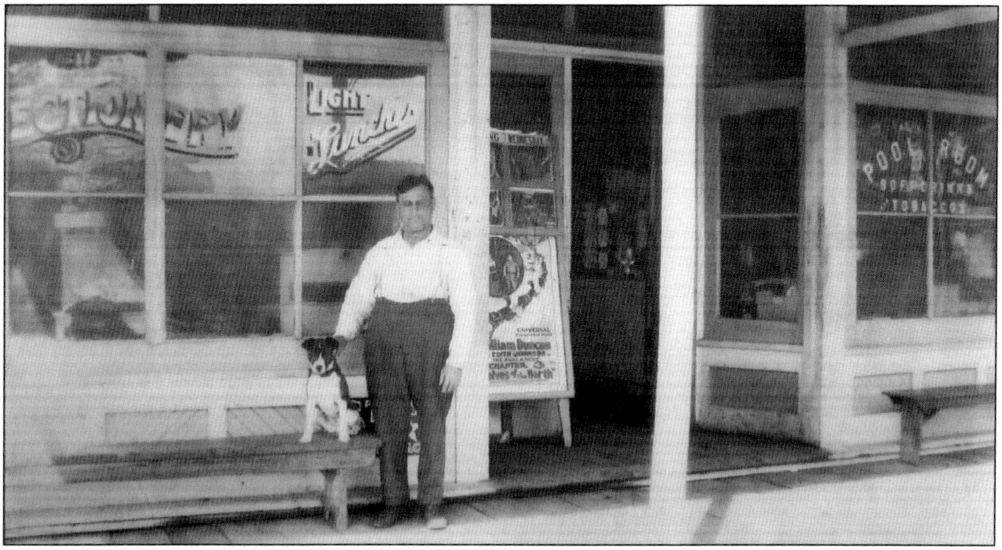

An unidentified man and his dog are standing in front of Howard's Confectionery, run by William Howard and his wife, Vella. Light lunches, soft drinks, cigars, tobacco, and candies were sold up front. A pool room was in back. Movies began to be shown upstairs in 1922. The sign advertises *Wolves of the North*, starring William Duncan and Edith Johnson, released in 1924. (Courtesy of the SWHS.)

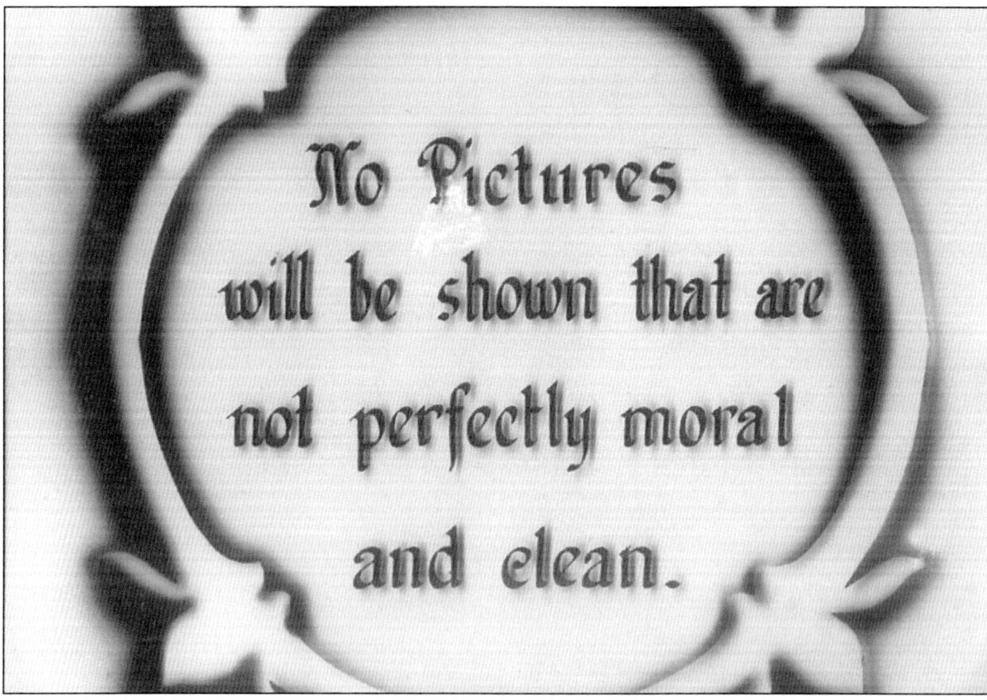

Lantern slides like this one were projected before the start of old movies. Cuthbert Gilliard operated a hand-cranked projector upstairs at Howard's Confectionery and pool hall during the early 1920s. Phillip Simon's daughter Evelyn played the piano for the silent movies in later years. Edward Howard showed one of Langley's first movies in the log schoolhouse. The film spilled onto the floor and had to be rewound. (Courtesy of the SWHS.)

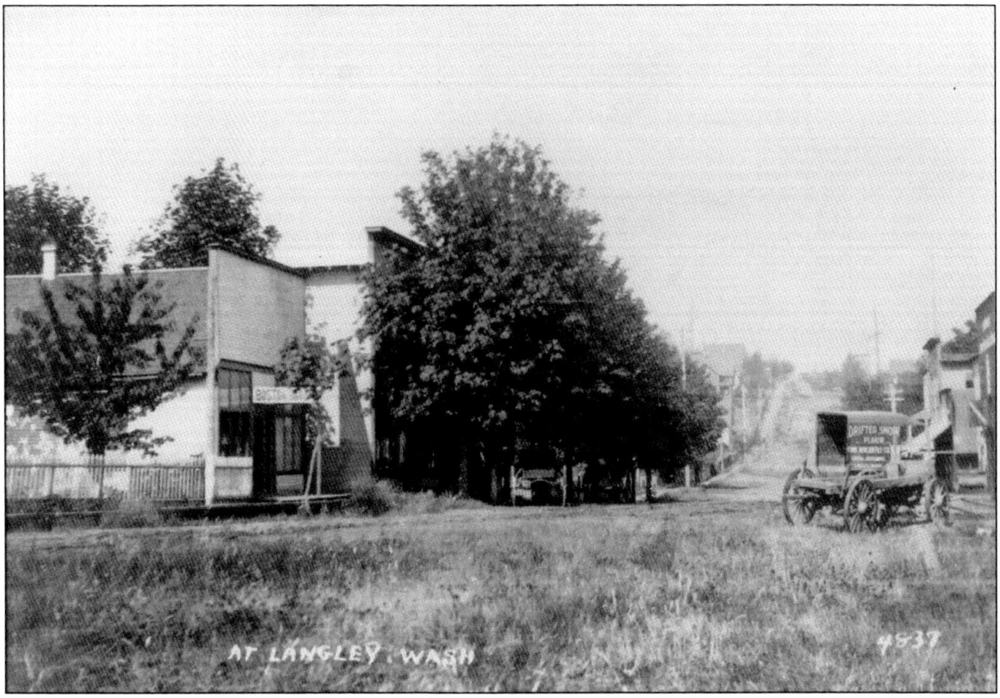

Joseph Primavera, his wife, Martina, and son, Victor, moved to Langley in 1917 and occupied the two-story house at the southwest corner of Second Street and Anthes Avenue. He established a shoe repair business there and bought the property in 1919. Primavera purchased the Boston Bakery (left) next to the Yeomen Building on First Street in 1922 and moved his family and leather goods business there. (Courtesy of the SWHS.)

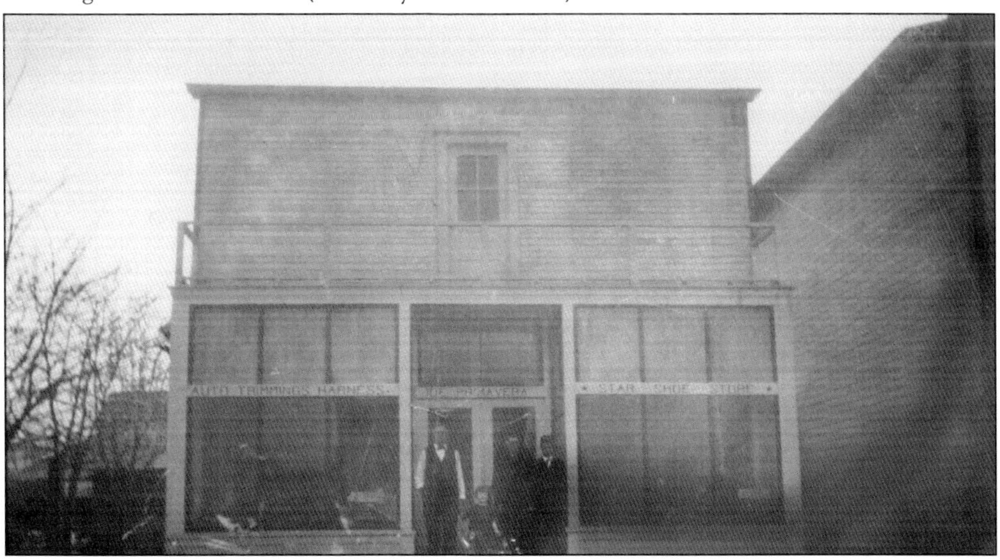

Joseph Primavera and his family are standing in front of the original Star Store on First Street in 1922. The sign across the front of the building reads, "Auto trimmings, harness. The Primavera Star Shoe Store." The name came from a popular manufacturer of shoes. Joseph sold the house on Second Street and Anthes Avenue, and the Primaveras moved into the building. (Courtesy of Anna Primavera.)

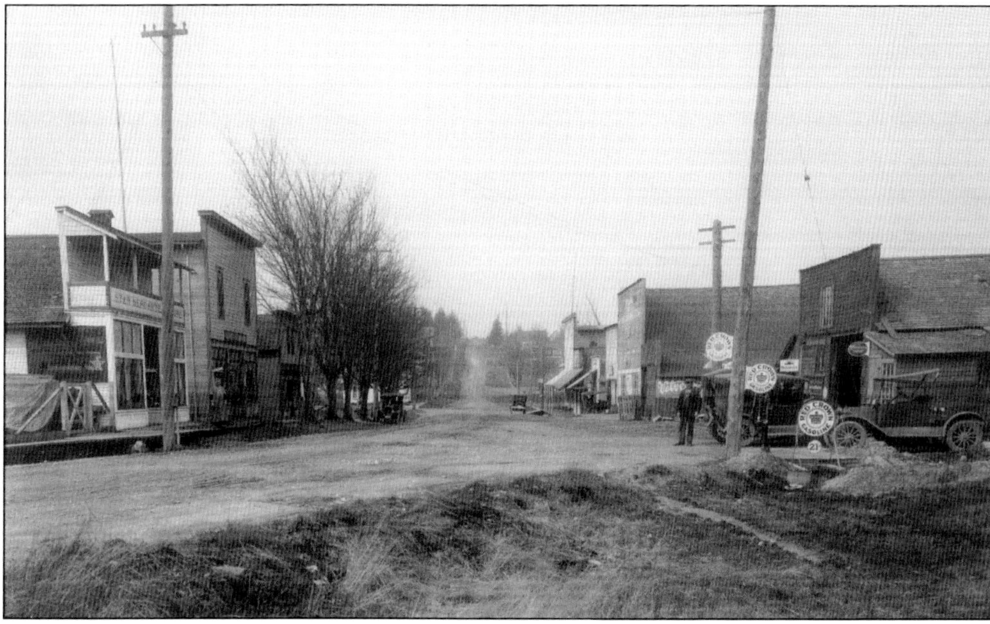

This is a view looking west on First Street in 1923. A roof has been added over the landing of the Star Mercantile Store (left). The lady in front of the Star Mercantile Store is Martina Primavera. The Yeomen Building next door houses the Whidby Trading Company. Across the street, Carl "Charlie" Lenz is standing in front of his garage, built in 1919. (Courtesy of the SWHS.)

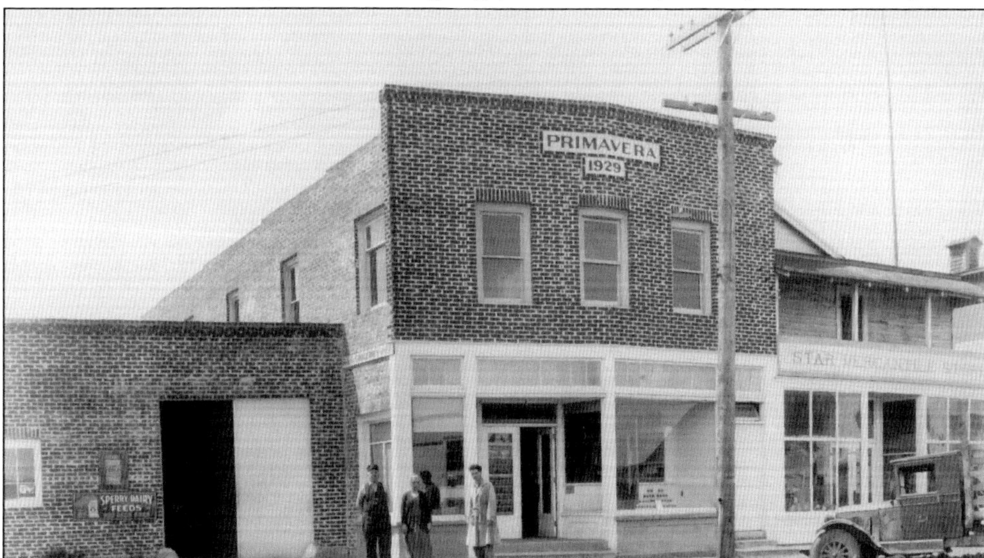

On the right is the original Star Mercantile Store. The truck parked in front of the original store was used by Victor to transport merchandise from Everett once a week. Joseph Primavera (left), his wife, Martina, and their son Victor are standing in front of the new two-story addition with brick facade constructed in 1929. The adjacent building with brick facade (left) served as a warehouse. (Courtesy of Anna Primavera.)

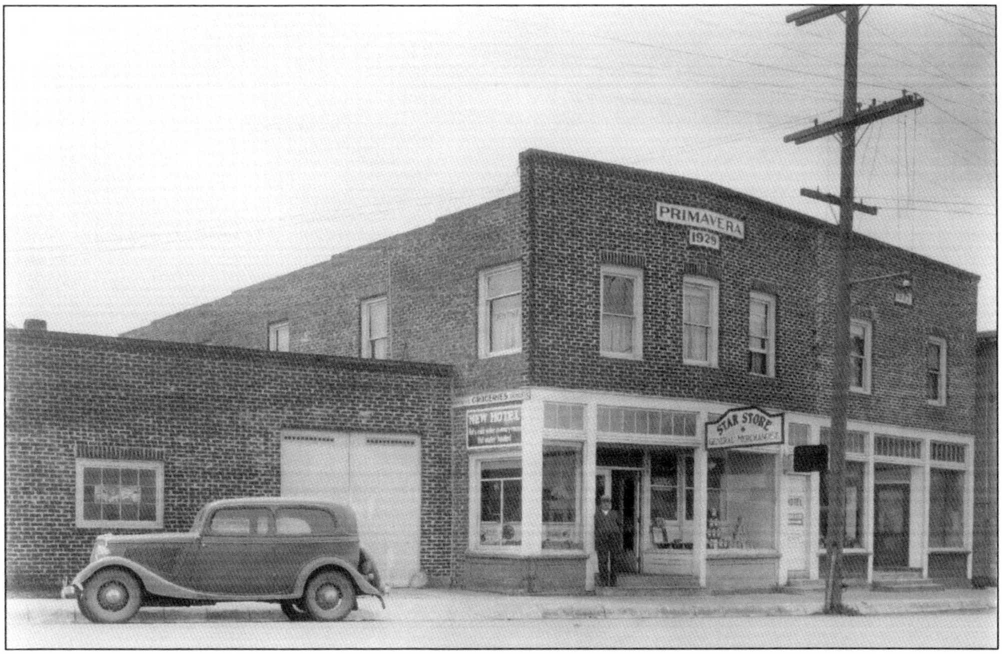

In 1933, the original Star Mercantile Store structure (right) was extensively remodeled and a new brick facade added. The remodeled store featured general merchandise and groceries; hotel rooms and a dentist's office were above. With the name shortened, the Star Store continues to be an impressive structure facing First Street. (Courtesy of Anna Primavera.)

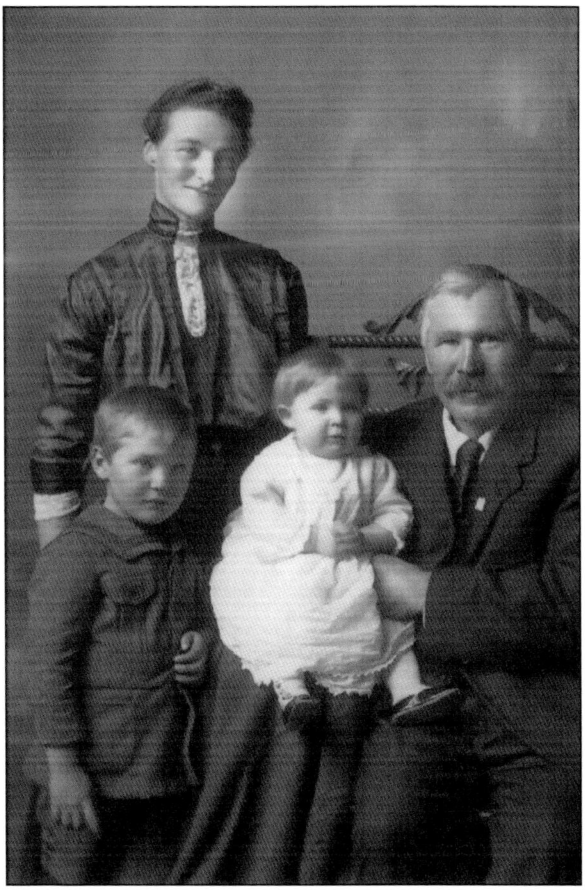

Fredrick and Florence Tiemeyer came to Langley with their children and settled in a house on Second Street behind the Star Store. The family members are, from left to right, David, Florence, Camilla, and Frederick. Fredrick ran a bakery next to the Star Store. His butterhorns cost a nickel and were very popular with the community children. (Courtesy of Anna Primavera.)

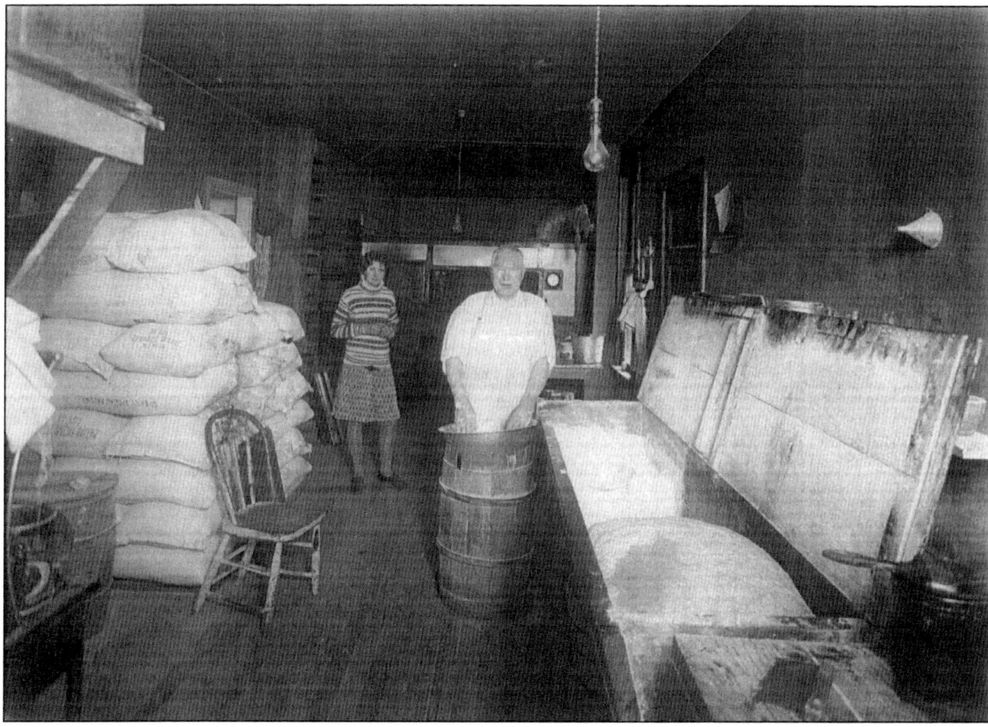

Frederick Tiemeyer did the baking, and goods were sold at a counter in front. Anna Peters lived with them for a time while attending high school. The Tiemeyers had a little barn and a cow. Anna would babysit in the morning while Florence milked the cow, then tended the bakery while Frederick had breakfast, then she headed off to school. (Courtesy of Anna Primavera.)

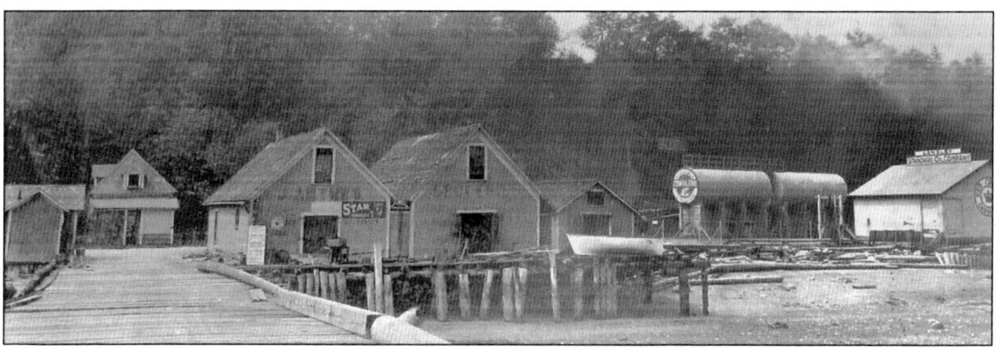

This photograph shows the Langley wharf around 1922. The Standard Oil Company bought property north of the wharf and constructed an office and storage tanks (right), demolishing the dance pavilion to make room for them. Barges unloaded oil that was piped along one side of the dock to the tanks. Claude Johnson managed the facility. (Courtesy of the SWHS.)

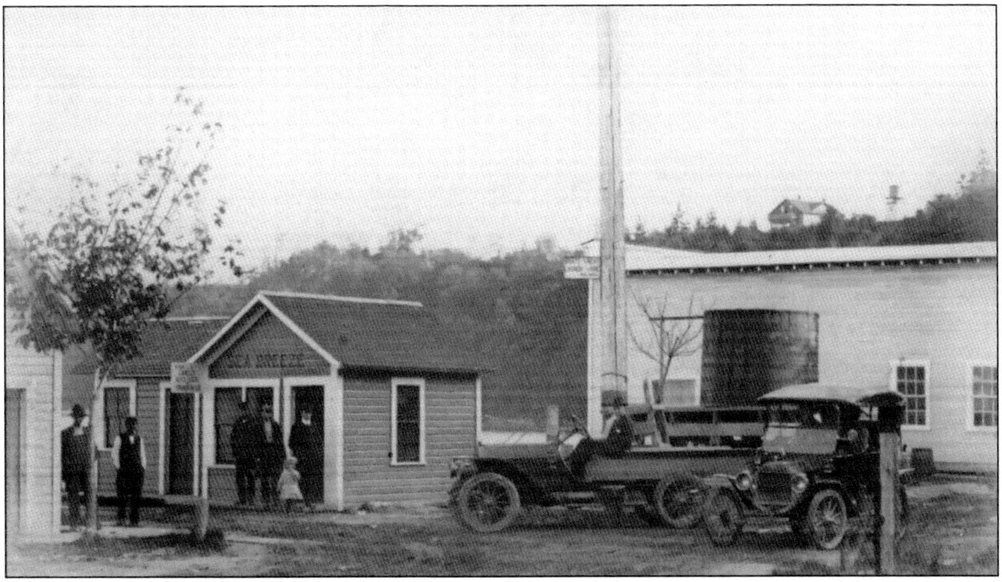

This photograph shows the Langley wharf area around 1923. In addition to owning the Sea Breeze Confectionery, Phillip Simon ran the Langley Auto Livery and Transfer Company and rented boats and launches. He also operated the generator supplying electricity during two mornings a week for laundry and at night until he blinked the lights, signaling he was going to bed. (Courtesy of Anna Primavera.)

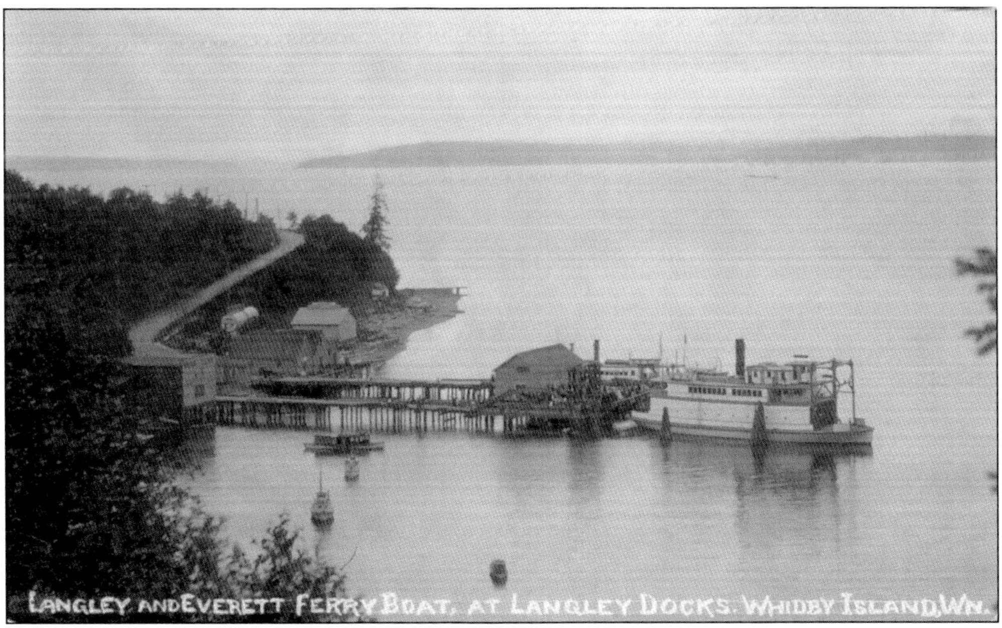

Increasing numbers of automobiles led to intense competition to build car ferries during the 1920s. In 1919, only two small ferries, the *Whidby I* and the *Central I*, served south Whidbey Island. The *Whidby II*, shown here at the Langley wharf, was christened on May 16, 1923, and began five round trips daily on the Everett-Clinton-Langley run with Bartlett Lovejoy as captain. (Courtesy of the PSMHS.)

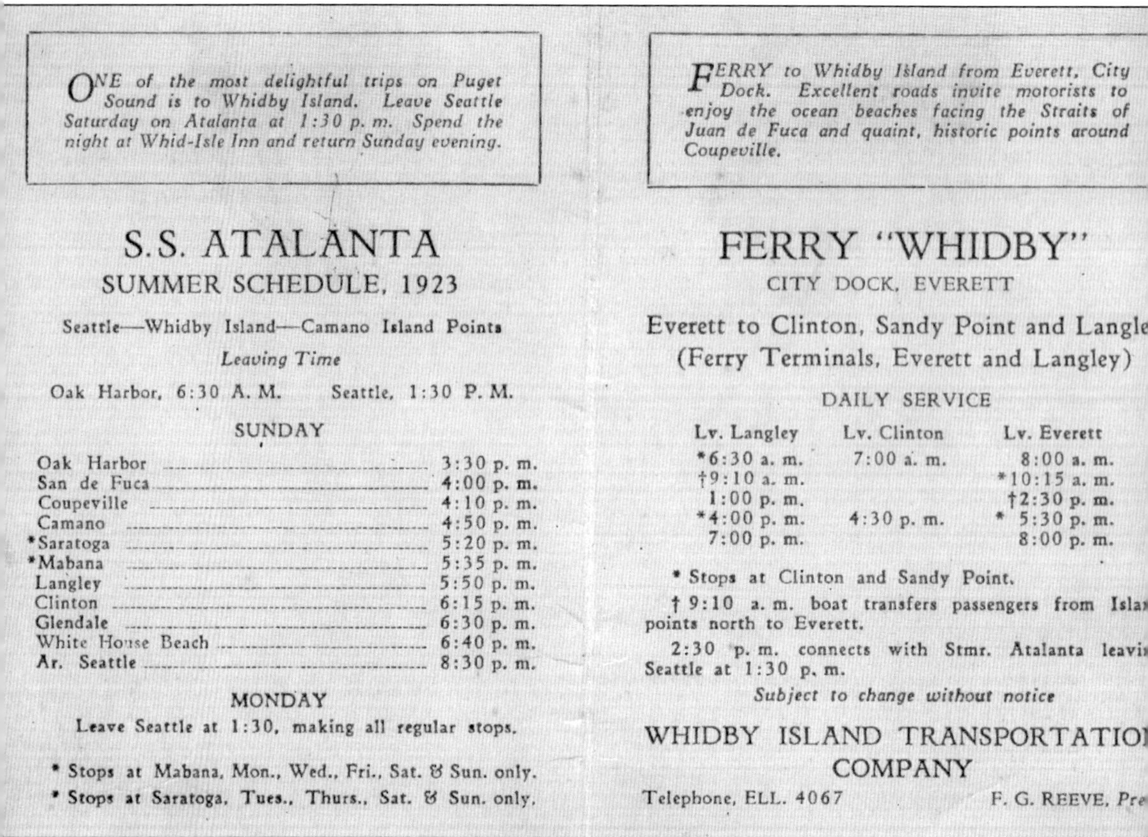

ONE of the most delightful trips on Puget Sound is to Whidby Island. Leave Seattle Saturday on Atalanta at 1:30 p.m. Spend the night at Whid-Isle Inn and return Sunday evening.

S.S. ATALANTA

SUMMER SCHEDULE, 1923

Seattle—Whidby Island—Camano Island Points

Leaving Time

Oak Harbor, 6:30 A. M. Seattle, 1:30 P. M.

SUNDAY

Oak Harbor	3:30 p. m.
San de Fuca	4:00 p. m.
Coupeville	4:10 p. m.
Camano	4:50 p. m.
*Saratoga	5:20 p. m.
*Mabana	5:35 p. m.
Langley	5:50 p. m.
Clinton	6:15 p. m.
Glendale	6:30 p. m.
White House Beach	6:40 p. m.
Ar. Seattle	8:30 p. m.

MONDAY

Leave Seattle at 1:30, making all regular stops.

* Stops at Mabana, Mon., Wed., Fri., Sat. & Sun. only.

* Stops at Saratoga, Tues., Thurs., Sat. & Sun. only.

FERRY to Whidby Island from Everett, City Dock. Excellent roads invite motorists to enjoy the ocean beaches facing the Straits of Juan de Fuca and quaint, historic points around Coupeville.

FERRY "WHIDBY"

CITY DOCK, EVERETT

Everett to Clinton, Sandy Point and Langle
(Ferry Terminals, Everett and Langley)

DAILY SERVICE

Lv. Langley	Lv. Clinton	Lv. Everett
*6:30 a. m.	7:00 a. m.	8:00 a. m.
†9:10 a. m.		*10:15 a. m.
1:00 p. m.		†2:30 p. m.
*4:00 p. m.	4:30 p. m.	* 5:30 p. m.
7:00 p. m.		8:00 p. m.

* Stops at Clinton and Sandy Point.

† 9:10 a. m. boat transfers passengers from Isla points north to Everett.

2:30 p. m. connects with Stmr. Atalanta leavi Seattle at 1:30 p. m.

Subject to change without notice

WHIDBY ISLAND TRANSPORTATIO COMPANY

Telephone, ELL. 4067 F. G. REEVE, Pre

The *Bee Line* replaced the *Whidby II* in 1924, joining the *Atalanta* and *Clatawa* making runs to Langley. Jacob Jensen sold the dock to Capt. Willis Nearhoff in 1926. In response, a group of businessmen formed the Langley Dock Company and acquired ownership of the property along the waterfront. Nearhoff sold them the dock in 1928. Ferry service to Langley was discontinued on December 17, 1929. (Courtesy of William Hunziker.)

Seven

Adjusting to Social Change *1930–1950*

Off the main road and suffering economic depression along with the rest of the United States, Langley barely held on during these two decades. The businesses that endured catered to the area's remaining farmers, loggers, and service providers. Down at the wharf, a canning business built to process strawberries and raspberries replaced the warehouses but lasted only a few years. Later, the Sea Breeze Tavern moved into the vacant cannery building.

The federal government's Works Progress Administration (WPA) stepped in to help with Langley's recovery. It funded a large pole-constructed building at the fairgrounds. When built in 1937, this was the largest such building anywhere in the United States. Albert Melsen helped to purchase a six-acre chicken farm to provide land and organized construction of the building. For years, he had been responsible for the creation of many of Langley's main buildings, including the Methodist church, the Olympic Club, the Clyde Theatre, and several homes. In addition, he was also Langley's longest-serving mayor.

In 1936, the WPA funded the building of the Deception Pass Bridge at the northern tip of Whidbey Island, connecting the island to the mainland. This scenic span high above the churning waters, along with new, larger car ferries on the Clinton/Mukilteo run, attracted car travel to the island. It was also a time in which Norman Clyde established a large garage, the Clyde Theatre, and an automobile showroom complete with an antique car collection.

During World War II, many families left the island for work and men reported for service. After the war, as the country recovered, fishing resorts opened to summer vacationers. Around South Whidbey, more than 20 resorts lured clients. One of these was the Sunrise Beach Resort near Langley's wharf. Several small cabins were for rent along with boats and fishing tackle. The fishing was excellent, and the resort provided an inexpensive vacation.

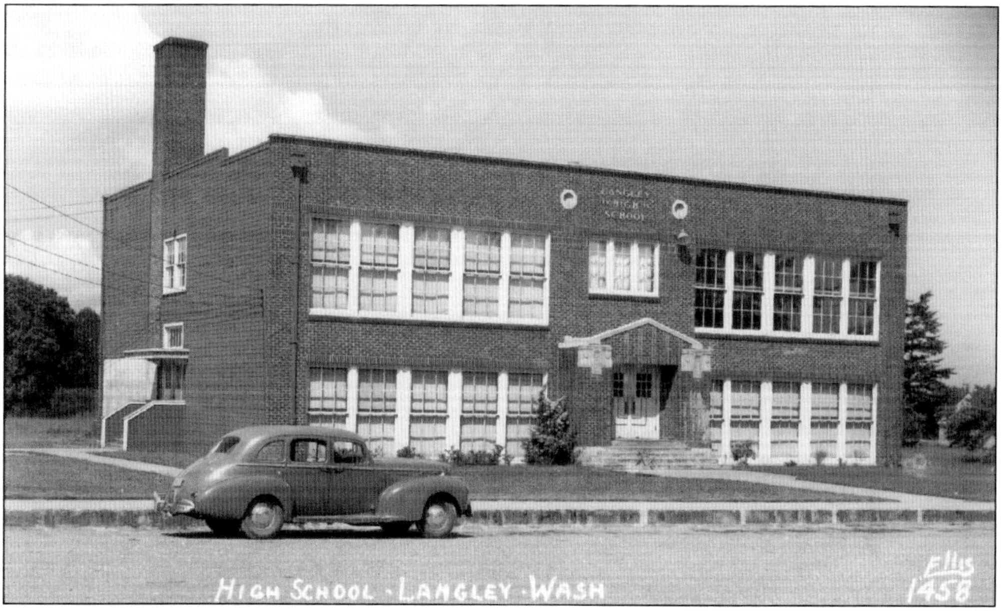

High school enrollment increased from 1929 to 1935, and a new high school was needed. Several communities, including Bayview and Mutiny Bay, vied for the new school, but the district acquired land adjacent to the existing Langley school, and a new brick high school, shown in the above photograph, was completed in 1935. The 1915 building south of the high school was demolished and replaced by a new brick building, which opened in October 1941. During construction, the upper grades met in the large, pole-constructed building (below) built by the WPA on the adjacent fairgrounds in 1937 to replace the school gymnasium as exhibit hall. (Both photographs by Ellis; courtesy of the SWHS.)

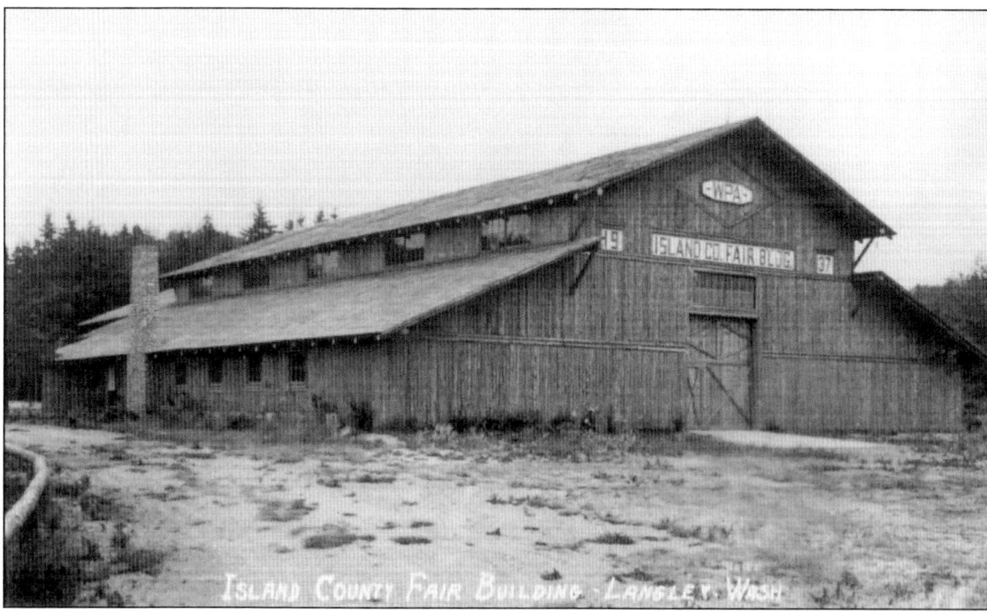

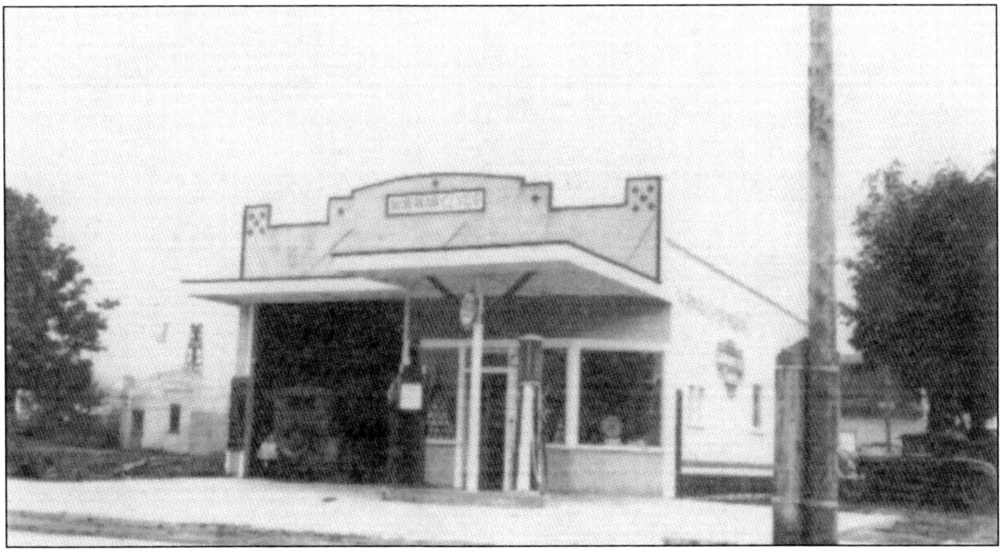

William Clyde came to Langley in 1925 from New Mexico and taught eighth grade at the Langley School. When both his wife and sister died, Clyde's son Norman came to Langley with his wife, Hazel, in 1927 to console him. After working for a year for Carl Lenz, in 1928, Norman Clyde built a garage on the east side of Anthes Avenue near the corner of Second Street. In 1935, he built a new garage (above) on the site of the former Jacob Anthes store at the corner of First Street and Anthes Avenue. The building in the alley behind the garage labeled "City Hall" in the photograph also housed the fire department. In 1937, at the height of the Great Depression, Norman constructed a theater (at left, below) next to his garage. (Both, courtesy of the SWHS.)

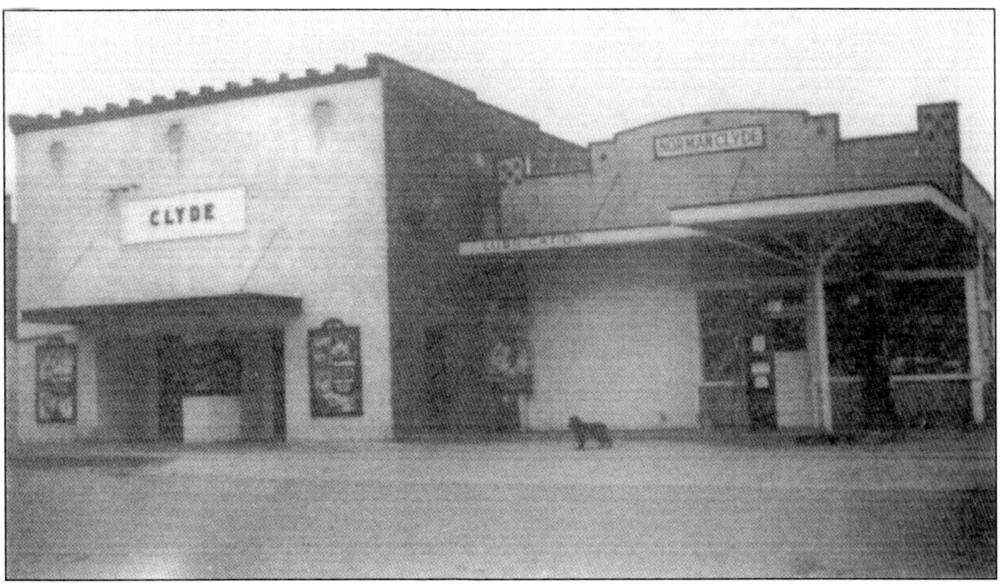

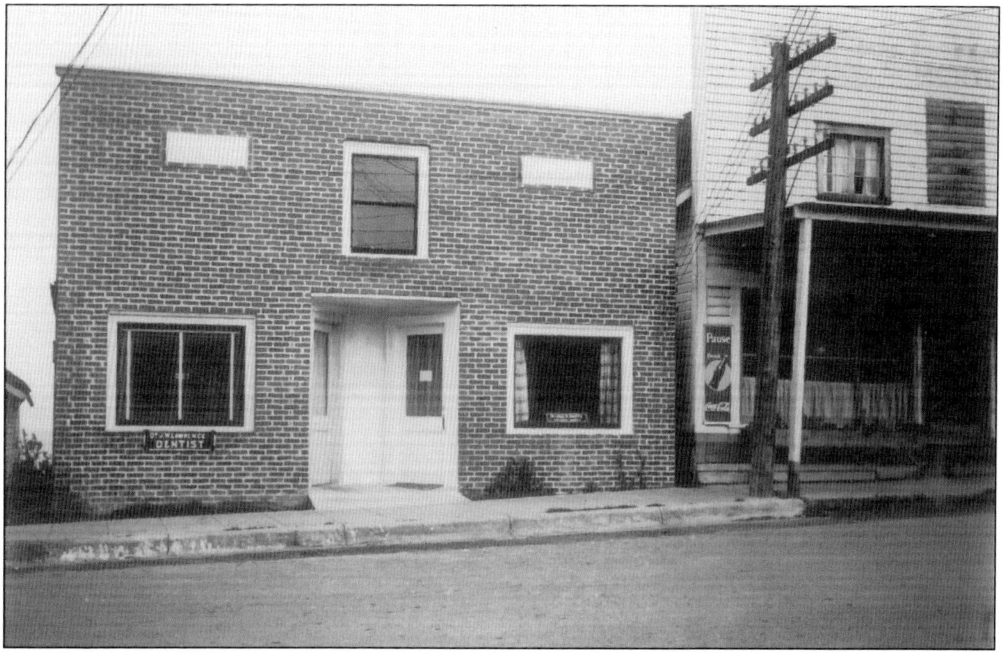

The blacksmith shop was replaced in 1939 by Richard Luhn, who built this brick-facade building to house his real estate and insurance business. Charlotte Hensley ran a restaurant from 1936 to 1937 in the former livery stable building to the right. She had a contract to feed the Puget Power and Light employees who stayed in the rooms above the Star Store. (Courtesy of Joan Handy.)

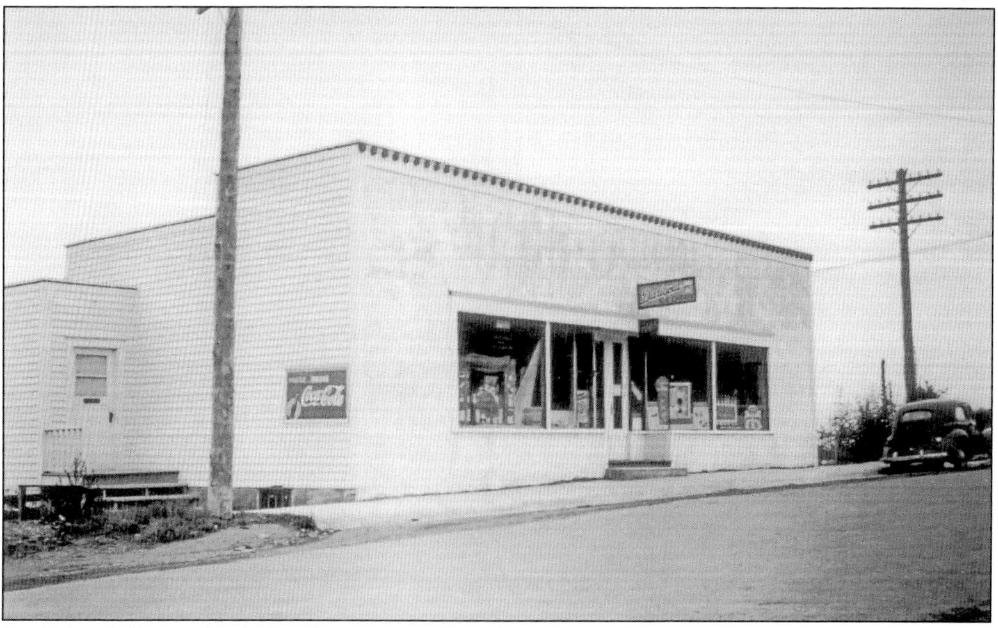

Dr. Orlando Brewer built this drugstore and residence around 1943 at the east end of First Street. After a short absence, Brewer returned to Langley with his third wife, Elinor, and stepson Donald. They lived across the street in a building that Dr. Brewer remodeled as a home and medical office. After they divorced in 1949, Elinor ran a bed-and-breakfast called the Edgewater Inn in their home. (Courtesy of Joan Handy.)

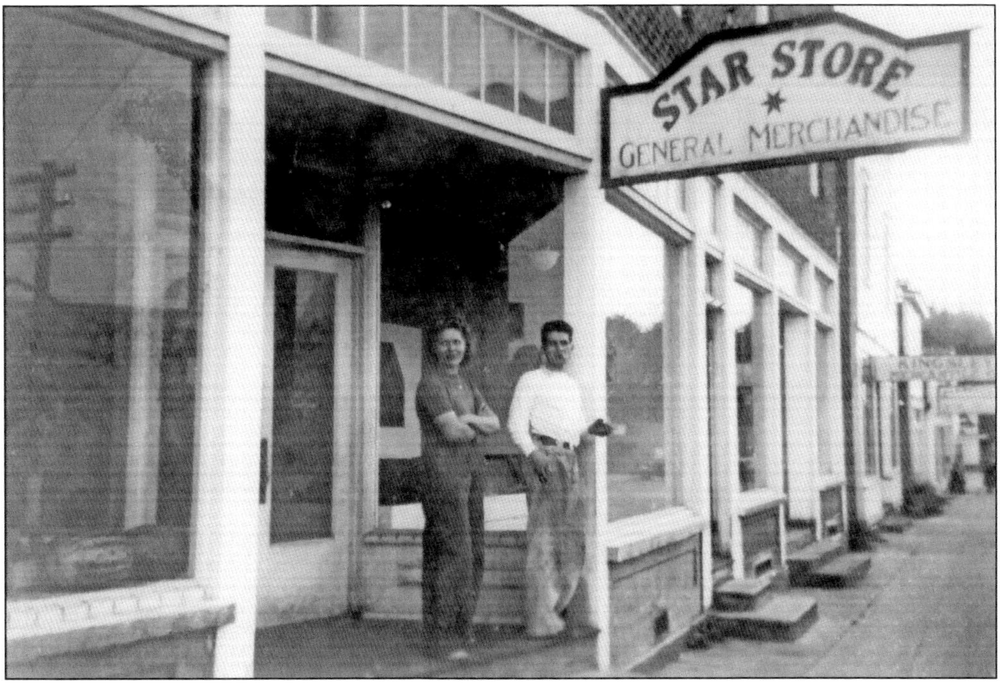

Anna Peters (left) worked in the Tiemeyer Bakery. She caught the eye of Victor Primavera, who made frequent trips to buy baked goods to sell in the Star Store next door. They married in 1938, and Victor inherited the Star Store when his father died in 1939. The newlyweds lived upstairs, and their first two children were born there. (Courtesy of Anna Primavera.)

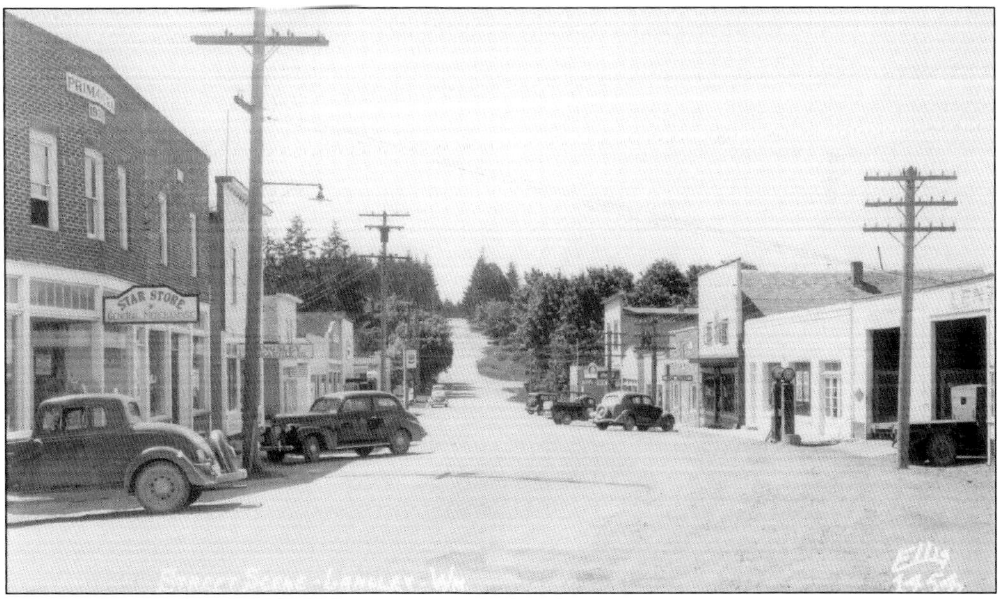

This photograph shows First Street looking west in 1940. The enlarged Lenz Garage (right) replaced the wooden garage built by Carl Lenz in 1919. Lenz hid his silver dollars in a bucket of oil. When the garage burned down in 1932, the bucket and money survived. The Kingsley Mercantile occupies the first floor of the Yeomen Building, next to the Star Store (left). (Photograph by Ellis; courtesy of Anna Primavera.)

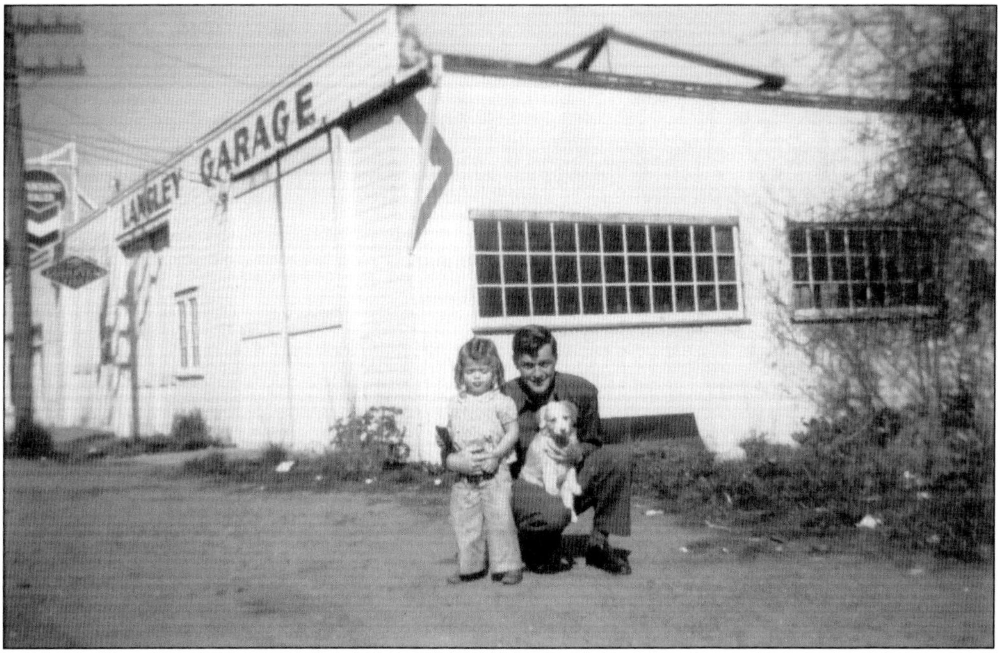

Joanne Primavera (left) and Jack Scriven are in front of the Langley Garage in this 1943 photograph. Martin Mortenson and his son-in-law, Edward Christoe, bought the Lenz Garage, renamed it, and added a DeSoto-Plymouth showroom. Mortenson ran a hardware store in the old livery stable, then across First Street next to the Clyde Theatre. (Courtesy of Anna Primavera.)

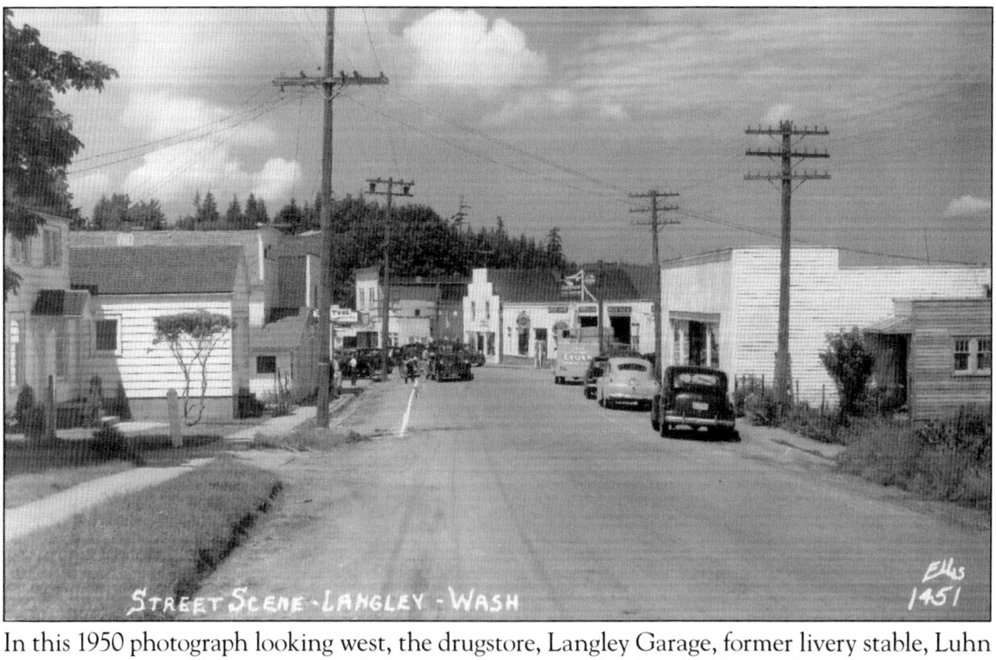

In this 1950 photograph looking west, the drugstore, Langley Garage, former livery stable, Luhn Building, meat market, and Dog House Tavern line the north side of First Street. John Braun, one of the founders of the Choochokam art fair, lived in the house at far left. (Photograph by Ellis; courtesy of John Ball.)

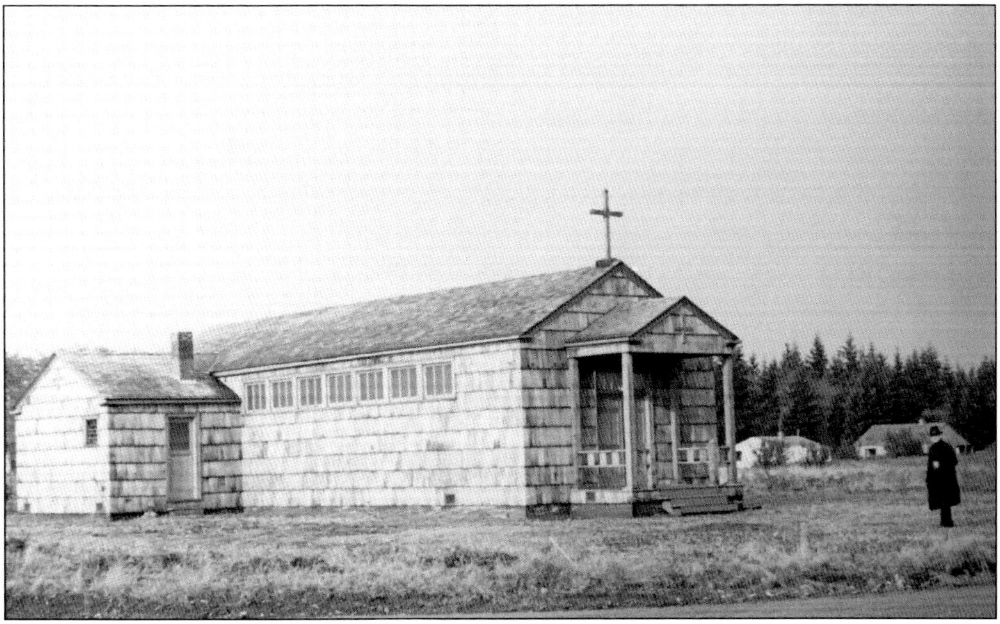

St. Hubert's Mission Church was built at the corner of Third Street and DeBruyn Avenue in 1935. It became a mission of the Oak Harbor Church in 1938 and a parish in 1966, with Fr. August Royer as pastor. Rev. John O'Brien from Oak Harbor celebrated the first mass in 1940. Additions to the building were made in 1991 and 2008. (Courtesy of the Archdiocese of Seattle.)

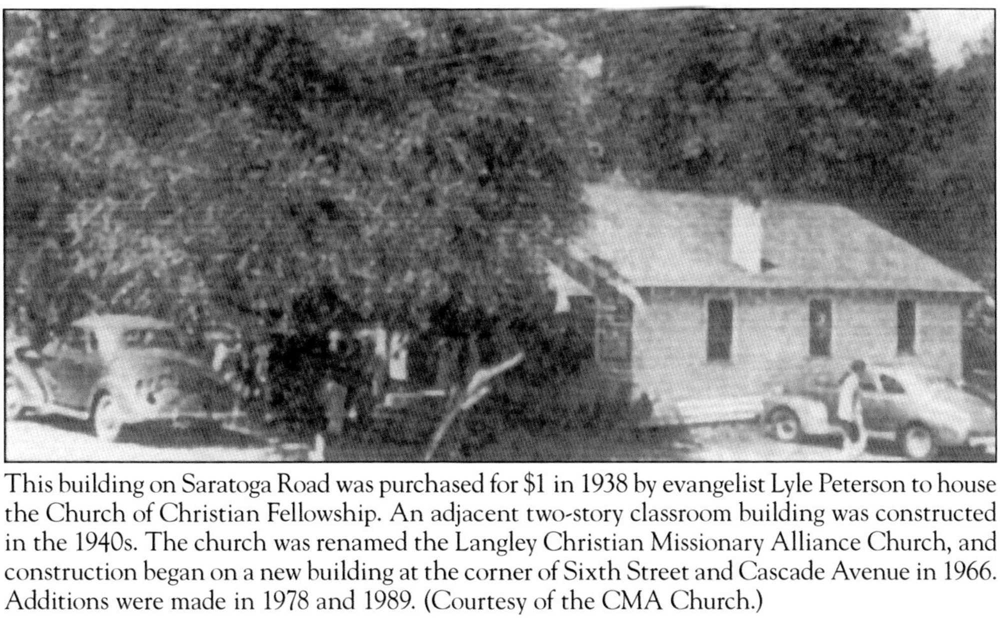

This building on Saratoga Road was purchased for $1 in 1938 by evangelist Lyle Peterson to house the Church of Christian Fellowship. An adjacent two-story classroom building was constructed in the 1940s. The church was renamed the Langley Christian Missionary Alliance Church, and construction began on a new building at the corner of Sixth Street and Cascade Avenue in 1966. Additions were made in 1978 and 1989. (Courtesy of the CMA Church.)

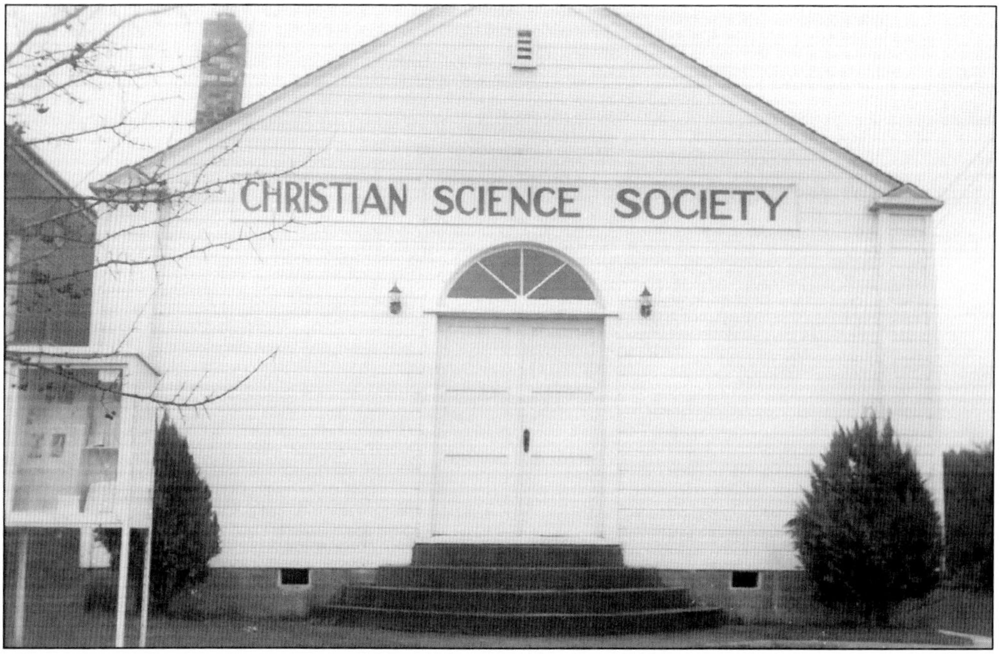

The Christian Science Society building (shown here around 1950) was built in 1941 west of the library on a lot purchased from Jacob Anthes in 1928 for $250. Services were held in the library prior to that. The building was sold in 1983 and has been occupied by several businesses since then. (Courtesy of Mark Kjellstrom.)

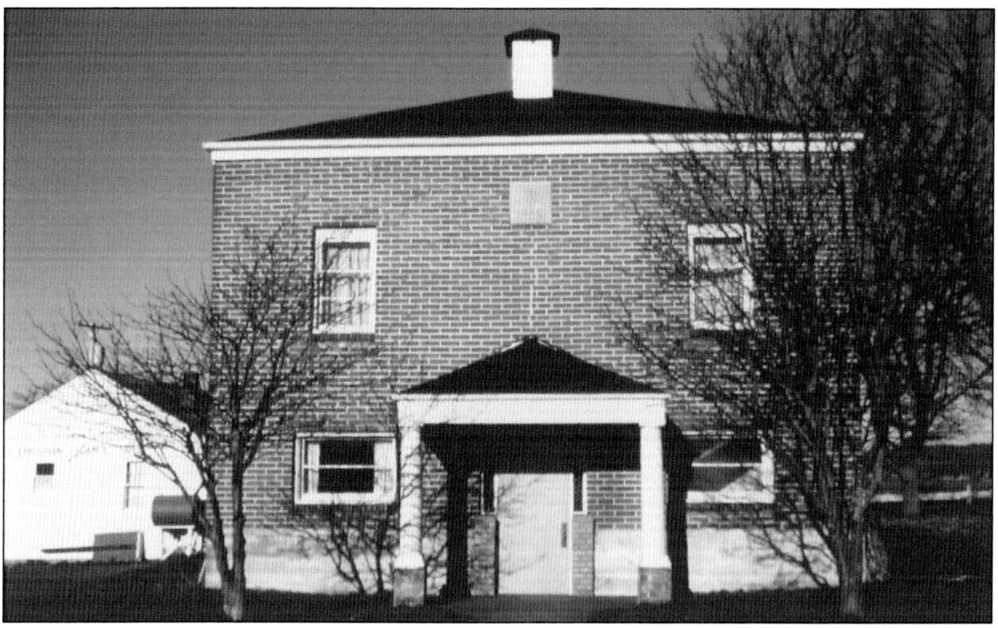

The Masonic temple on Second Street (shown here in 1991) was built in 1948 next to the library on a lot donated by Jacob Anthes, himself a Mason. Albert Melsen was lead contractor. The Masons had been meeting on the second floor of the Yeomen Building on First Street. The city purchased the temple in 1992 and remodeled it into the current Langley City Hall. (Courtesy of Michael Boyd.)

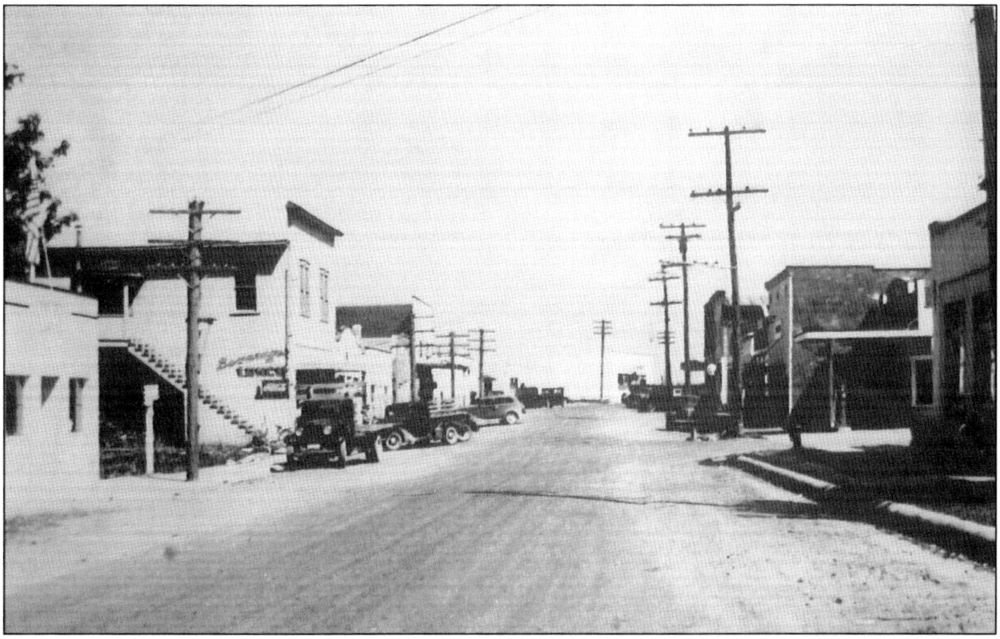

This view of First Street is looking east around 1940. A new post office (left) was built in 1939 by Ernest Noble Jr. on the site of the hotel that burned down in 1921. His mother lived in an apartment in the rear until her death, after which it was occupied by the postmaster, Emma Cloke. It replaced the former post office building, which subsequently became the Moonraker bookstore. (Courtesy of Roger Steele.)

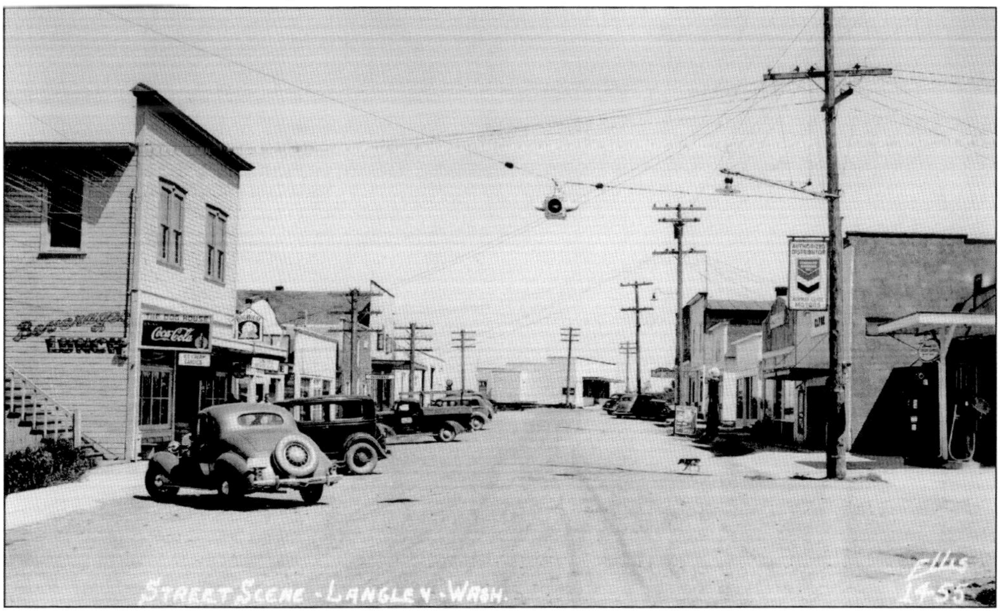

This c. 1942 photograph of First Street looking east shows Howard's Confectionery (left), which was renamed the Dog House Tavern by William Howard's wife, Vella, in 1933 following repeal of Prohibition. Gas could be purchased at the Norman Clyde Garage (right), the Langley Garage up the street, and from pumps in front of Mortenson's hardware store next to the Clyde Theatre. (Photograph by Ellis; courtesy of the SWHS.)

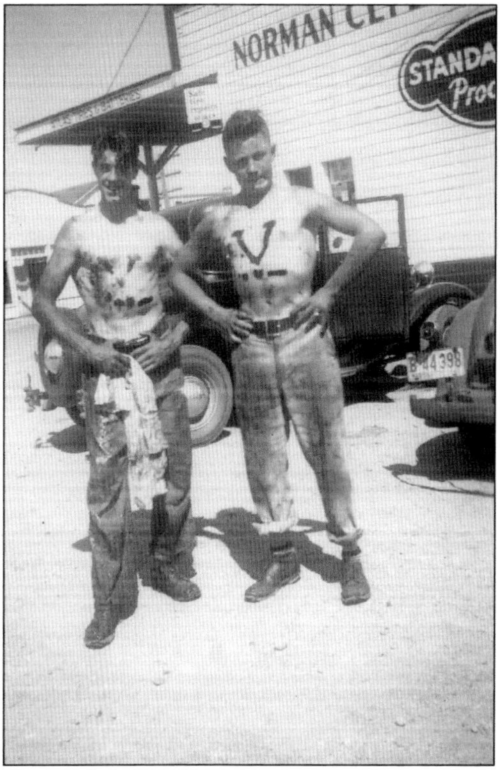

Joe Zylstra (left) and Richard Clyde are standing on Anthes Avenue with "V" for victory in Morse code painted on their chests in roofing tar. After a stint in the Navy, Clyde returned to Langley. He purchased the garage from his father in 1954 and changed the name to Clyde Garage, running it until he sold it in 1988. (Courtesy of Richard Clyde.)

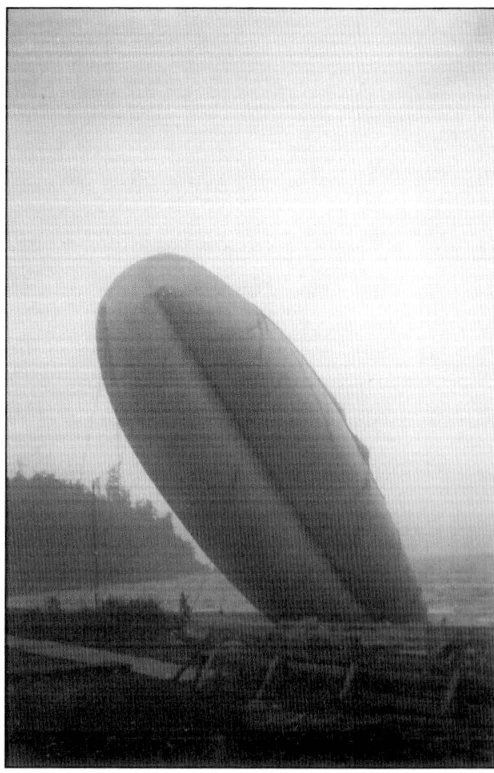

A barrage balloon broke away from its mooring and landed at Sandy Point in 1942. Langley residents watched for enemy planes during World War II from an observation tower at the southeast corner of Park Avenue and Third Street. None were apparently observed, but in 1944, a Canadian transport plane crashed on the ridge across from the cemetery, killing all on board. (Courtesy of Richard Clyde.)

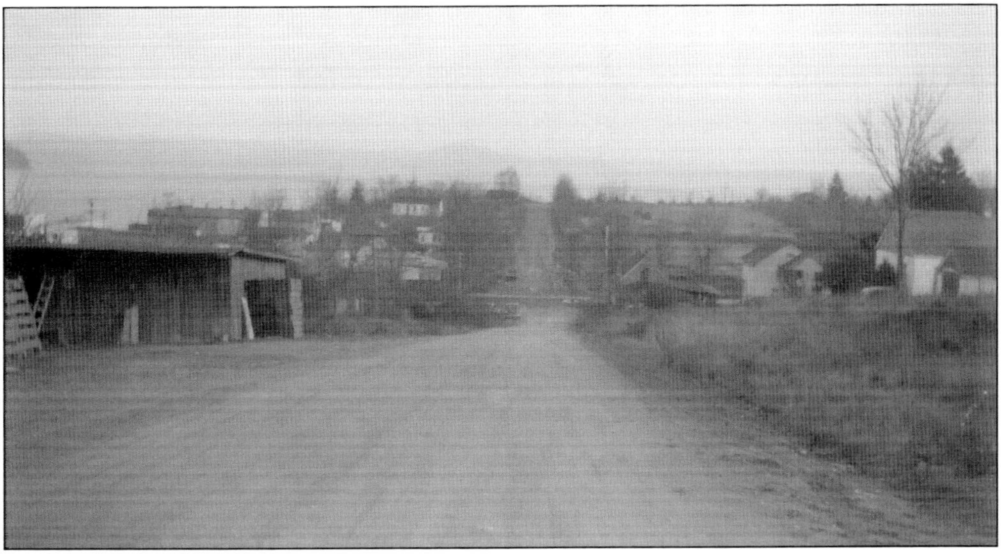

This c. 1942 photograph of Second Street looking east shows the white Christian Science Society building (left of center) and adjacent library at the top of the hill. The building at left is part of the lumberyard purchased from Harvey Maule by Charles Burk in 1932. Customers entered from Second Street, made a loop, purchased supplies, and exited back onto Second Street. (Courtesy of Frances Johnson.)

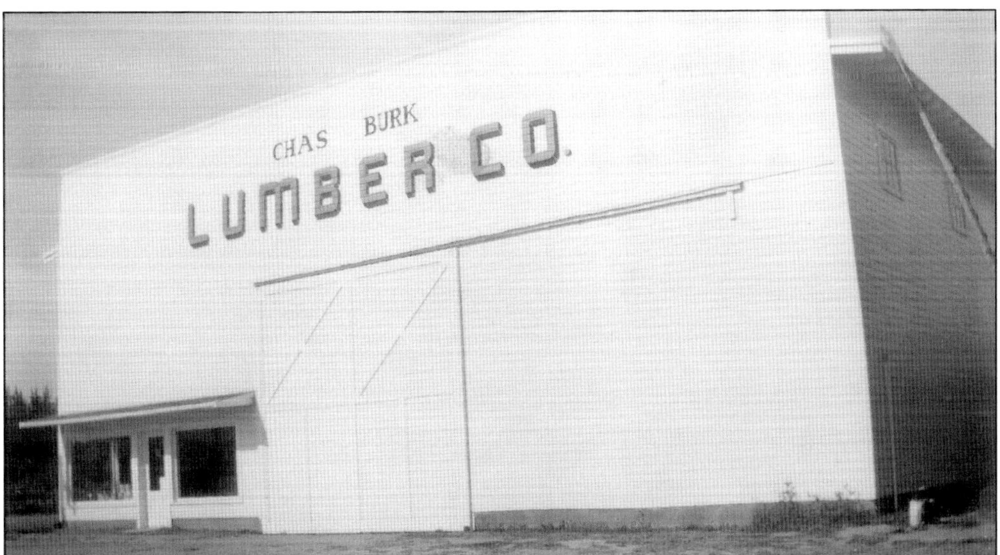

In 1944, Charles Burk purchased the property at the corner of DeBruyn Avenue and Second Street, and he moved his lumberyard to that location in 1945. This property had once been the farm of Langley's banker, James Curtis Langley. In 1955, Burk built a brick home at the southeast corner of Second Street and Park Avenue. (Courtesy of Jean Bjorn.)

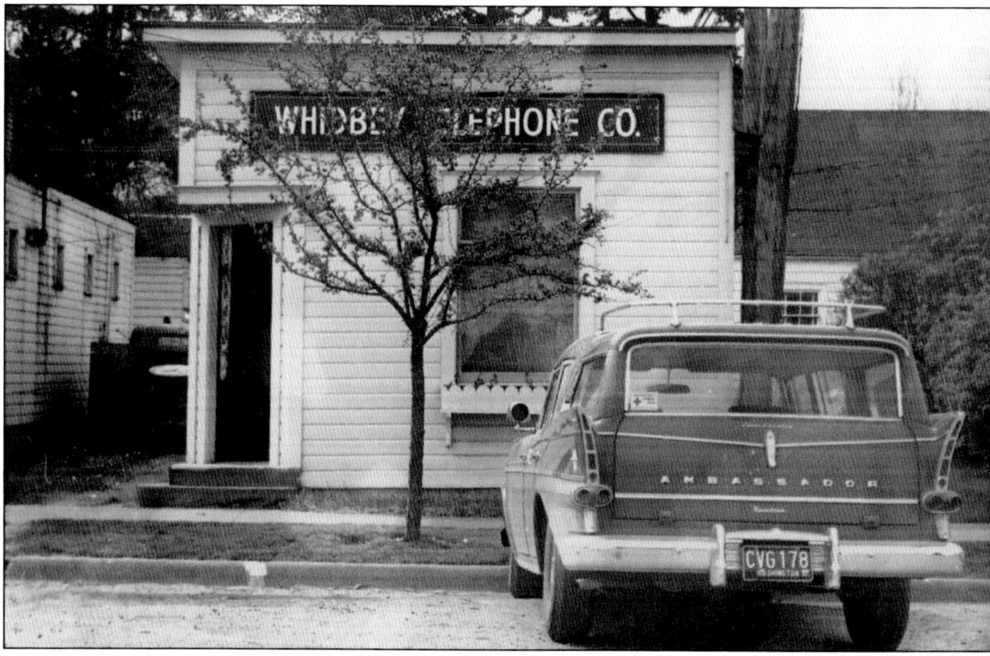

David Henny purchased the telephone company from Ernest Noble in 1953 and changed the spelling to Whidbey Telephone Company. In 1961, the central office was moved to its present location at Bayview. The old telephone office building was relocated across from the fairgrounds, where it housed a number of businesses. (Courtesy of Robert Noble.)

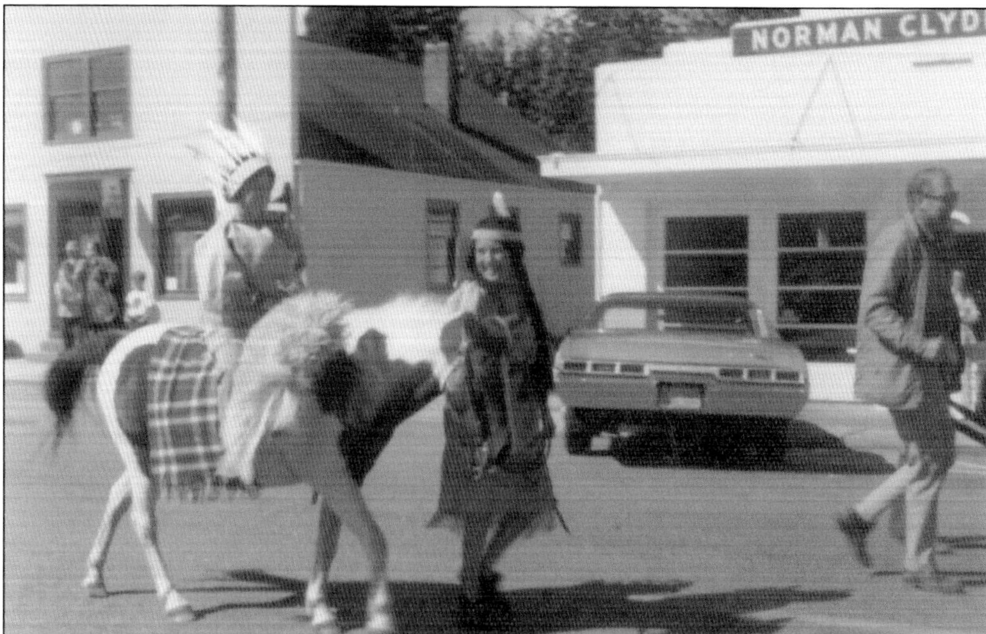

In 1940, Norman Clyde erected a building, seen here on the right in 1973, on the site of the former Funk Mercantile. He sold appliances, then Nash automobiles. The building across the alley (at left) was built by Julius Dettrich as a beauty parlor and barbershop in 1939, replacing a building occupied by Leslie Hensley that burned down in 1932. (Courtesy of Richard Clyde.)

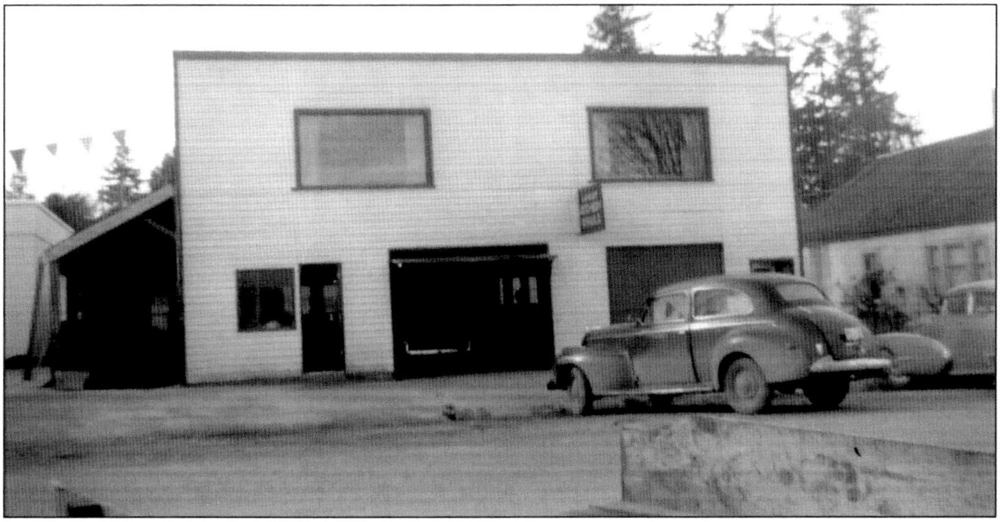

In 1950, Lloyd Carter built the Langley Auto Rebuild, shown here, on Anthes Avenue next to Julius Dettrick's building (far right). When fumes from the paint bay became too noxious for the apartment above, a lean-to was added on the south side of the building as a paint booth. Carter operated it for about three years. (Courtesy of Lloyd Carter.)

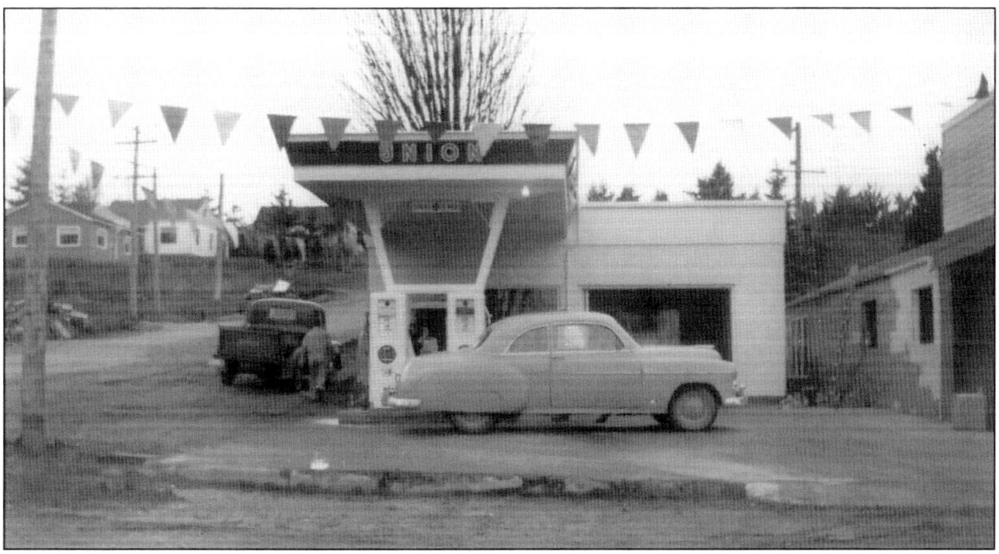

Lloyd Carter built this Union gas station in 1951 at the corner of Anthes Avenue and Second Street next to his Auto Rebuild shop, which can be seen at the far right of the photograph. The area of the gasoline pumps was later enclosed, and the building subsequently housed a number of businesses, including a ceramics shop, laundry, antique store, barbershop and beauty parlor, art gallery, and software business. (Courtesy of Lloyd Carter.)

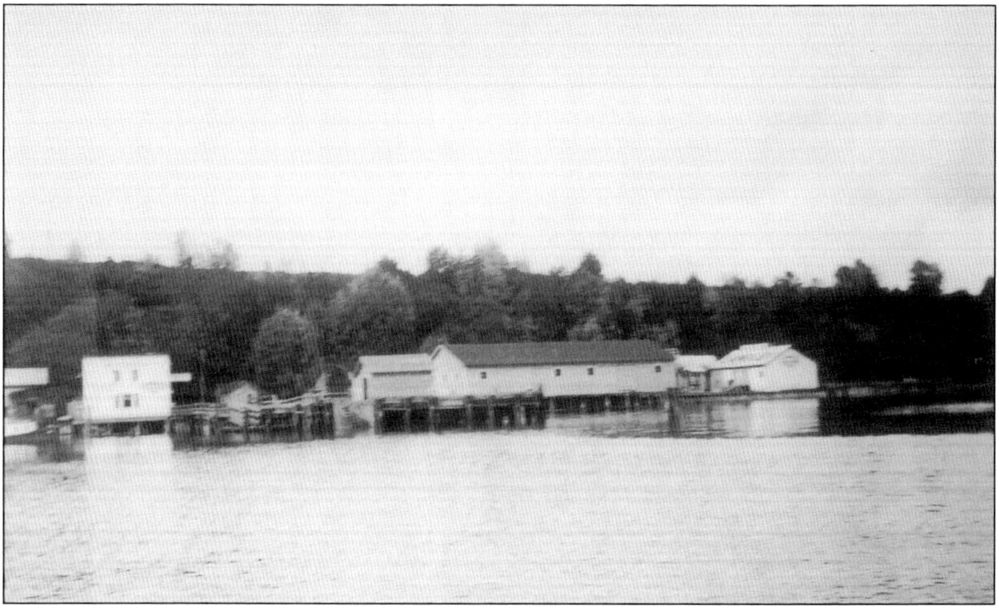

A berry-packing plant (center) was built in 1930, replacing several old warehouses. Strawberries from all over the island were bought to Langley and packed in large barrels that were barged to Everett and Seattle, providing seasonal work for Langley residents. This operated until 1941, when a drop in prices forced the plant's closure. (Courtesy of Joan Handy.)

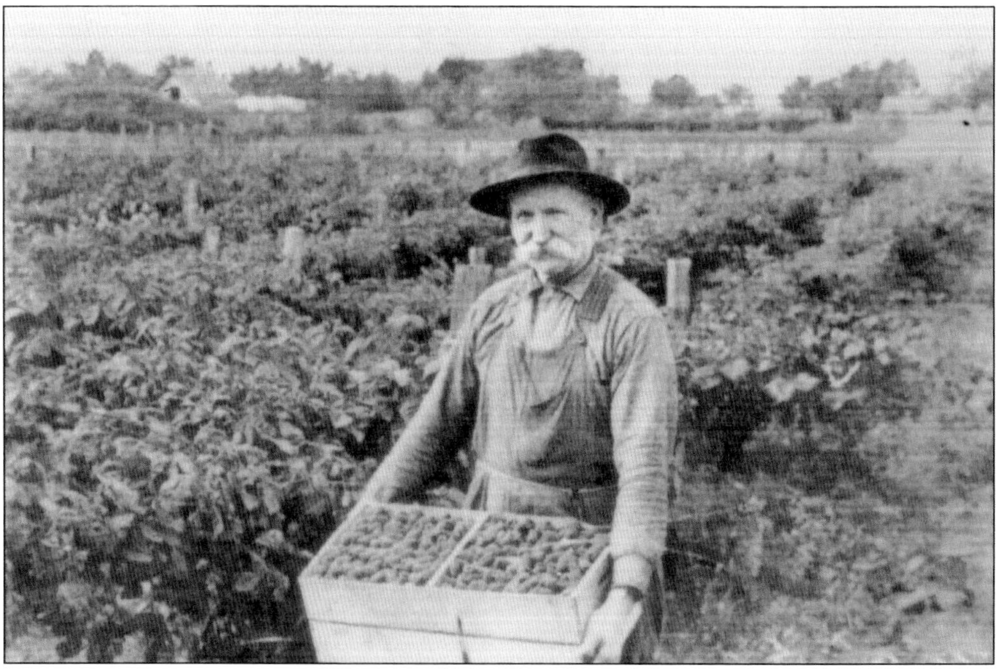

Growing raspberries and strawberries was a big industry on the south end of Whidbey Island during the 1920s and 1930s. Isaac "Ike" Bainter owned some of the best fields. Bainter came to Langley in 1906 with his wife, Kittie, a Tklinget, and their children, Lucy, Flora, Daniel, and May. He purchased a large house and the land that is now the Northview subdivision. (Courtesy of the SWHS.)

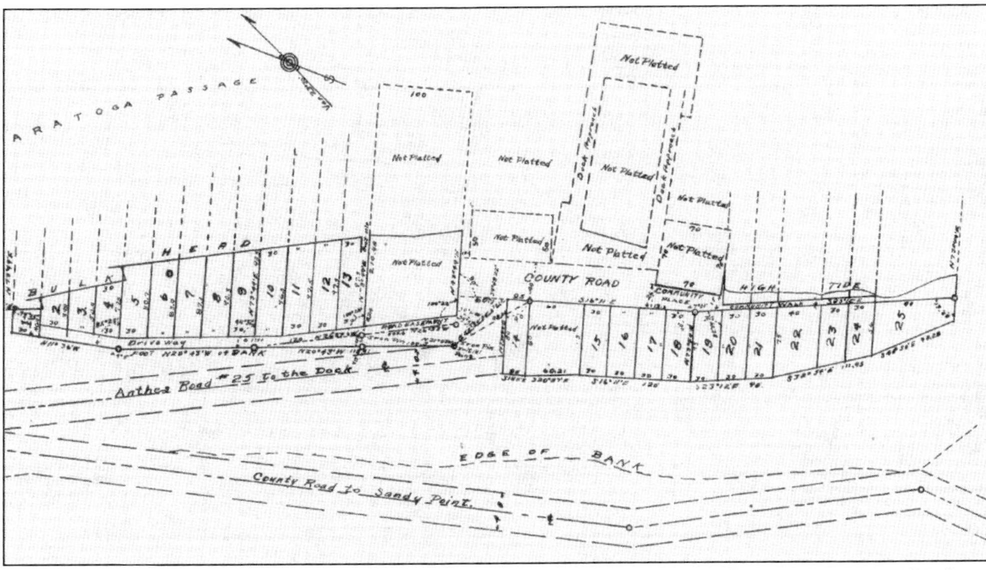

The Langley Dock Company platted its holdings on the waterfront into lots in 1936. In 1939, faced with diminished opportunities for economic development of the area, the dock and tidelands were sold to the town of Langley for $1, and the Langley Dock Company was disbanded on August 16, 1939. (Courtesy of the City of Langley.)

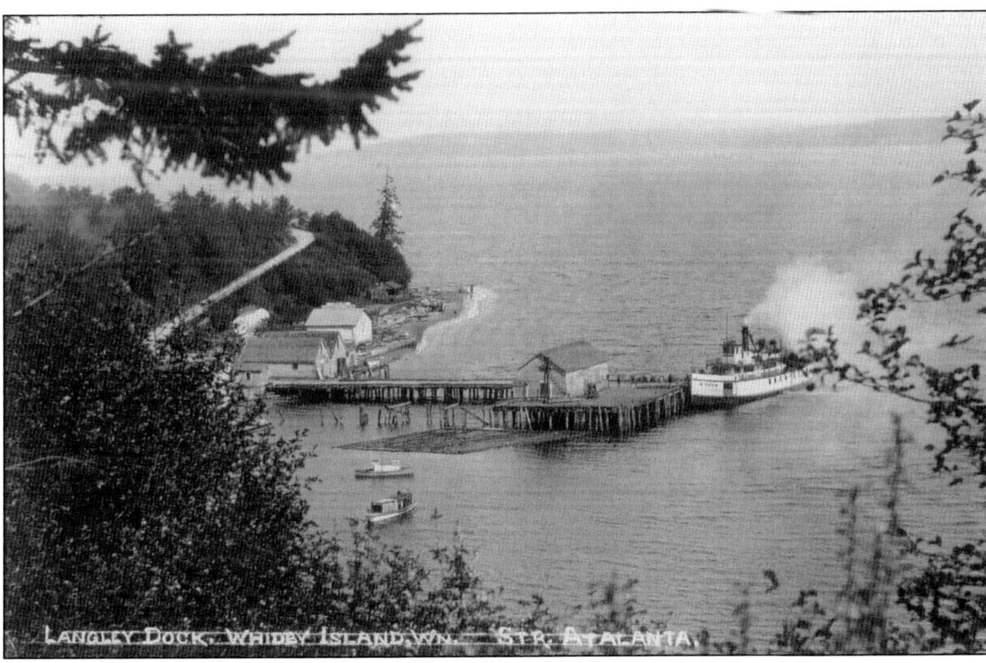

This photograph shows the *Atalanta* at the Langley dock around 1929. Funds for maintenance of the dock were scarce during the Great Depression, and a WPA crew supervised by John Farmer of Bush Point replaced the south leg of the dock in 1939 at a cost of $10,000. It had a float that permitted moorage for smaller craft. (Courtesy of Roger Steele.)

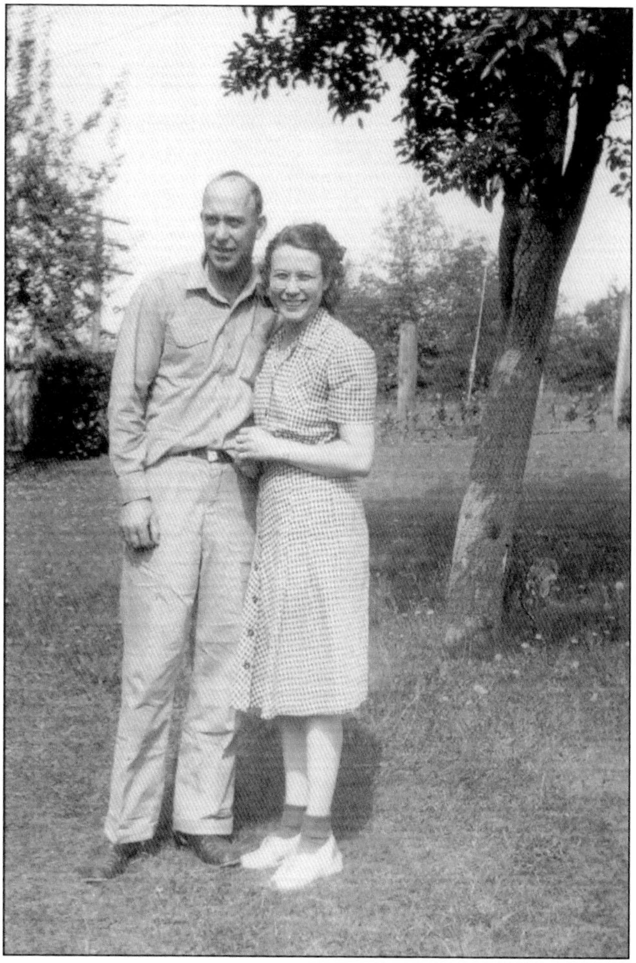

In 1941, Arvid and Leone Hansen, pictured here, bought lots 10 and 11 in the Sunrise Beach Addition. With the help of Leone's father, Ernest Atkinson, they began constructing cabins north of the Standard Oil facility that would become the Sunrise Beach Resort. Arvid also owned the building that housed Ferrell's Fountain on First Street. (Courtesy of Virginia Lindsey.)

The Sunrise Beach Resort cabins are pictured here around 1942. Each cabin had a small bedroom and cooking facilities. Firewood, placed in the spaces between cabins, was accessible through a little door. Fishing resorts were popular, and the Sunrise Beach Resort was one of approximately 20 such vacation spots on South Whidbey. (Courtesy of Virginia Lindsey.)

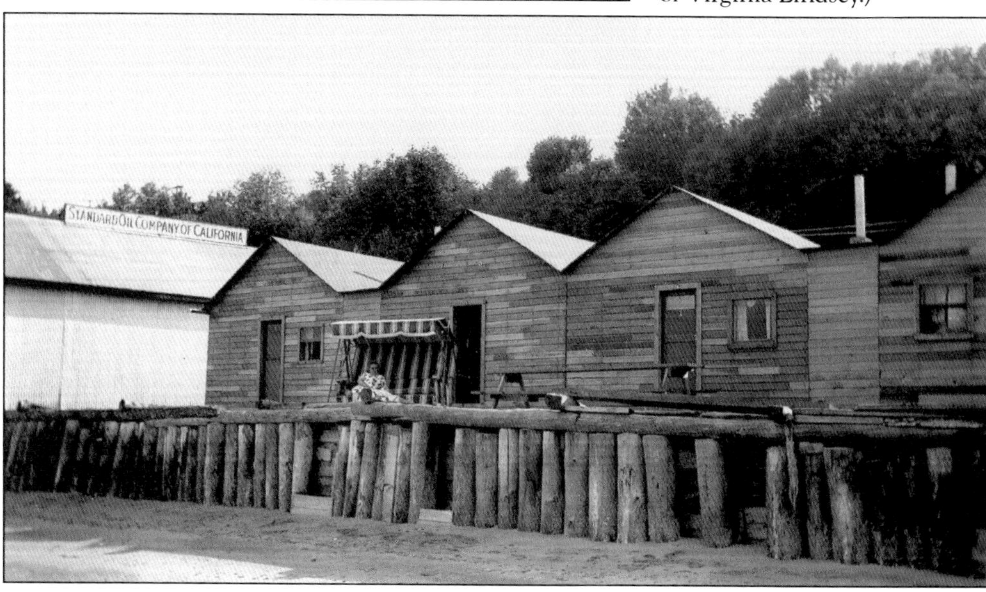

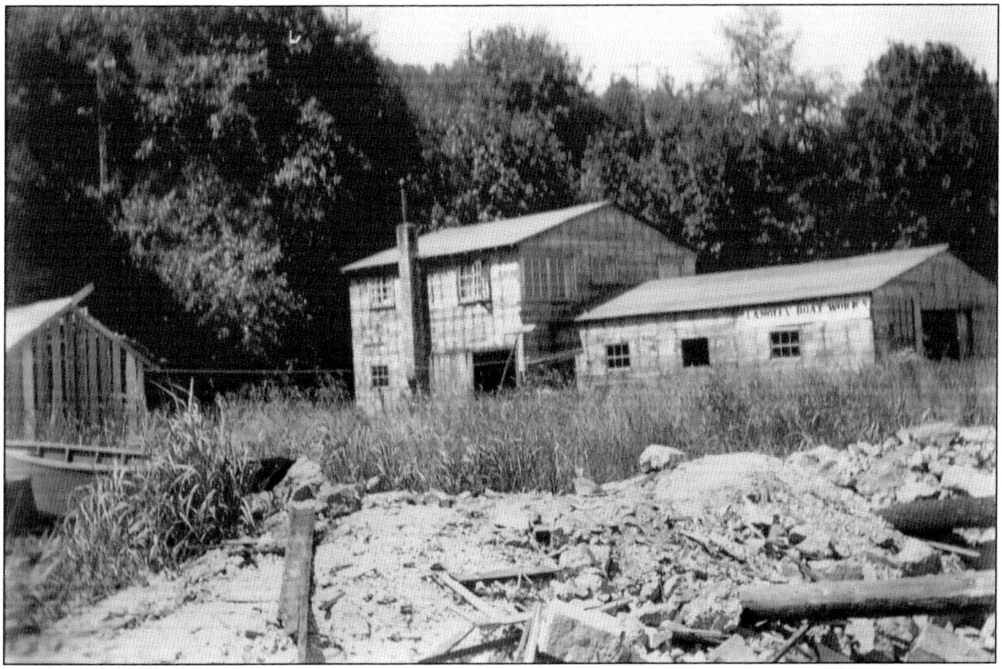

The Langley Boat Works was housed in a two-story building north of the cabins. The above photograph, taken from the beach, shows how it looked when purchased by the Hansens. They converted it into an office on the ground floor and living quarters for their family above. The below photograph shows the structure after the renovation. There was an additional bathroom next to the office for use by guests in the smaller cabins. Fish were plentiful. People could rent a cabin, fishing gear, and a boat for very little money. (Both, courtesy of Virginia Lindsey.)

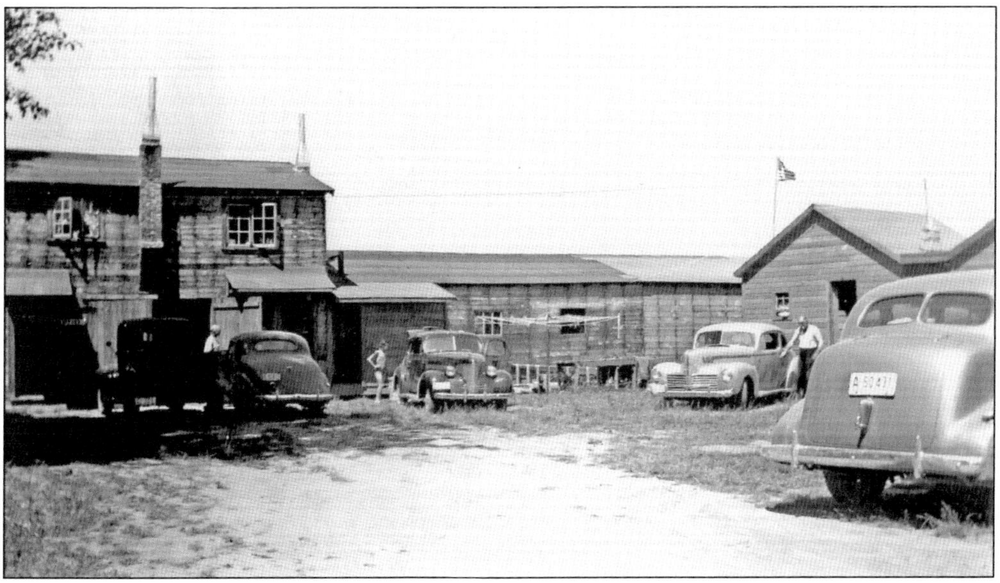

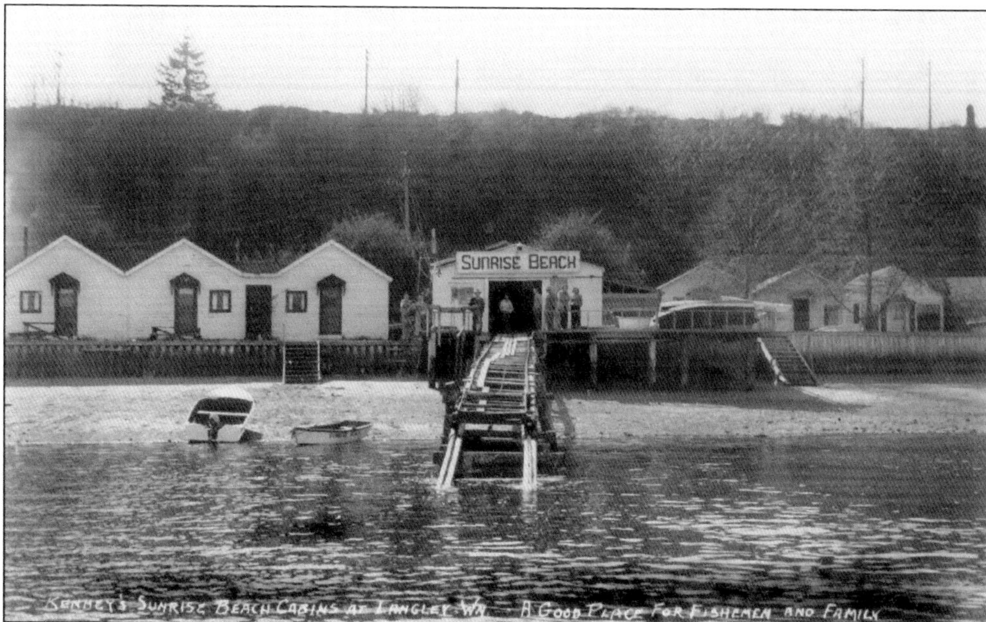

The cabins were painted white, and awnings were constructed over the doors. In 1944, the Hansens sold the Sunrise Beach Resort to the Kaastrups, who sold it to Walter Kenney in 1945. The Kenneys built an additional three cabins (right) north of the old Langley Boat Works building. (Courtesy of Terry Schmidt.)

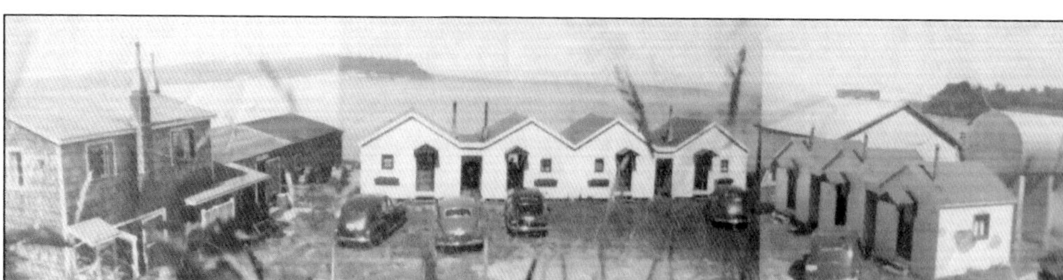

In 1959, Harold and Florence Haun purchased the Sunrise Beach Resort, and they operated it until 1975. They modernized the cabins and installed gasoline facilities. Nichols Brothers Boat Builders of Freeland bought the resort property for its Langley operation in 1979. The resort buildings were removed except for the old Langley Boat Works building (left), which was retained. (Courtesy of Florence Haun.)

Eight

Struggle for Survival 1950–1970

South Whidbey gradually changed its character through these next two decades. Logging slowed as the supply of timber decreased and those employed in the industry left town. Reflecting trends across the country, some residents expressed a new awareness of preserving the natural forests. Pollution from the Everett harbor and other causes greatly diminished the salmon runs, and both commercial and sports fishing languished.

Along Langley's First Street, a few businesses catering to locals held on, but many storefronts stood empty. Despite this economic downturn, the town made some progress. In the 1950s, a four-unit motel began to house tourists on the corner of Sixth Street and Cascade Avenue. Good Cheer, a donation thrift shop, opened in 1962. St. Hubert Catholic Mission was elevated to a parish church in 1966, and parishioners constructed a new building on Langley's west side. Across town, the Christian Missionary Alliance Church moved to its new home at Cascade Avenue and Sixth Street. A real estate agent named Robert Smith bought up the properties along the north side of First Street from the Dog House Tavern east and began renovating. Down at the wharf, Bernard and Marjorie Hein purchased the old brush plant and opened the Langley Marina, serving recreational boaters and the clients of the Sunrise Beach Resort.

In the late 1960s, the first flight of "hippies" wafted into town. They had relatives or close friends on South Whidbey, and word of mouth brought more newcomers from Seattle, California, and the Midwest. These "back to the landers" were attracted by the island's rural character and cheap rents. Small farms, vegetable gardens, and shared housing enabled an inexpensive alternative lifestyle, exactly what the 1960s generation was searching for. Some lived in school buses, others in renovated chicken coops. For $75 per month, one could rent an old house plus 50 acres. In 1969, government funding helped build Brookhaven, a low-income housing community. Mostly, the "old timers" welcomed this new wave of energy that would catalyze the revival of their town.

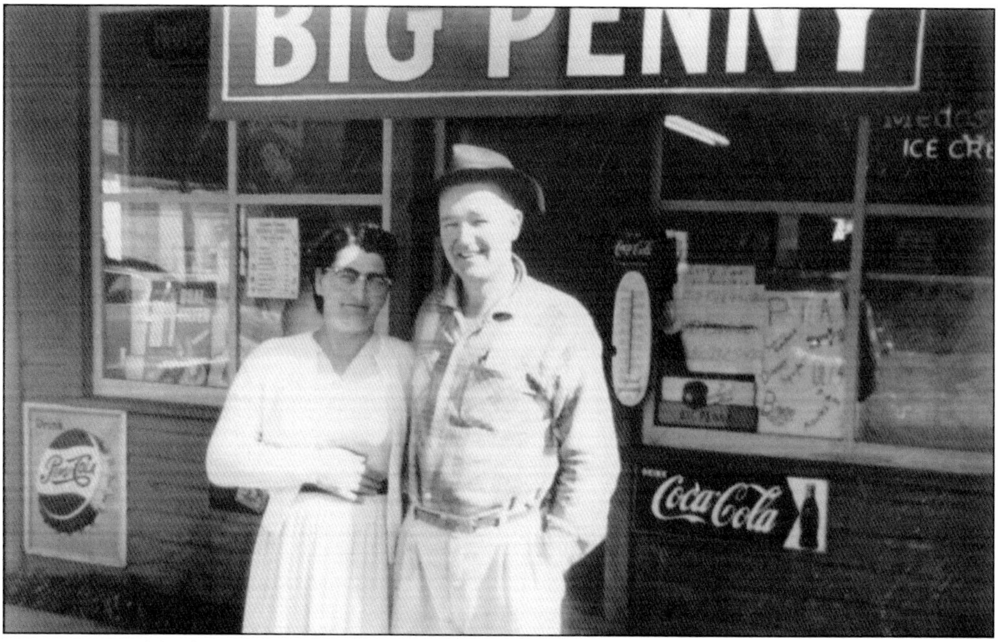

Margaret "Mildred" and Albert Anderson, seen here in 1959, operated the Big Penny store, in the old Norman Clyde Garage building on Anthes Avenue, from 1954 to 1964. It was a grocery store, and Mildred served hot lunches in the back. The store was previously owned by Edward Kyler and Albert Monet. (Courtesy of Margaret Anderson.)

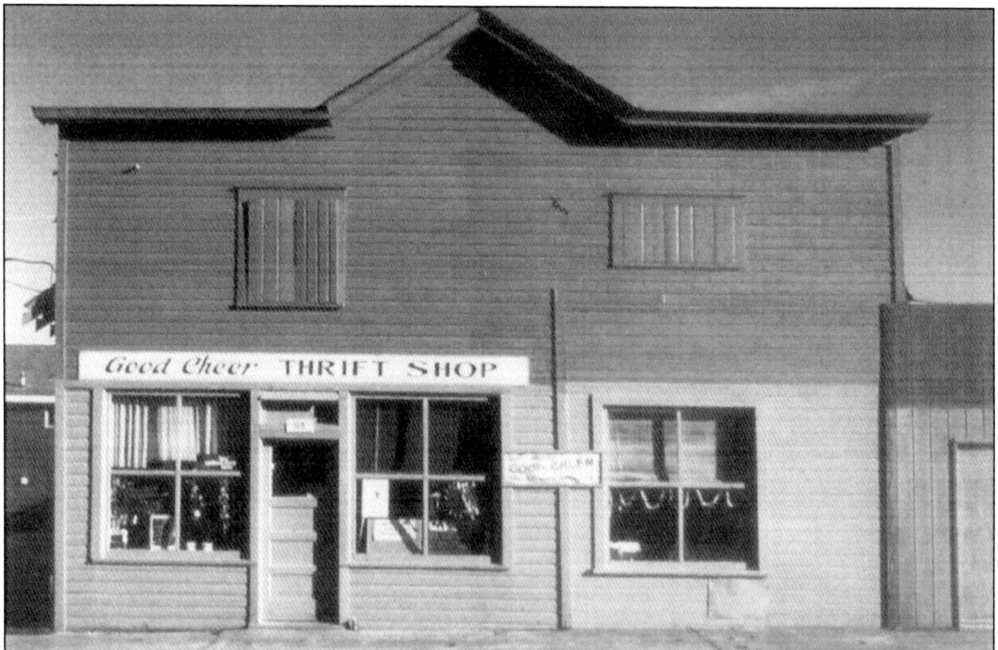

The Andersons sold the building to Good Cheer in 1969 to house its thrift shop. Good Cheer began in 1962 and was formally organized in 1963. It was located for a short time in the old post office building owned by Ernest Noble on First Street before moving into this building in 1966. (Courtesy of Good Cheer.)

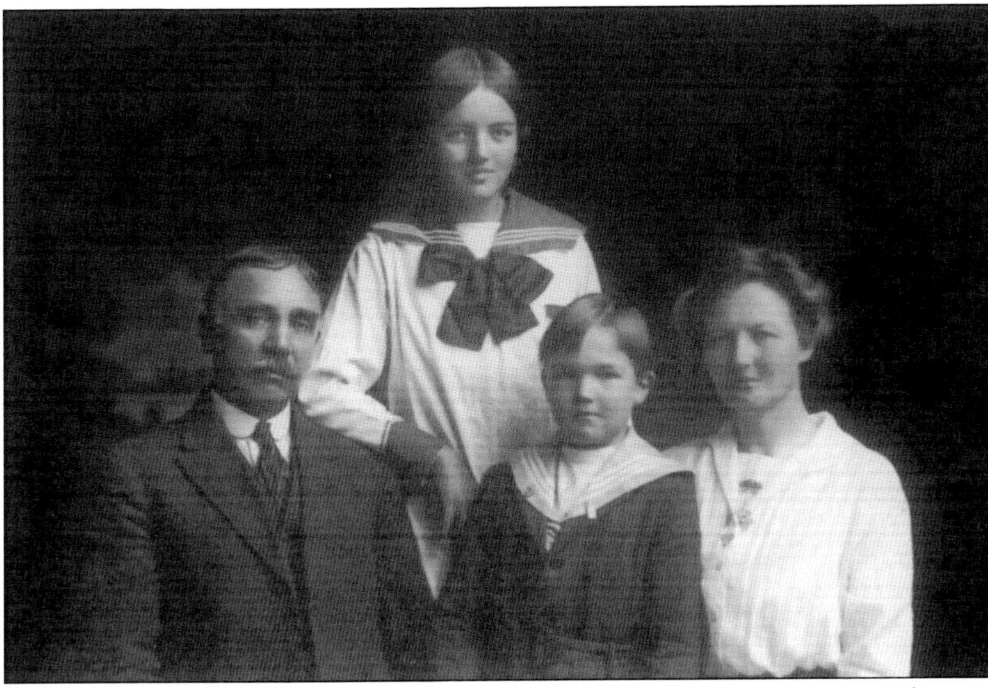

The Anders Anderson family came to Langley from Montana in 1906. The family members are, from left to right, Anders, Ester, Albert, and Bertina. They stayed in the two-story house across Second Street from the Anthes bunkhouse while Anders built a small house south of town next to the cemetery. Albert was born there in 1910; he married Margaret Hagglund in 1937. (Courtesy of the SWHS.)

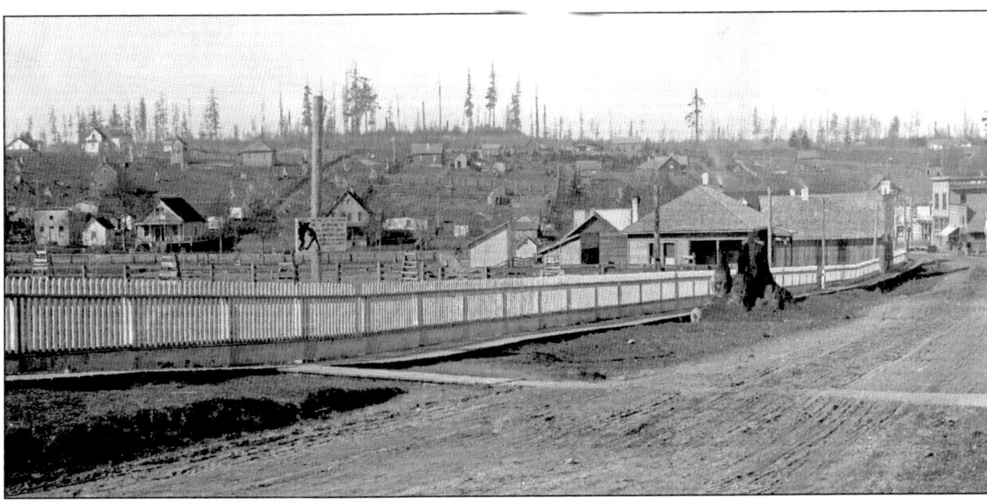

This view looking west shows First Street around 1920. The two-story house (third from left) at Second Street and Anthes Avenue housed early arrivals, such as the Andersons, while they found permanent homes. It later served as a high school, a newspaper office, the Primaveras' home and shoe repair business, a brush packing plant, and a lumberyard. It was demolished in 1968 to make room for the octagonal Whidbey Record Building. (Courtesy of the SWHS.)

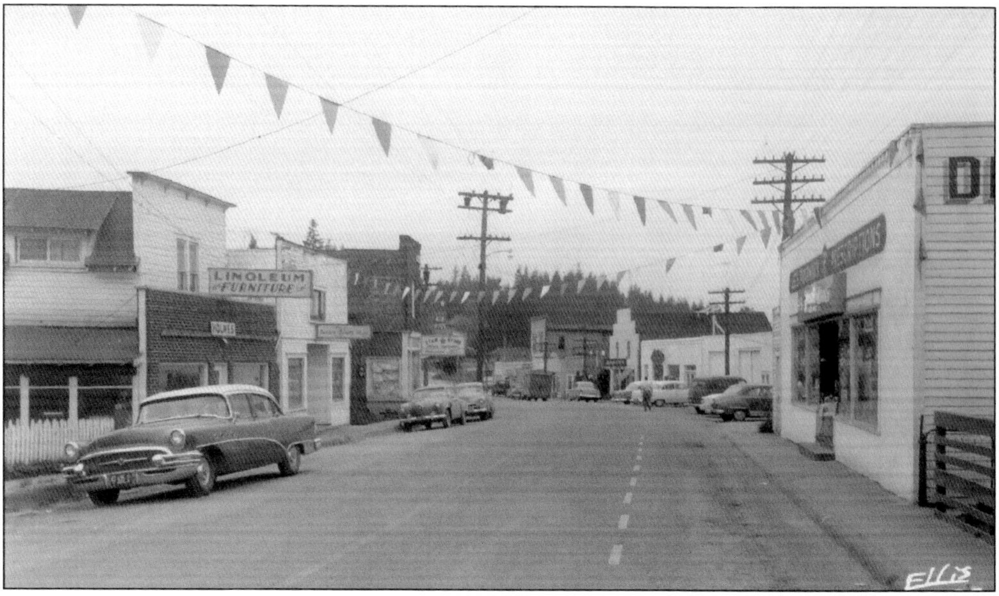

This photograph shows First Street looking west around 1955. The drugstore (right) was purchased by Leo Lee in 1955 from Dr. Brewer's ex-wife, Fern, and renamed Lee's Langley Drugs. The building across the street, formerly owned by Dr. Brewer, was turned into Linoleum and Furniture store by Carl Drake. When Carl's son, Delbert, was killed in Korea, Carl sold it to the Mahans. (Photograph by Ellis; courtesy of Anna Primavera.)

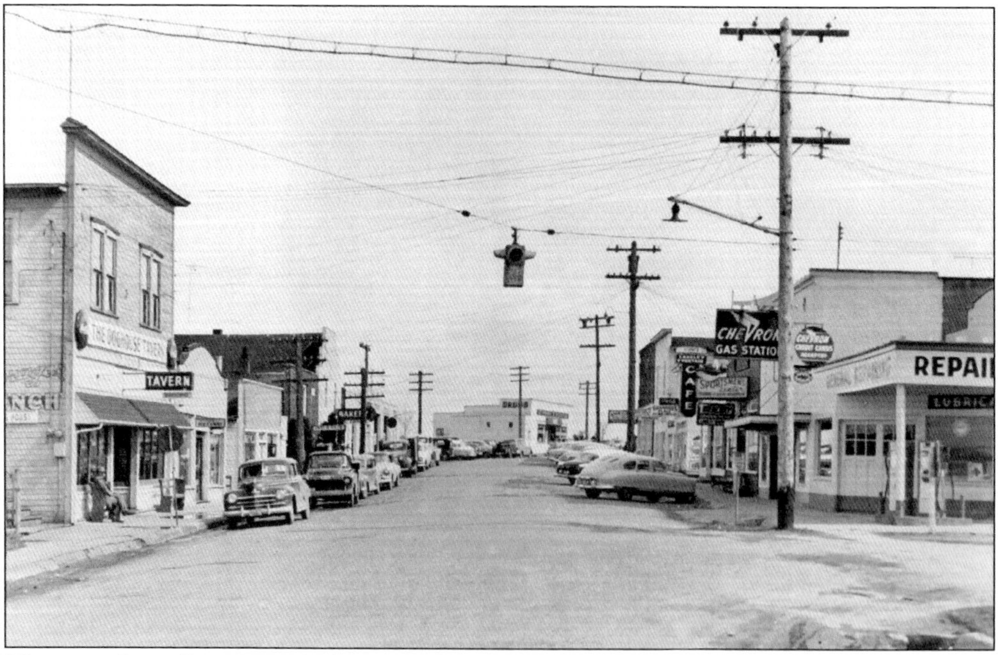

This view shows First Street looking east from Anthes Avenue around 1955. Next to the Clyde Garage and Clyde Theatre (right) was the former Mortenson hardware store, purchased in 1952 by Bernard Hein, who sold outboard motors. The sign on the storefront reads, "Sportsmen's Center. Fishing and Resort Information." Next door was Stuart's Fountain and Café. (Courtesy of Marion Henny.)

Around-the-island motorboat races began in 1954, with boats leaving from Holmes Harbor. The starting point was moved to Langley in 1958. A number of social events preceded and followed the race. Fredrick and Carl Frei won the race in 1958 with a time of two hours and fifty-five minutes. Two courses for different-sized boats, laid out in 1961, are shown on this map. (Courtesy of Robert Noble.)

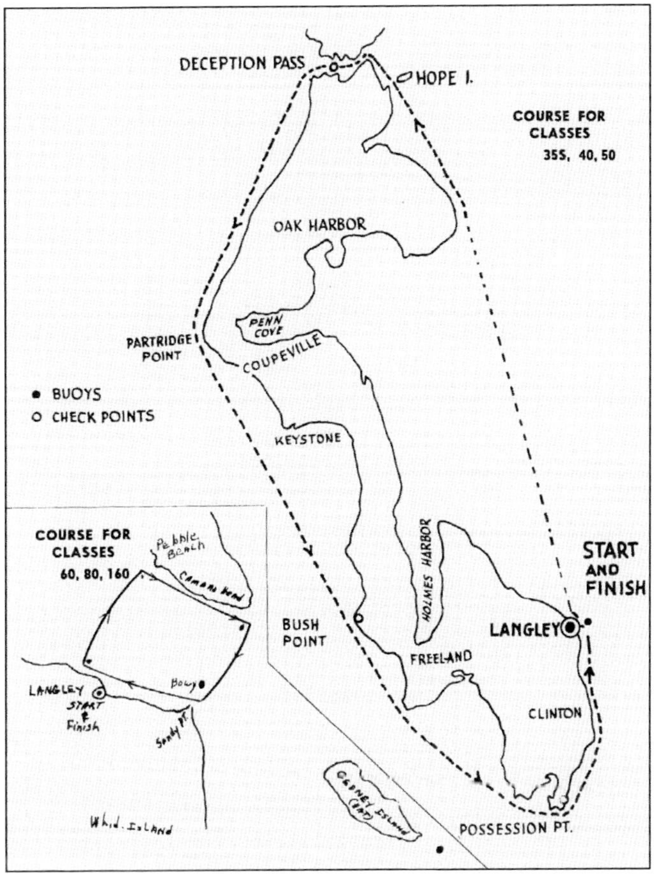

In 1959, Bernard "Barney" Hein and his wife, Marjorie, sold their hardware store on First Street and renovated the empty brush plant, converting it into the Langley Marina (left), which opened in May 1960. They built second-story living quarters and a 150-foot-long dock and installed a gas pump and underground tanks. (Courtesy of Florence Haun.)

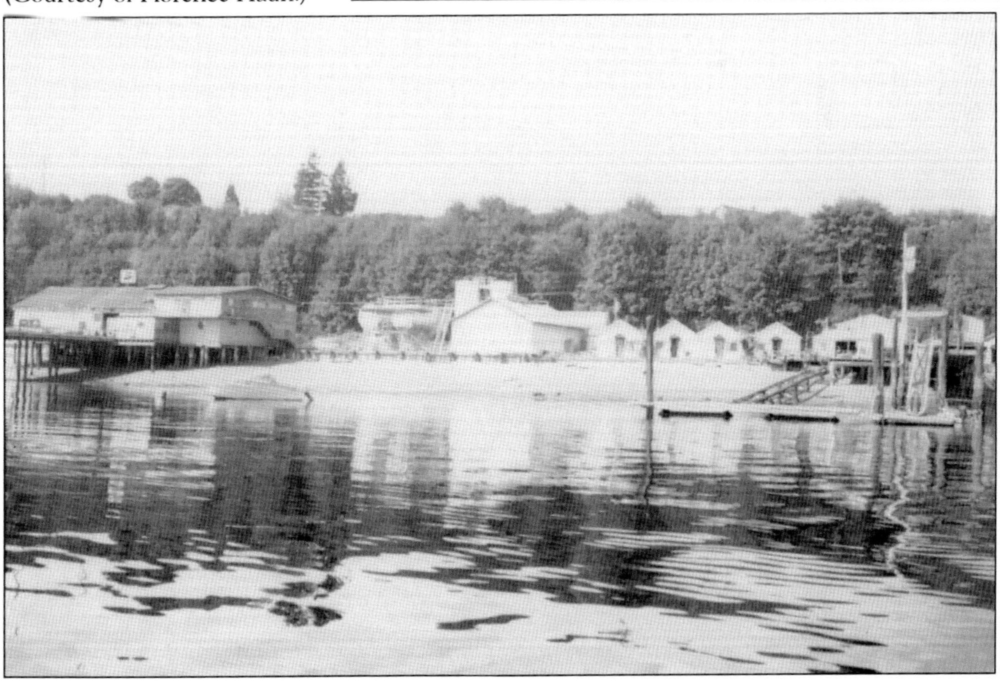

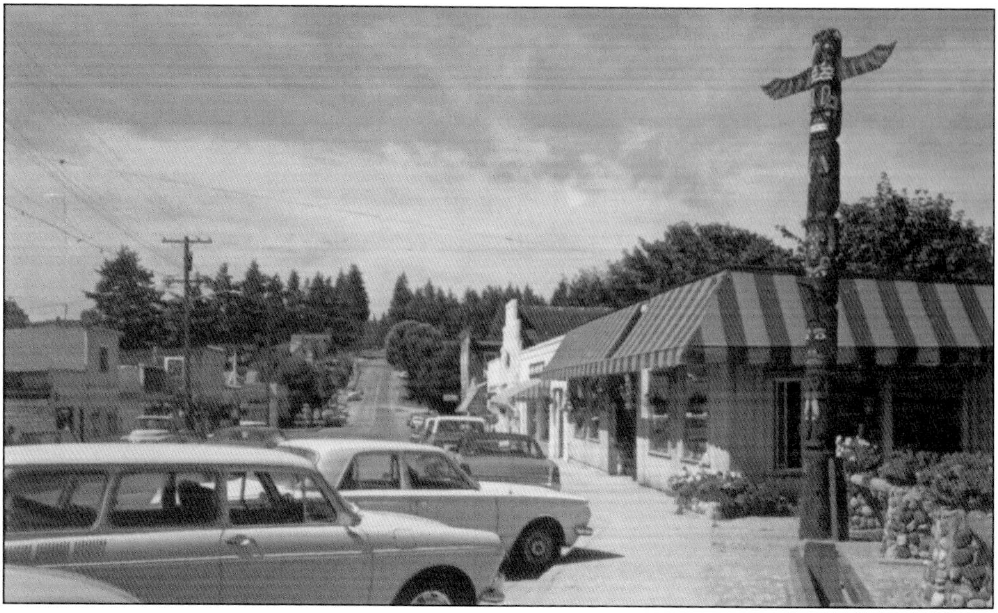

In 1965, Robert Smith purchased the buildings on the north side of First Street, from the Dog House Tavern to the open space next to the Lee's Drugs, and began revitalizing the block. The Langley Garage (right) was converted into retail spaces, including some run by Smith's relatives. In 1966, a totem pole carved by Mike Arnold was placed in the small park that Smith deeded to the town in 1969. (Courtesy of John Ball.)

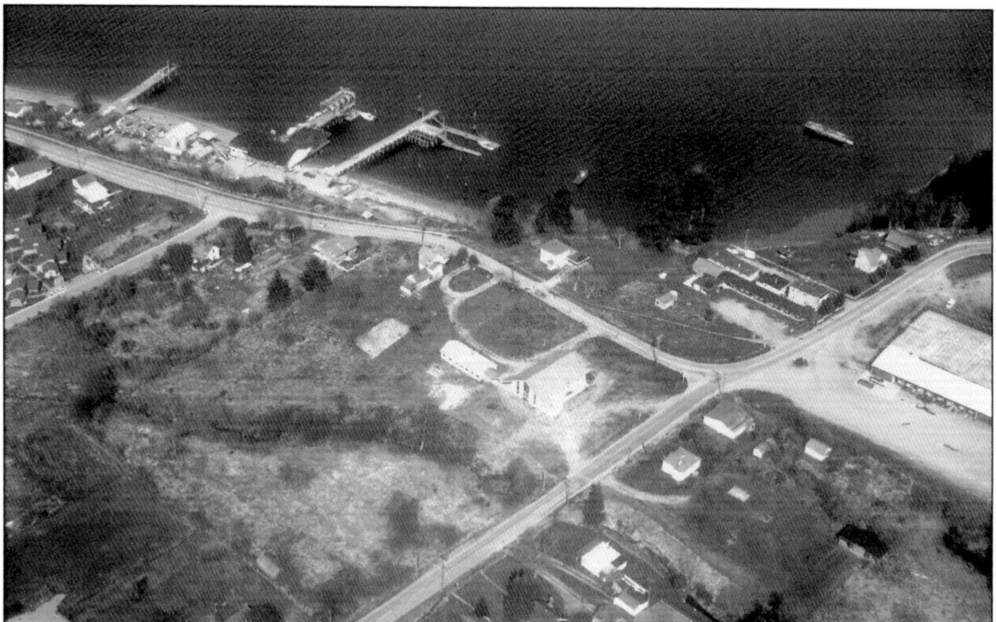

This 1971 aerial photograph shows a town dock with two mooring floats (left of center) constructed in 1963 by the Washington State Parks and Recreation Commission and the Langley Marina and Sunrise Beach Resort docks. A Christian Missionary Alliance Church building (center), constructed in 1966, replaced the former church on Saratoga Road. The adjacent chicken coop, called Leghorn Hall, served as classrooms. (Courtesy of Ben Breedlove.)

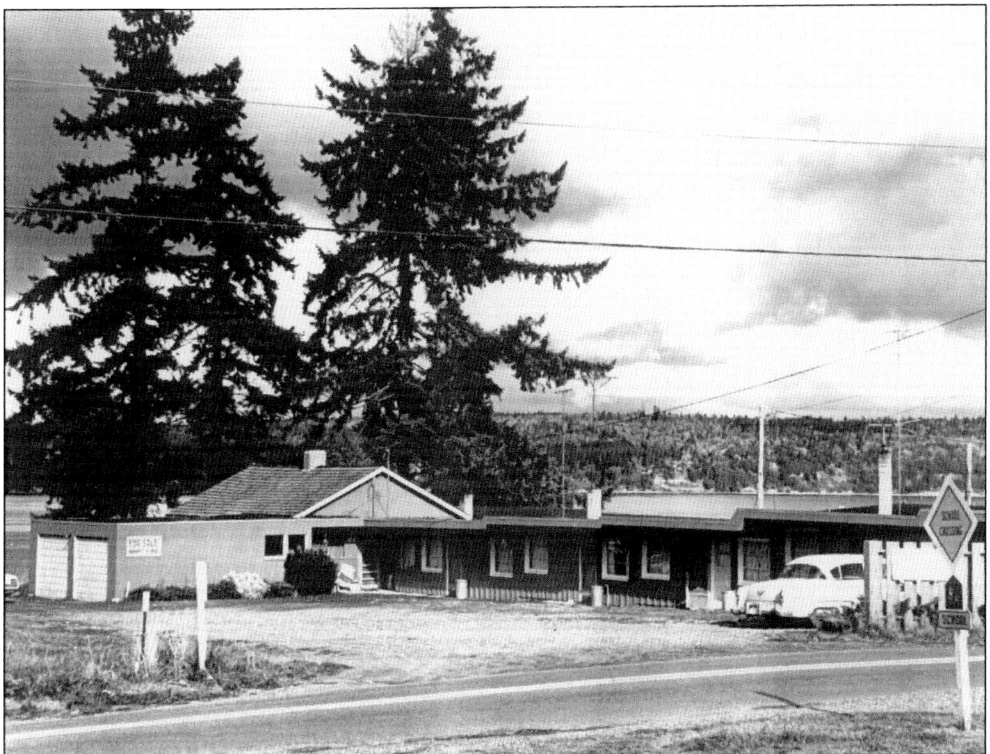

The four-unit Langley Motel and adjacent house were built in the 1950s on Cascade Avenue overlooking Saratoga Passage, across from the school bus barn. The motel units were later converted to apartments. The complex was restored to a motel in 2002 by the present owner, Todd Soli. (Courtesy of Gary Piper.)

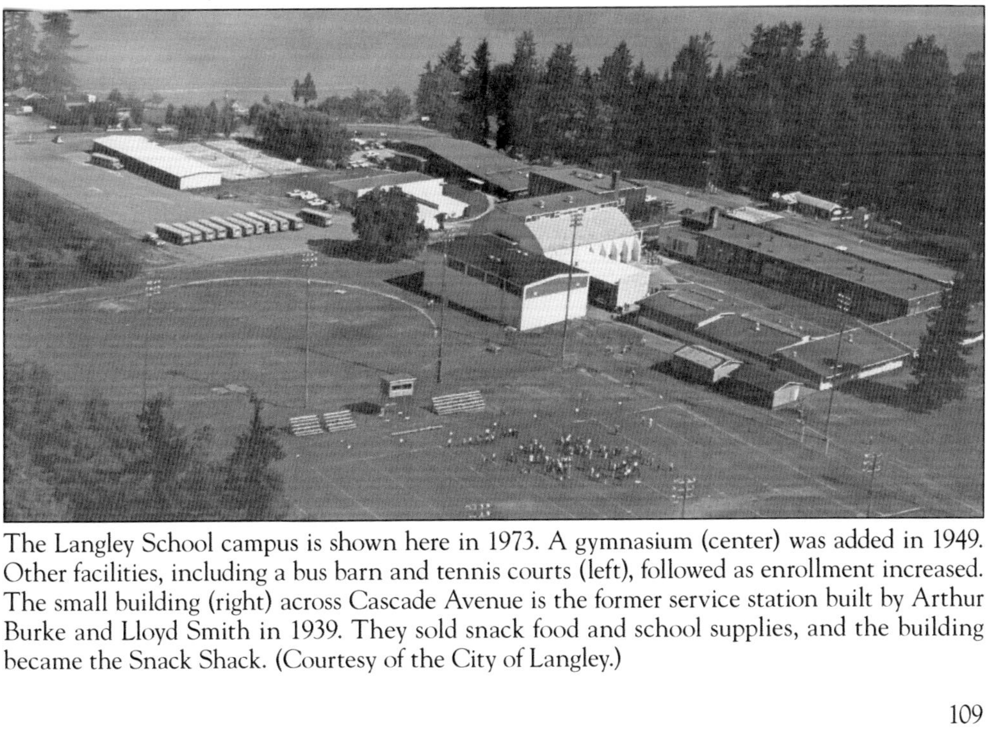

The Langley School campus is shown here in 1973. A gymnasium (center) was added in 1949. Other facilities, including a bus barn and tennis courts (left), followed as enrollment increased. The small building (right) across Cascade Avenue is the former service station built by Arthur Burke and Lloyd Smith in 1939. They sold snack food and school supplies, and the building became the Snack Shack. (Courtesy of the City of Langley.)

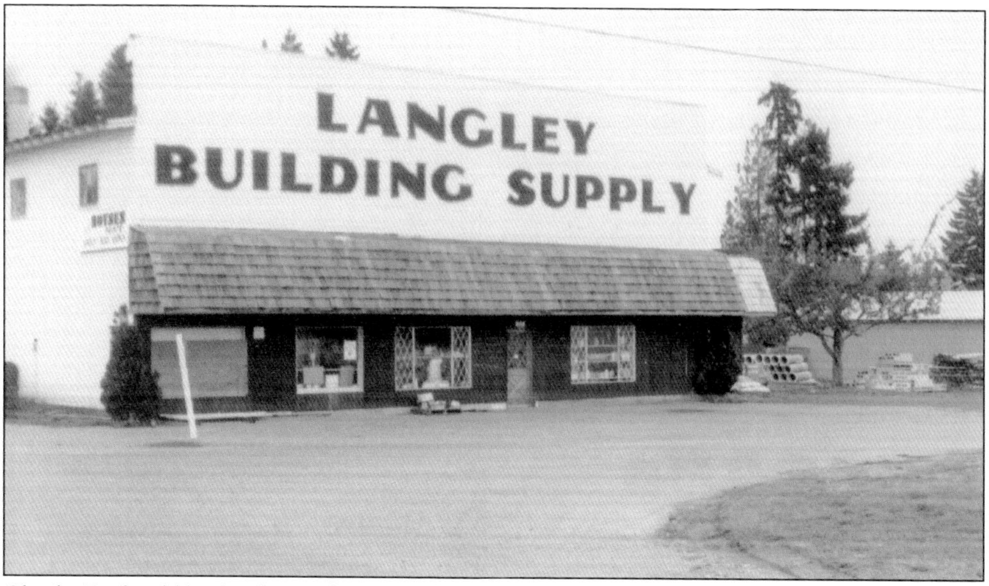

Charles Burk sold his lumberyard at Second Street and DeBruyn Avenue to Phillip and Jean Bjorn in 1971. They remodeled it and renamed it Langley Building Supply. The Bjorns' son-in-law, Bob Frause, installed the letters. Small storage units were later added behind the main building. The building at right was constructed to house a thrift store. (Courtesy of Jean Bjorn.)

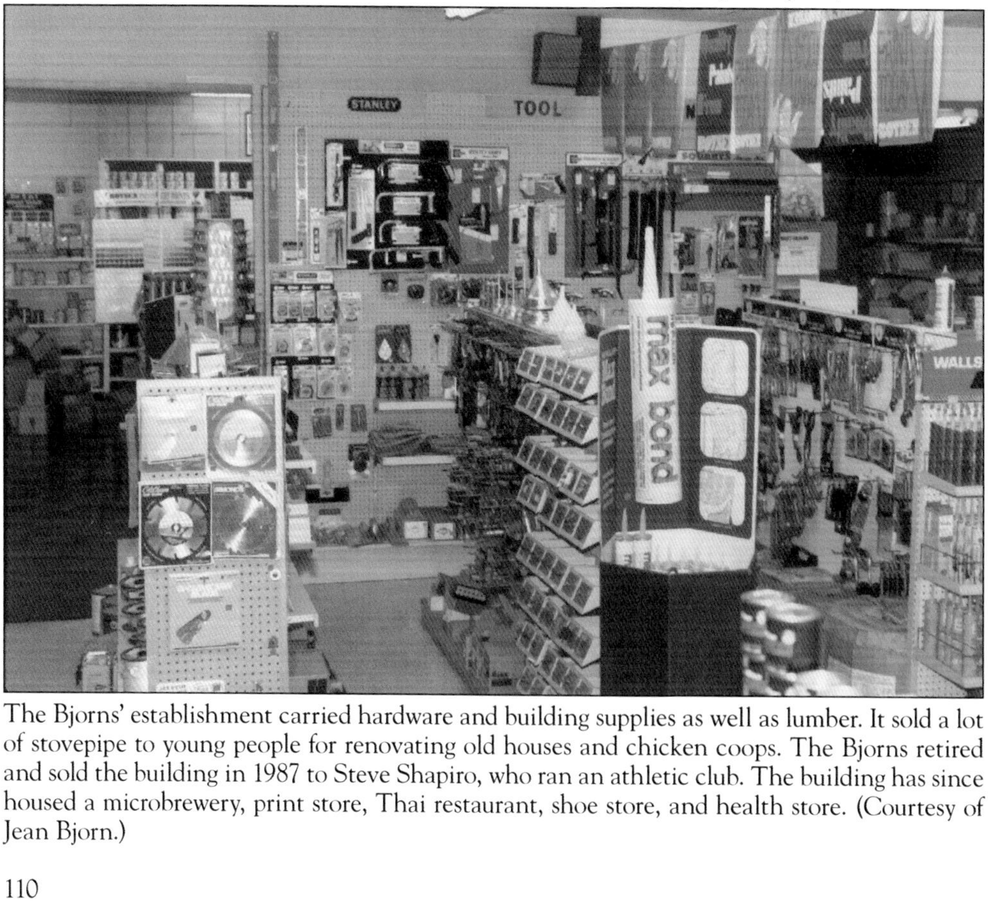

The Bjorns' establishment carried hardware and building supplies as well as lumber. It sold a lot of stovepipe to young people for renovating old houses and chicken coops. The Bjorns retired and sold the building in 1987 to Steve Shapiro, who ran an athletic club. The building has since housed a microbrewery, print store, Thai restaurant, shoe store, and health store. (Courtesy of Jean Bjorn.)

Nine

REJUVENATION *1970–1990*

Cooperation, and a sense of community, thrived. With this came a bakery, women's clinic, and the Soup Coop, a restaurant and food cooperative. Island Strings offered music classes, while the Island Theater produced plays. Josh and Glenn Hauser turned the old post office building into the Moonraker bookstore. Blake Willeford purchased the Clyde Theatre.

The town was officially designated a city in 1975. The following year, to protect the buildings along First Street, the city constructed a sea wall and Sea Wall Park. Next, the town installed a sewer system. Beginning in 1976, Bob Sabatini rallied many people to produce a series of live musical extravaganzas called "Fools" productions. To encourage sale of their work, visual artists staged the "100 Bucks Flat" shows upstairs in the Dog House Tavern. Local merchants began an artists' street fair. John Braun named it Choochokam, a Hopi word meaning "a gathering of stars."

The prosperity of the 1980s and 1990s brought many visitors to South Whidbey. Langley's hardware stores and garages retreated out to the main highway, replaced by businesses catering to tourism. In 1989, the Inn at Langley opened, followed by the Saratoga and Boatyard Inns. Down at the wharf, a new dock with moorage for recreational boaters was under way. Nichols Brothers Boat Builders, South Whidbey's largest commercial enterprise, replaced the Sunrise Beach Resort property with a facility to outfit and test its commercial boats.

These changes set the stage for the Langley of today, still bounded by breathtaking views of the Cascade Mountains, Camano Island, and the waters of Saratoga Passage. Gray and orca whales visit, prompting anyone who notices them to sound the "whale bell." Community activities include performances at Whidbey Island Center for the Arts, gallery openings, Mystery Weekend, movies at the Clyde, art fairs, the Island County Fair, and some of the shortest parades ever staged. Although Langley never thrived in the way that Jacob Anthes envisioned, it has grown into a unique blend of locals, visitors, artists, businesspeople, families, and retirees. Langley is still blessed with a strong sense of community and remains very much a village by the sea.

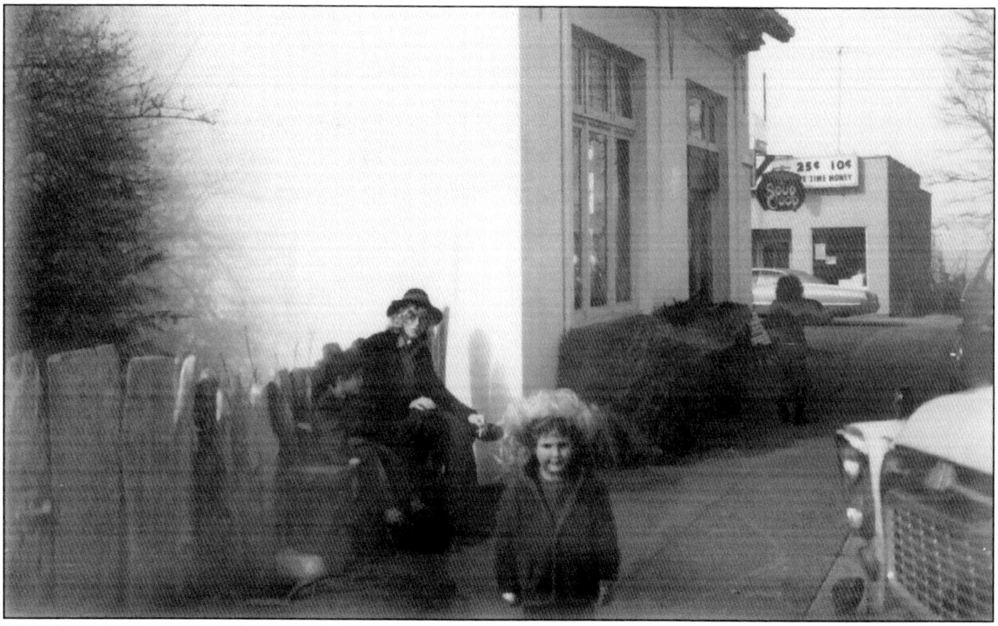

The Langley State Bank was sold to People's Bank and moved to a new building at the corner of Second Street and Anthes Avenue in 1970. A food cooperative and restaurant called the Soup Coop opened in 1972 in the former bank building and became a hangout for the hippies that lived in the area. (Courtesy of Brian McKenna.)

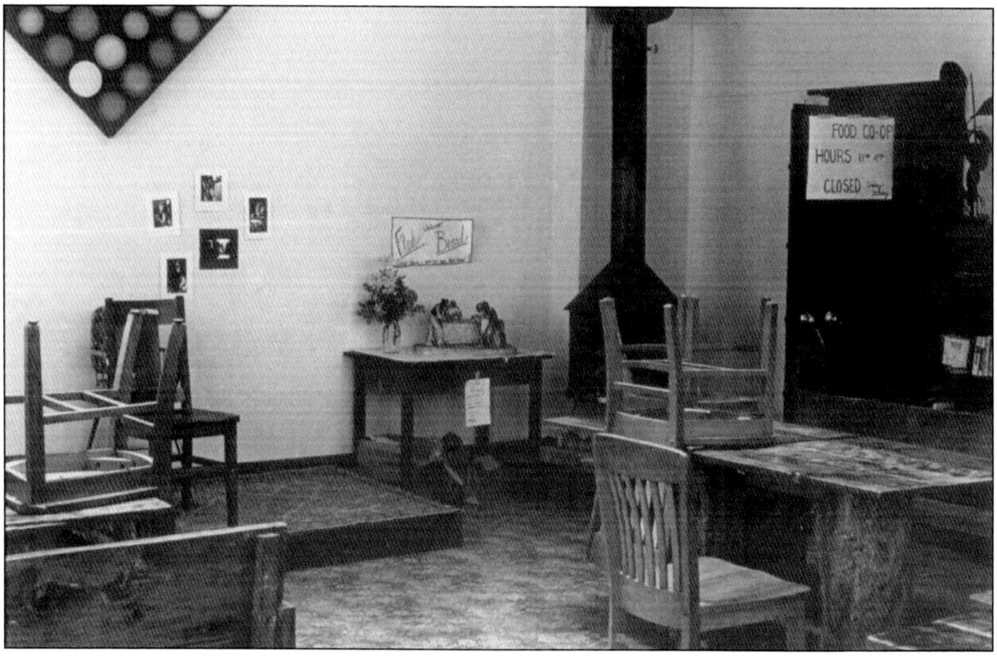

Food from the co-op was dispensed from the former bank vault (right). A small stage was used for musical performances. The original goal was to provide a community center where people of different lifestyles could meet. The establishment only lasted a few years, but it started a racing event down First Street called the Soup Box Derby that continues today. (Courtesy of Brian McKenna.)

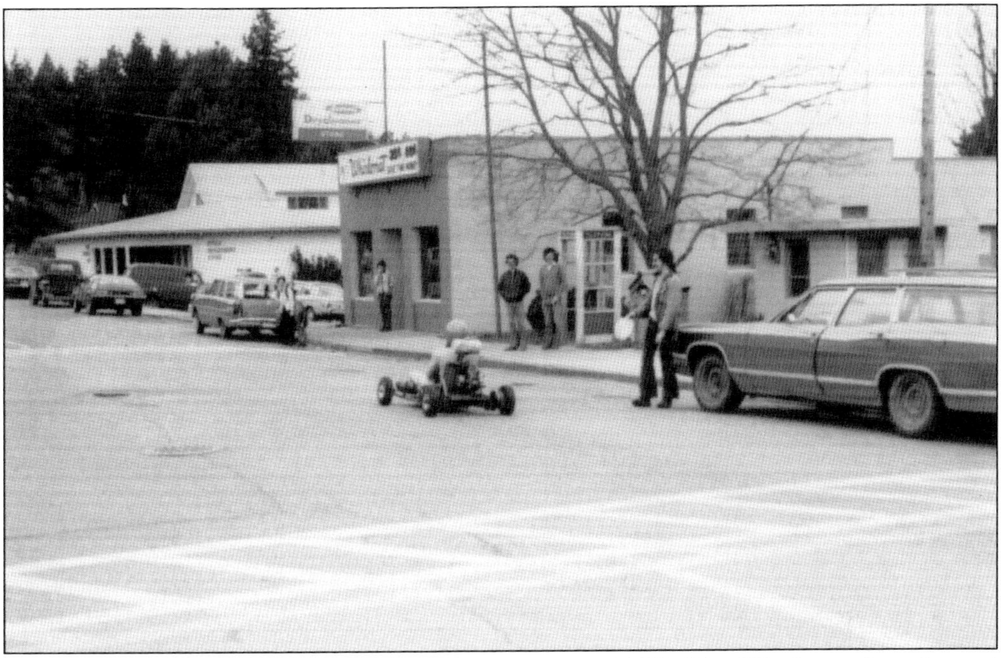

This photograph shows First Street, looking west, around 1974. The Whirlomat Laundry and Dry-Cleaning store occupies the former post office, across the street from the Soup Coop. The Jones Department Store (left) occupies the former Roderick McLeod house west of the Whirlomat. Vincent and Matilda Jones purchased the department store from the Duncans in 1956 and enlarged it in 1962. (Courtesy of Brian McKenna.)

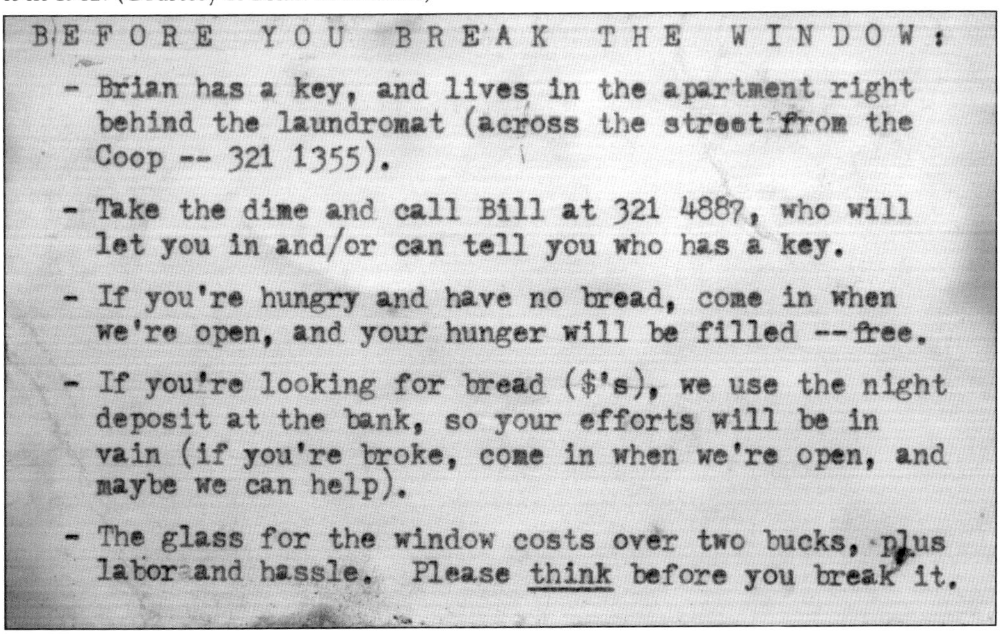

BEFORE YOU BREAK THE WINDOW:

- Brian has a key, and lives in the apartment right behind the laundromat (across the street from the Coop -- 321 1355).
- Take the dime and call Bill at 321 4887, who will let you in and/or can tell you who has a key.
- If you're hungry and have no bread, come in when we're open, and your hunger will be filled --free.
- If you're looking for bread ($'s), we use the night deposit at the bank, so your efforts will be in vain (if you're broke, come in when we're open, and maybe we can help).
- The glass for the window costs over two bucks, plus labor and hassle. Please <u>think</u> before you break it.

This sign in the window of the Soup Coop offered a warning to potential burglars. Brian McKenna, who managed the Soup Coop, lived in the apartment in the back of the Whirlomat building. The structure had been the home of the postmaster before the post office relocated to a new building on Second Street in 1960. (Courtesy of Brian McKenna.)

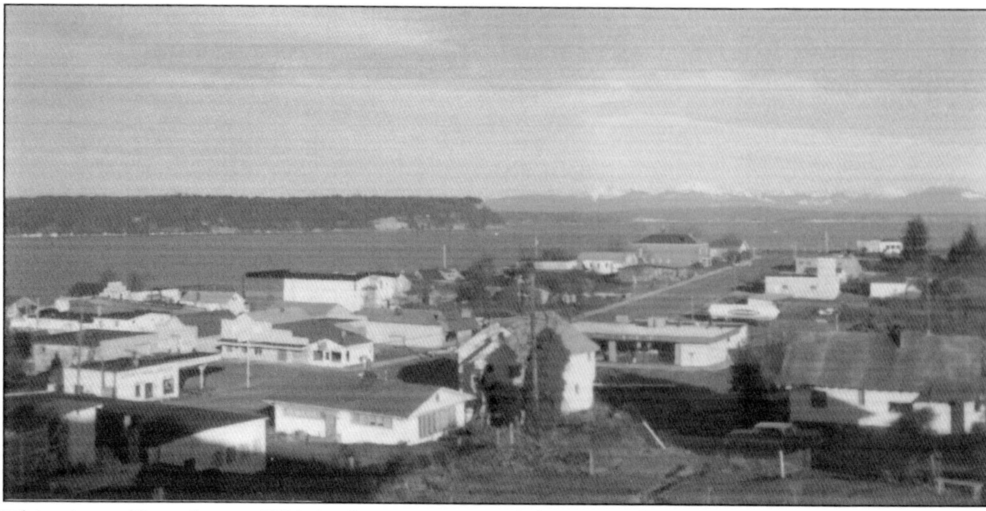

This view of Langley in 1971, looking east toward the Cascade Mountains, shows development along Second Street. The library and the Masonic temple are prominent features on the north side, and at the far end, of the street. The Chevron gas station across the street from the library, and the People's Bank at Second Street and Anthes Avenue, anchor the south side. (Courtesy of Anna Primavera.)

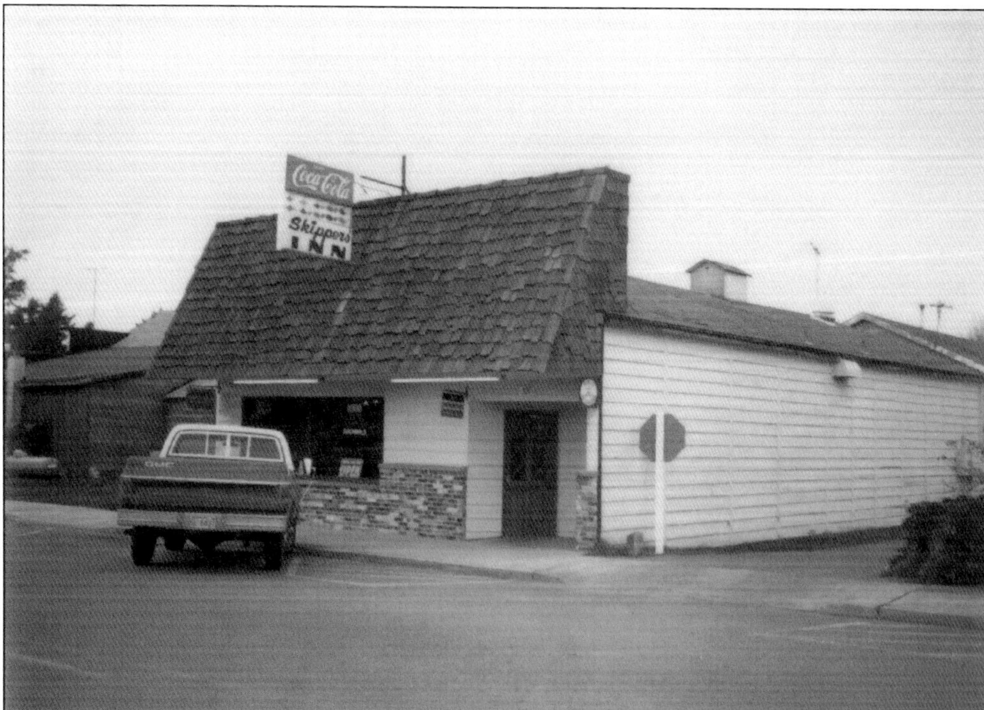

This building on Second Street, constructed by Wally and Sally Frick as a hardware store, was transformed into Skipper's Inn and Langley Café and Second Street Bar, establishments that became favorite hangouts for locals. Herbert and Marilyn Helsel purchased it in 1988 and remodeled it into a number of retail spaces, including Herb's Clock Shop. The alley along its length became known as Frick Lane. (Courtesy of the City of Langley.)

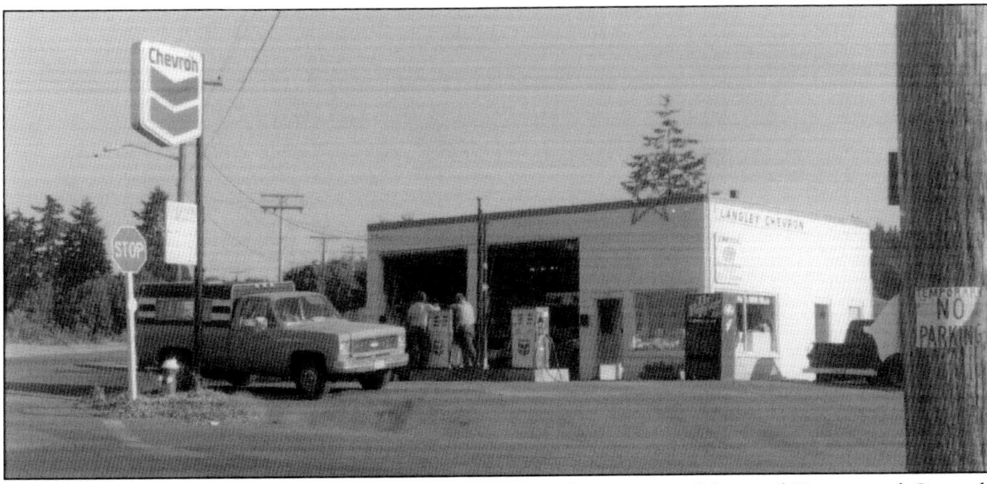

Norman Baker operated this Chevron gas station at the corner of Second Street and Cascade Avenue in the 1970s. It became the Mater-Lube of Langley, Inc., before being demolished in 1992 to make room for the Harrison House, which opened in 1994 and was renamed the Saratoga Inn a few years later. (Courtesy of Ross Chapin.)

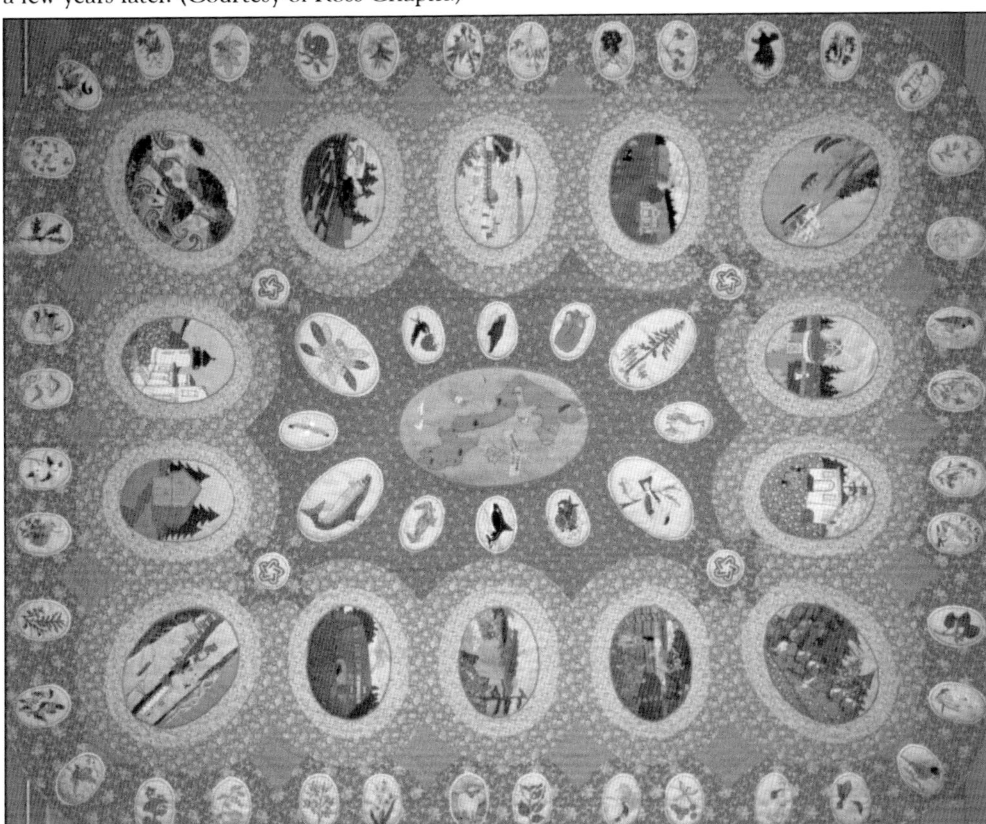

This quilt illustrating South Whidbey's history was raffled in 1978 as a fundraiser for the Wellspring Clinic, a family planning clinic housed in the former auto body shop on Anthes Avenue. Prior to this, women had to go off-island to get care. The clinic was eventually taken over by Washington State Planned Parenthood Association and moved to Oak Harbor. (Courtesy of Marjorie Dente.)

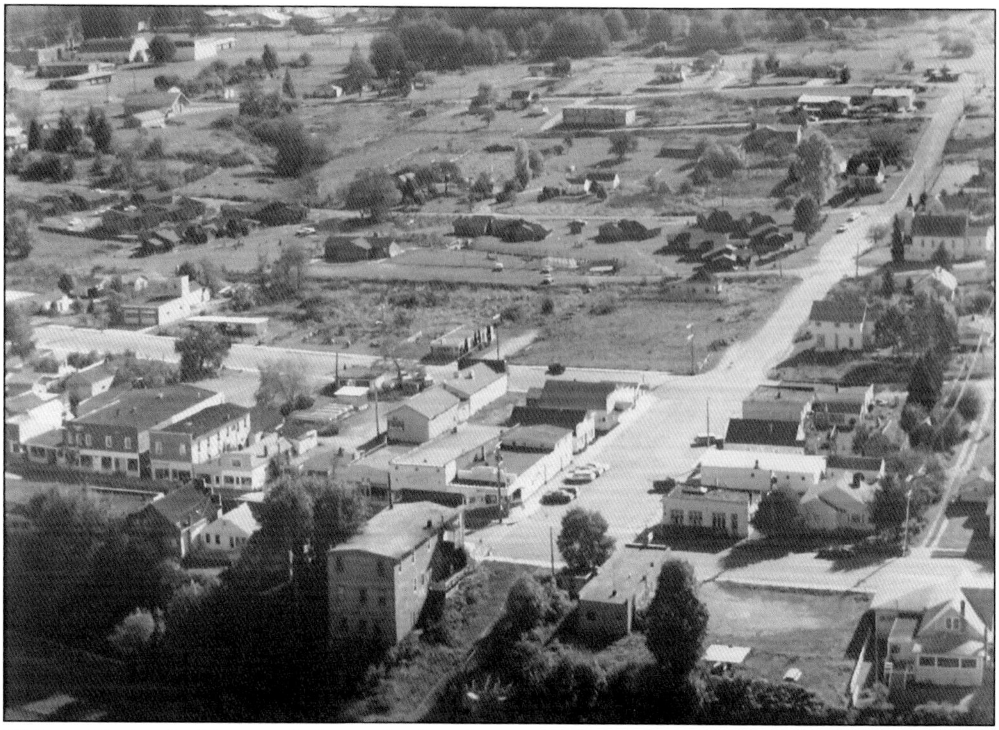

This aerial view looking south shows Anthes Avenue in 1969. The 40-unit, government-subsidized Brookhaven housing complex (center) between Third and Fourth Streets was completed in 1969. The site once hosted a circus. To earn entrance to the show, kids filled water buckets for the elephants. The firehouse with a drying tower is seen on Second Street next to a small shed. (Courtesy of Neil Colburn.)

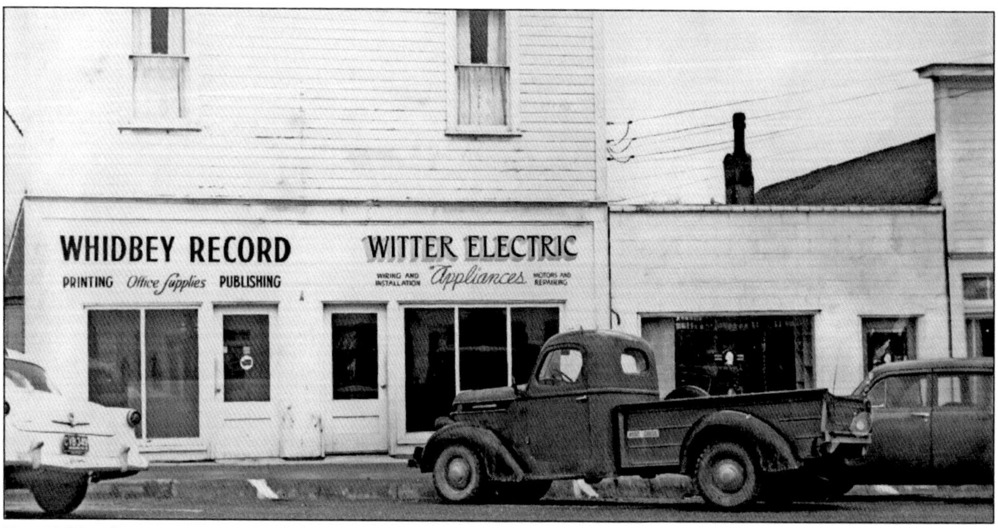

By 1970, the two-story building constructed in 1914 by the Brotherhood of Yeomen next to the Star Store was aging. The first floor housed numerous businesses over the years. The upper floor served as a meeting hall for civic organizations and as a residence during the 1940s. Victor Primavera purchased the building in 1970 and demolished it. The Liquor Store and former post office are at the right. (Courtesy of the SWHS.)

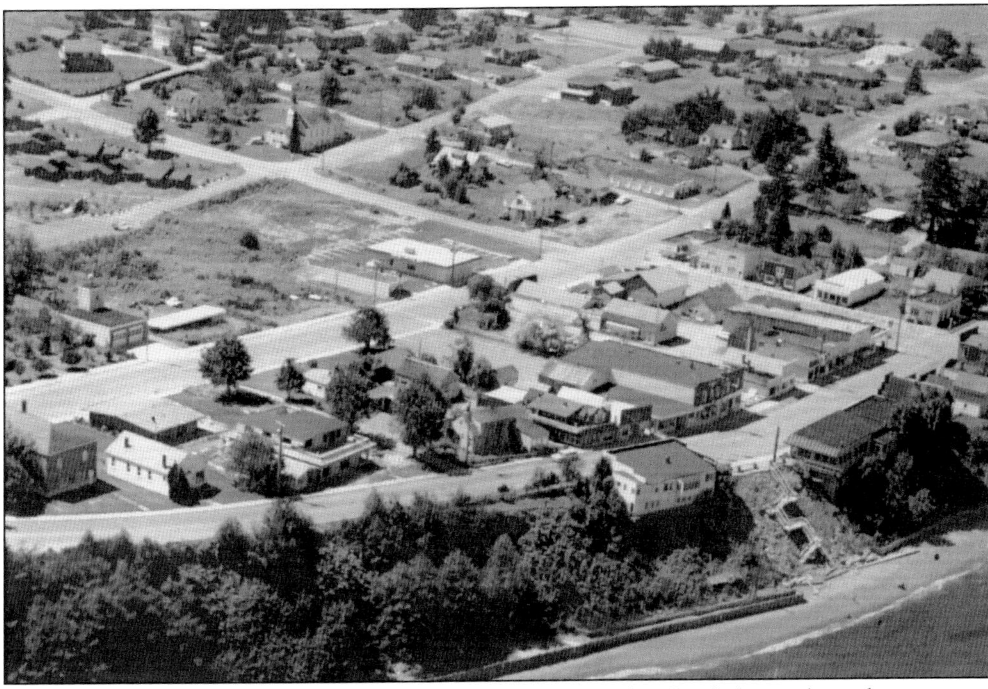

This aerial photograph was taken around 1970. The People's Bank (center), at the corner of Second Street and Anthes Avenue, was built in 1970. The small adjacent building housing the Puget Power and Light office was built earlier. The Masonic temple, the Christian Science Society building, and the Langley Clinic building are clustered on the left-hand side of the photograph, on the south side of First Street. (Courtesy of the City of Langley.)

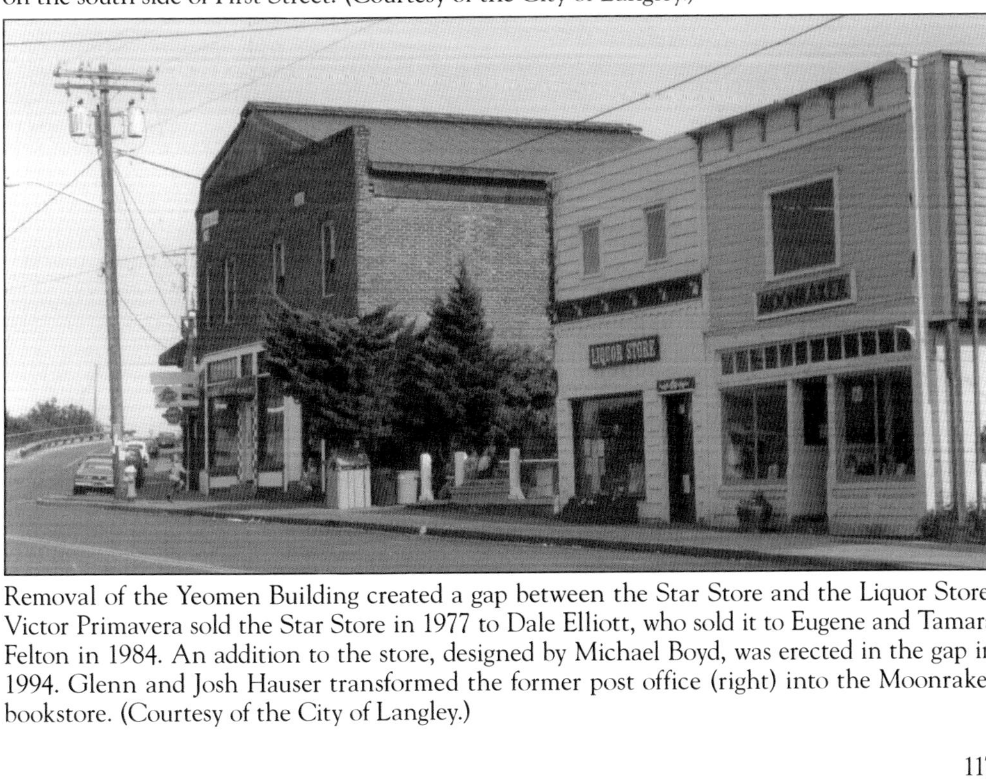

Removal of the Yeomen Building created a gap between the Star Store and the Liquor Store. Victor Primavera sold the Star Store in 1977 to Dale Elliott, who sold it to Eugene and Tamara Felton in 1984. An addition to the store, designed by Michael Boyd, was erected in the gap in 1994. Glenn and Josh Hauser transformed the former post office (right) into the Moonraker bookstore. (Courtesy of the City of Langley.)

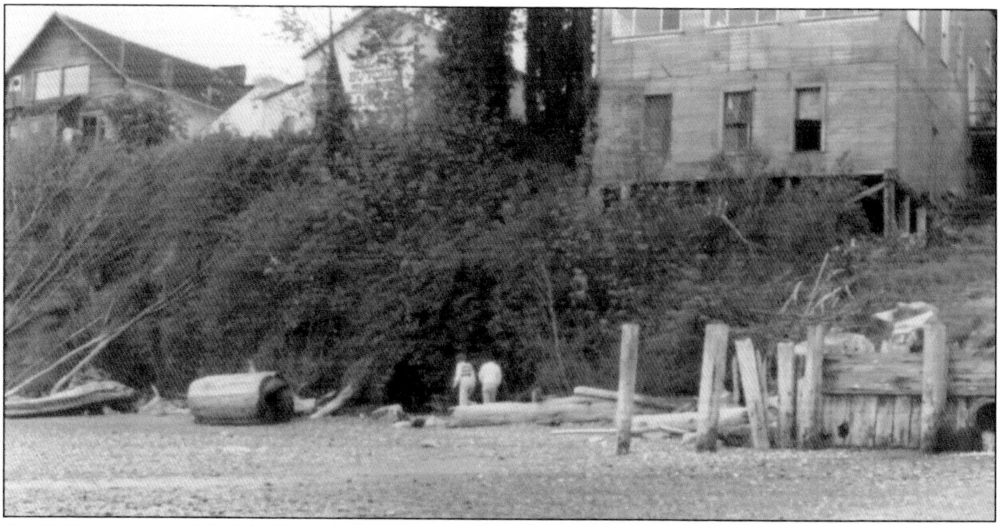

By 1975, erosion of the bluff was approaching the back of Dog House Tavern (upper right). When the town was founded, there had been enough land behind the buildings along the north side of First Street for children to play games and horses from the livery stable to be tethered. Jacob Anthes had even maintained an option for a road there. (Courtesy of the Langley City Hall.)

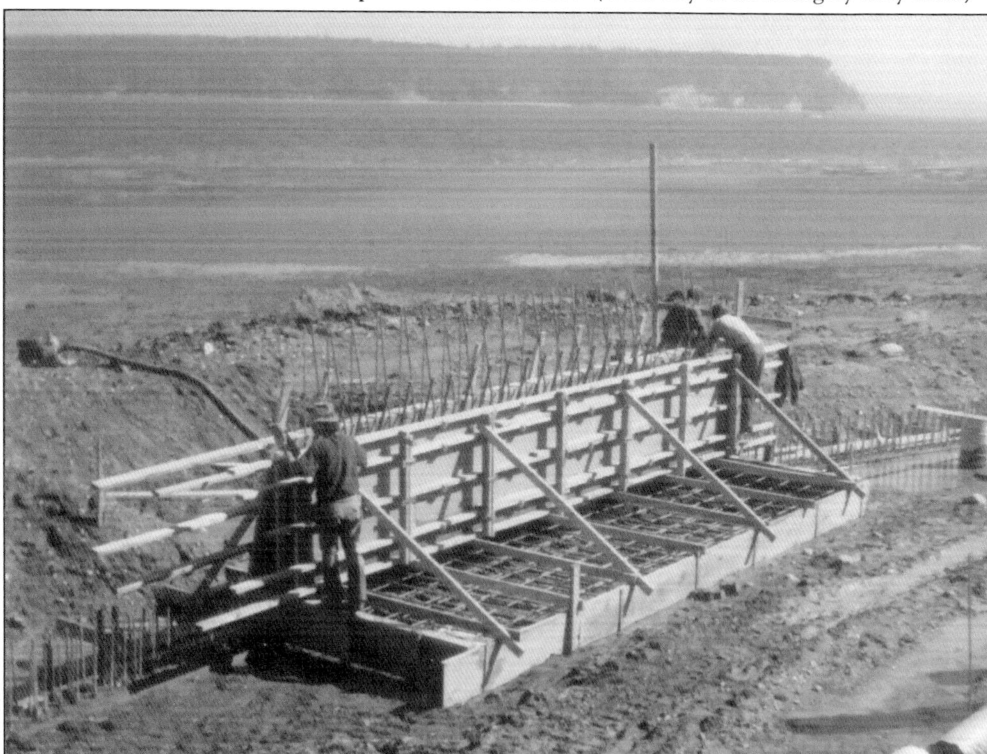

Construction of a sea wall began in 1975, some distance out from the shoreline. A concrete base was poured and topped with panels imprinted with Native American designs. When completed, the wall extended from below the Jones Department Store to the north end of the Sunrise Beach Addition. (Courtesy of the Langley City Hall.)

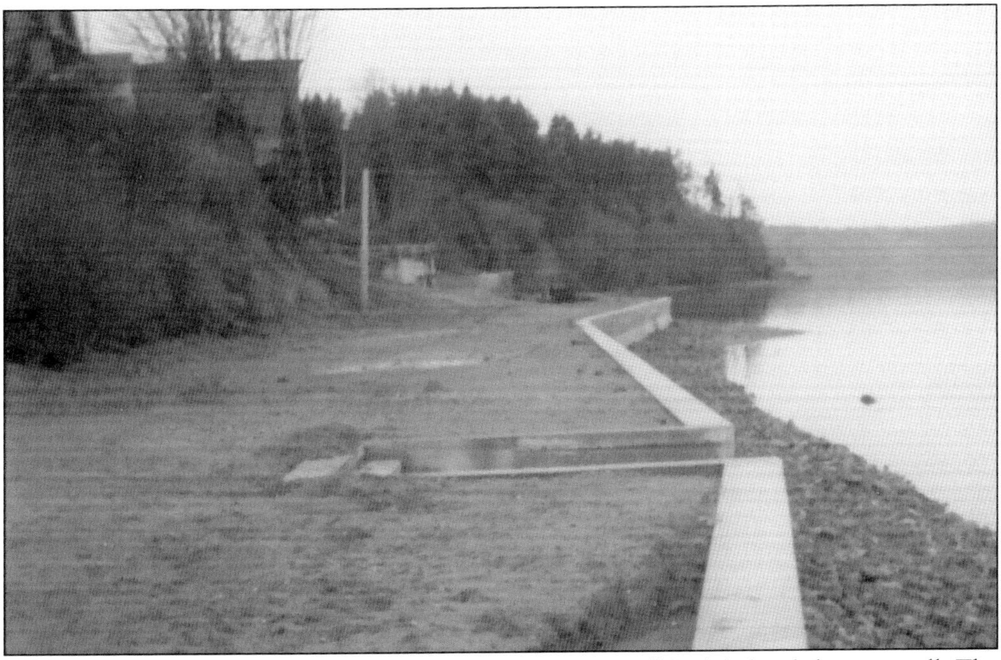

Rocks and dirt were barged and trucked in to create Sea Wall Park behind the new wall. The totem poles from First Street were placed here, and lighting, picnic tables, and memorial benches were added. (Courtesy of the Langley City Hall.)

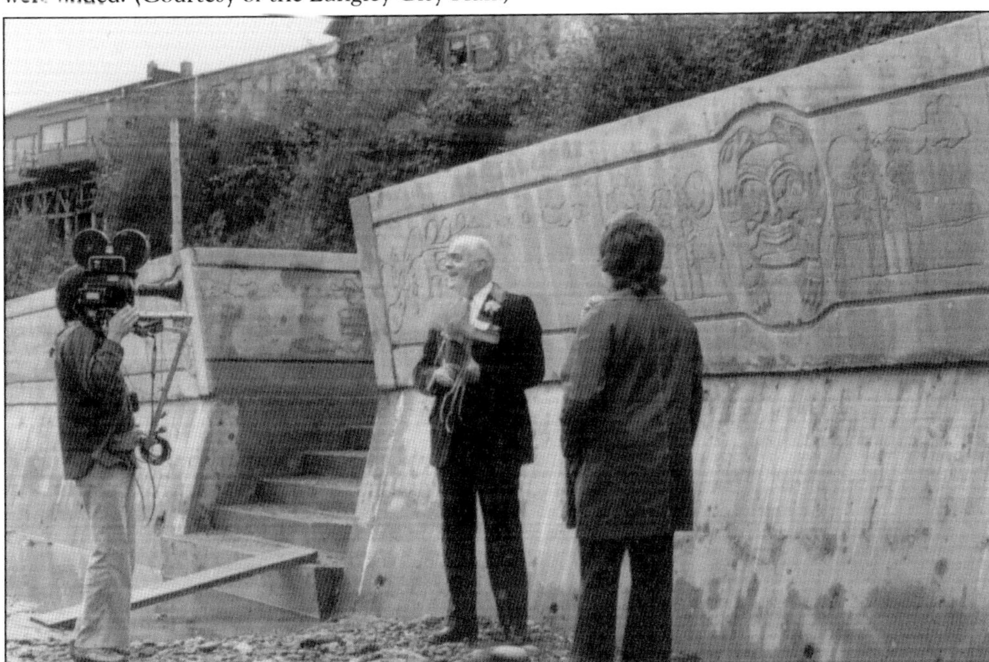

Mayor Donald Manchester (center) is pictured at the 1976 dedication of the new sea wall. The event was recorded by a KOMO 4 news cameraman. The mayor's wife, Peggy, broke a bottle of champagne on the wall, and a reception followed in the restaurant at the rear of the Dog House Tavern. (Courtesy of the City of Langley.)

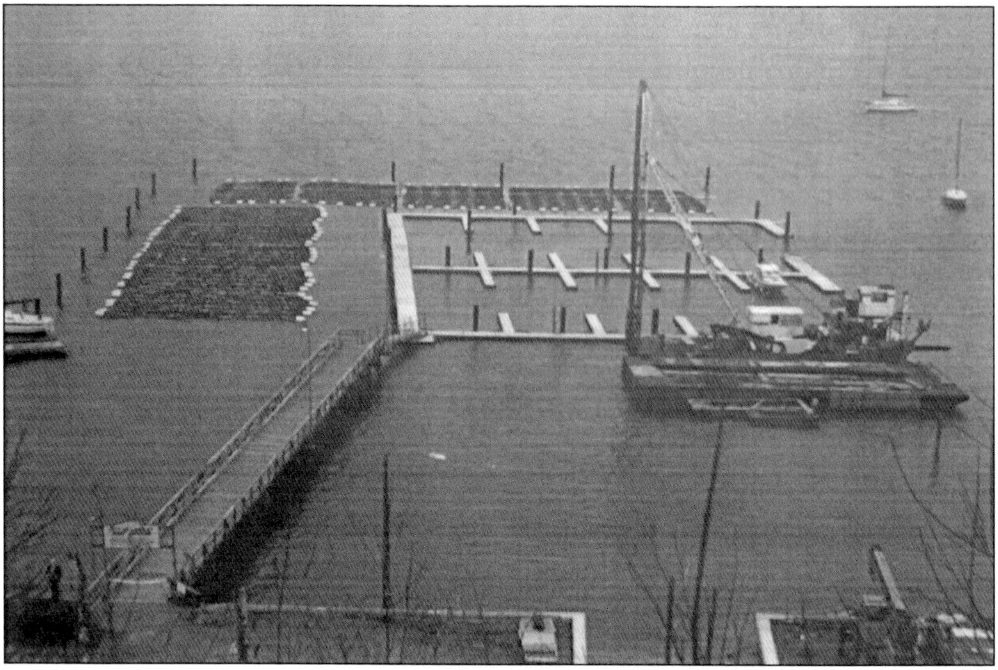

Mayor Donald Manchester dedicated a new Langley dock in 1979, following closure of the old dock for safety concerns. A floating breakwater composed of automobile tires protected the new 38-slip facility. The tires sank and the floats fell apart in 1983, leaving Langley without a boat moorage facility. (Courtesy of the City of Langley.)

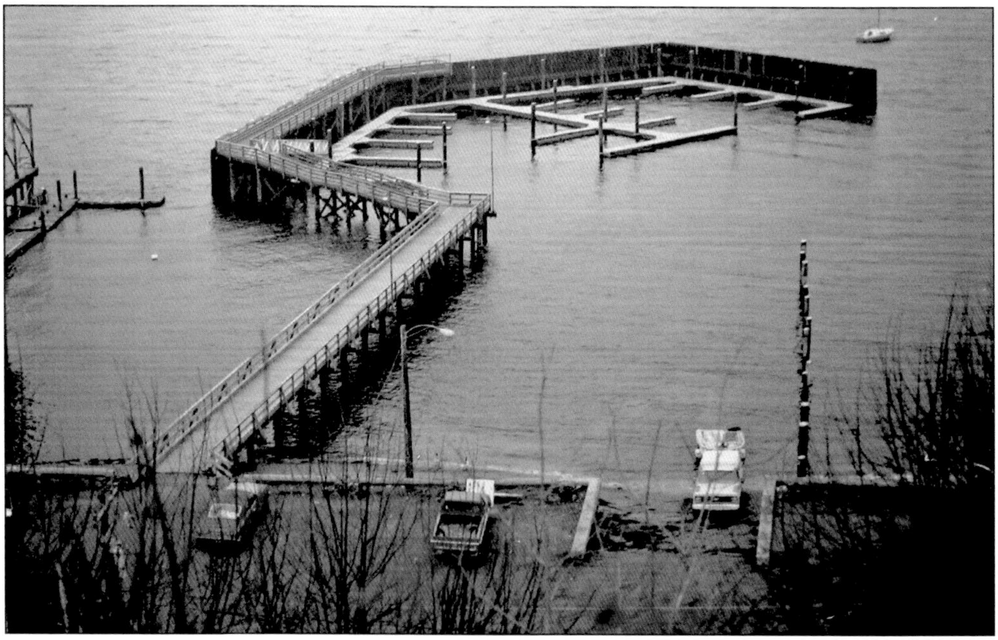

A new dock with a wooden piling breakwater and 35 slips was constructed and dedicated on May 10, 1986. State representative Mary Margaret Haugen broke a bottle of champagne at the dedication, presided over by Mayor Delores Cobb. This dock and surrounding property was sold to the Port of South Whidbey in 2009. (Courtesy of the City of Langley.)

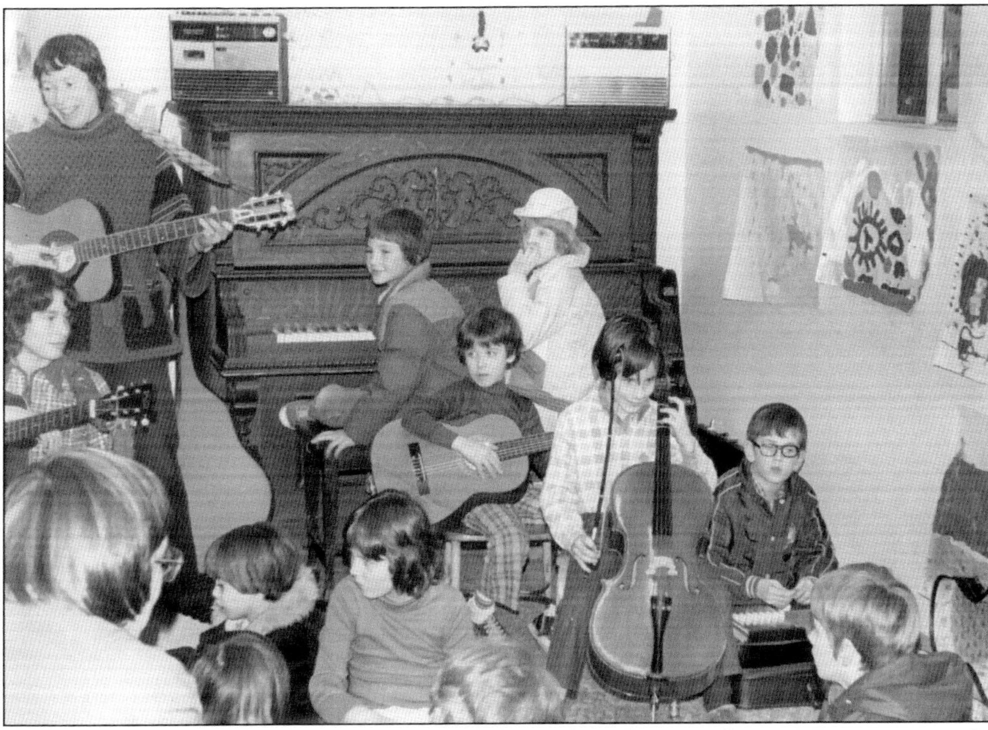

In 1974, Linda Good (with guitar, left), Paula Pugh, and Linda Morris began a music program for elementary students called Island Strings based on the Suzuki method. Practices were held in the physical education storage room. Students and their teachers have performed in many venues for decades. (Courtesy of Linda Good.)

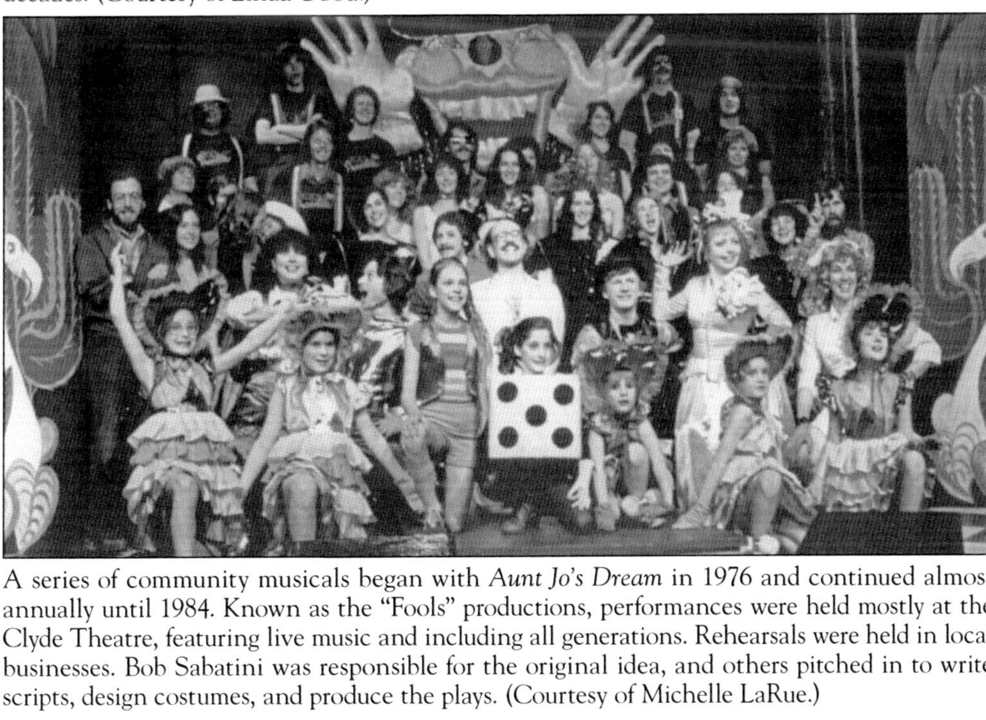

A series of community musicals began with *Aunt Jo's Dream* in 1976 and continued almost annually until 1984. Known as the "Fools" productions, performances were held mostly at the Clyde Theatre, featuring live music and including all generations. Rehearsals were held in local businesses. Bob Sabatini was responsible for the original idea, and others pitched in to write scripts, design costumes, and produce the plays. (Courtesy of Michelle LaRue.)

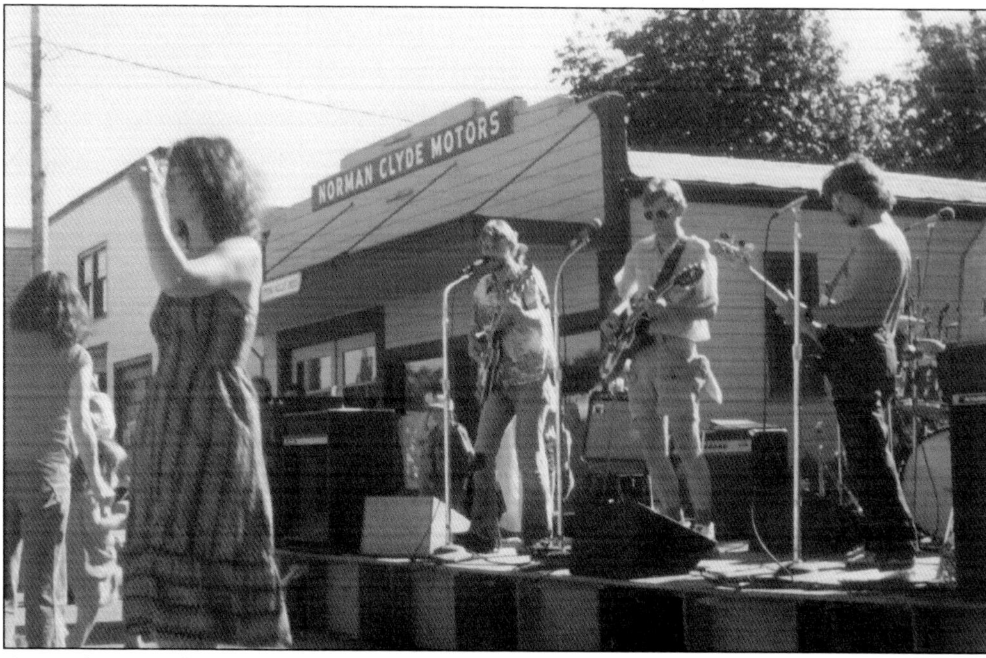

An art fair named Choochokam was begun by John Braun in 1975 to showcase local artisans. It features live music by local musicians. Members of the Fool Proof Band playing in front of Norman Clyde's showroom are, from left to right, David LiCastro, Michael LiCastro, and Fred Dente. The event has grown and continues today. (Courtesy of Susan and Randy Scofield.)

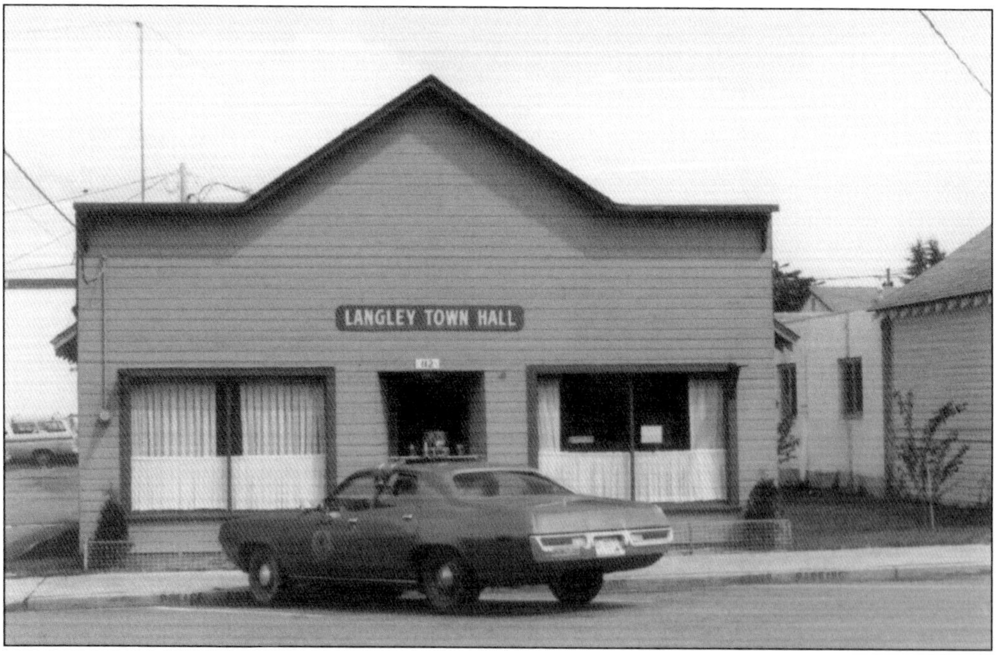

This building at the corner on Anthes Avenue and McLeod Alley served as town hall and police station until 1992, when the town hall moved to the former Masonic temple on Second Street. Langley became a city in 1975. The last of the maple trees planted by Jacob Anthes grew in front of the building until it was removed in the 1980s. (Courtesy of the Langley City Hall.)

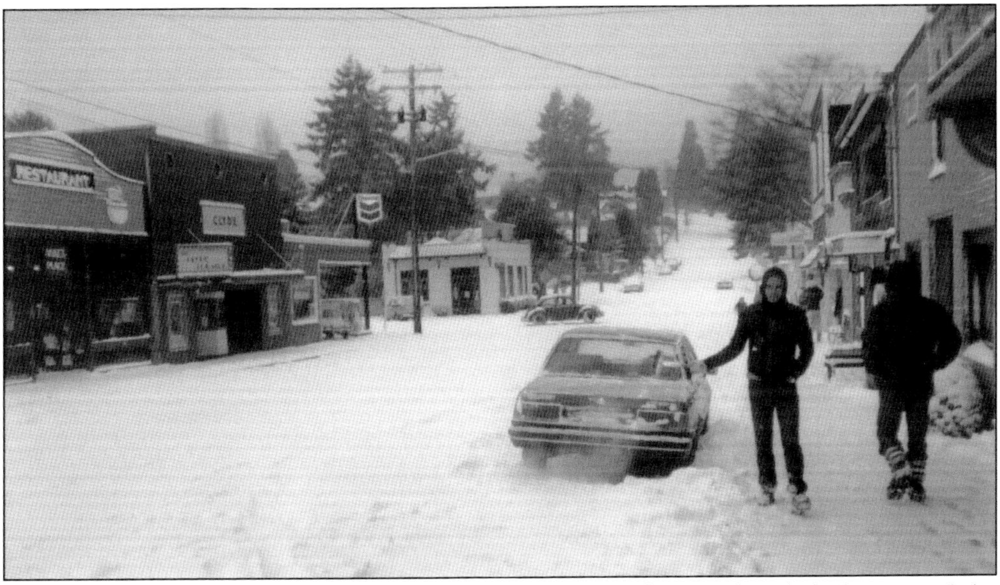

Shown here is First Street, looking west, during the winter of 1985. The Clyde Garage and the Clyde Theatre are across Anthes Avenue from the former bank and Soup Coop (center). Over the years, the building next to the Clyde Theatre housed Motenson's Hardware, Hein's Marine Store, Hizey's Farm Store, Brian McKenna's B-Street Restaurant, Al's Place, and Mike's Place. It was demolished in 1991 and replaced with a two-story building. (Courtesy of Brian McKenna.)

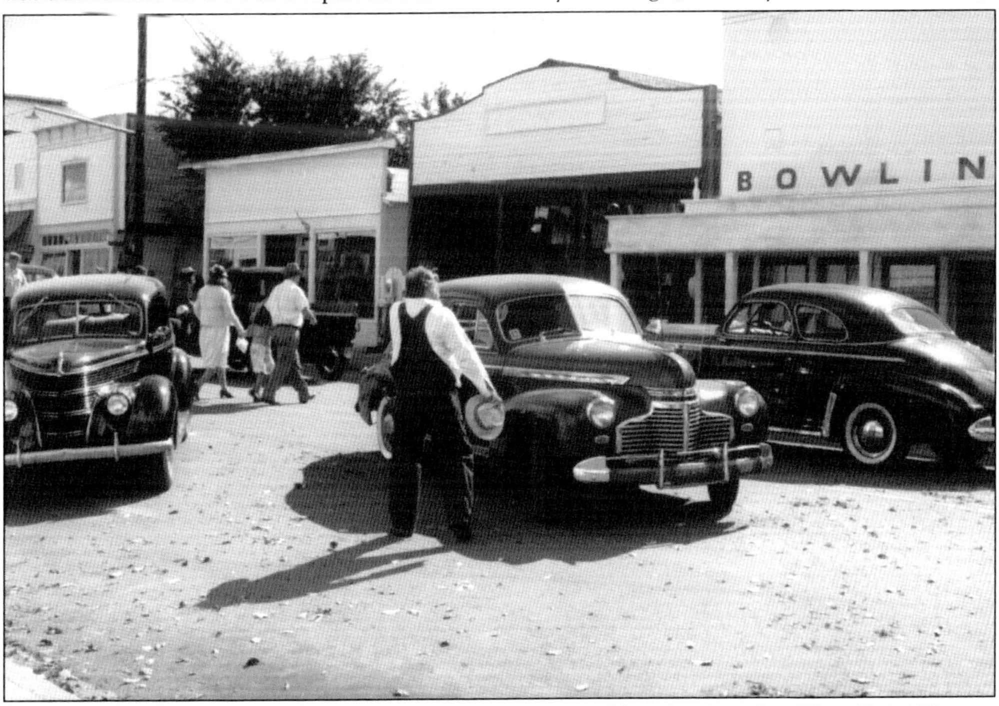

In 1985, a movie called *Dixie Lanes*, set in the 1940s, was filmed in Langley. The Clyde Theatre (right) was "the Bowling Lanes." Many people from the community were extras. The production company requested that the buildings along First Street be painted white. It ran out of money, leaving business owners to repaint their storefronts. (Courtesy of Ron Childers.)

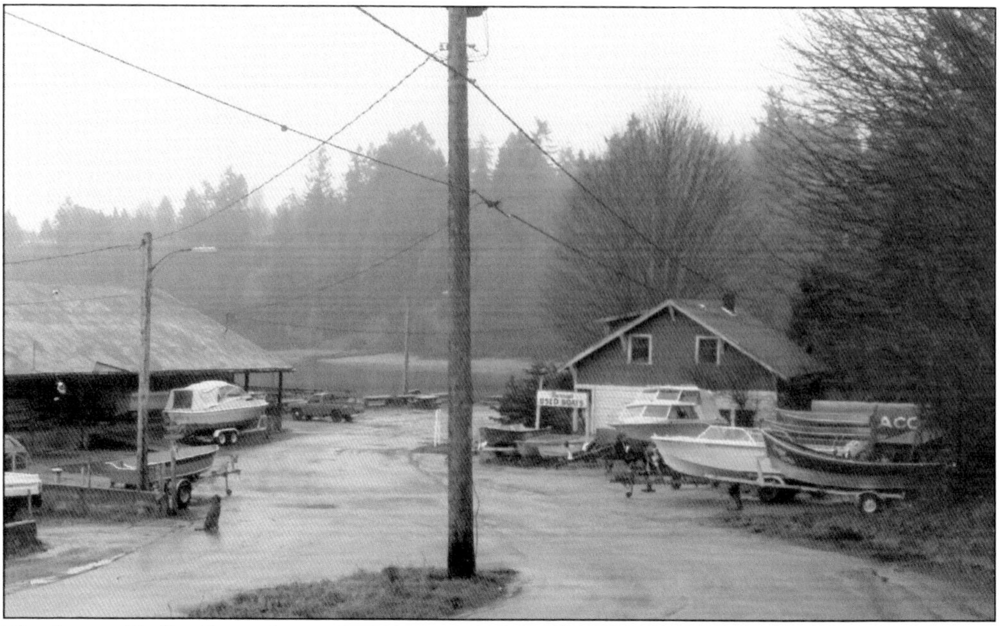

The former Phillip Simon house (right) was purchased by Bernard Hein, who owned the Langley Marina facility across the road. The house had been allowed to deteriorate and was condemned. Robert Drake purchased it in 1985 and remodeled it from the ground up. The Drakes lived in the house and rented rooms there. (Courtesy of Christina Drake.)

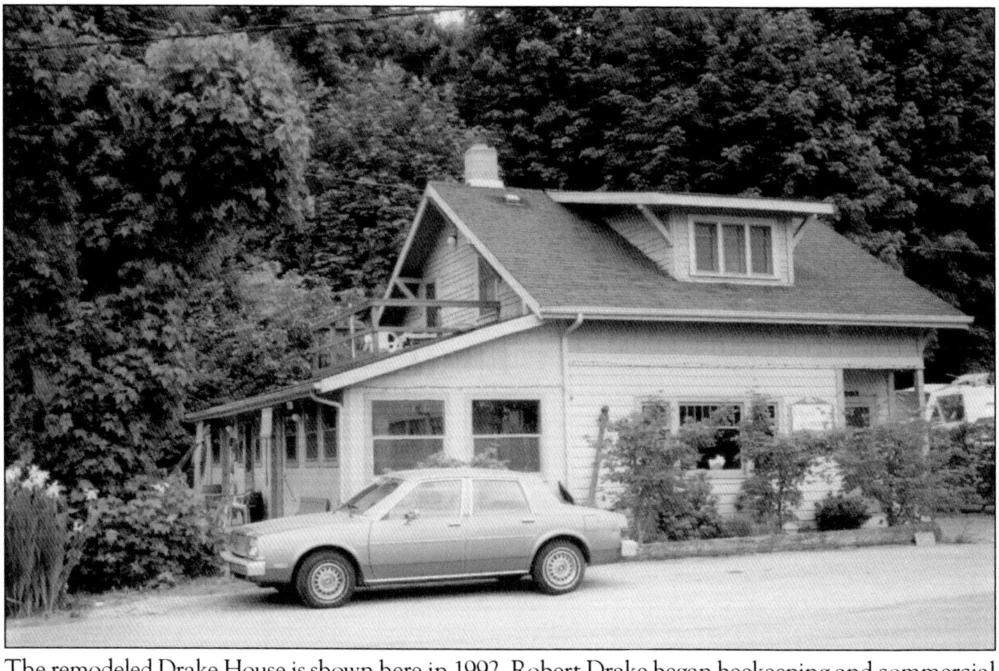

The remodeled Drake House is shown here in 1992. Robert Drake began beekeeping and commercial fishing after retiring from a career as a school principal. He was an original co-owner of Nichols Brothers Boat Builders, helping Frank Nichols construct their boat-building works in Freeland. He also loved Dixieland music and hosted "Mardi Gras parties to end all Mardi Gras parties" at Drake's Landing. (Courtesy of Christina Drake.)

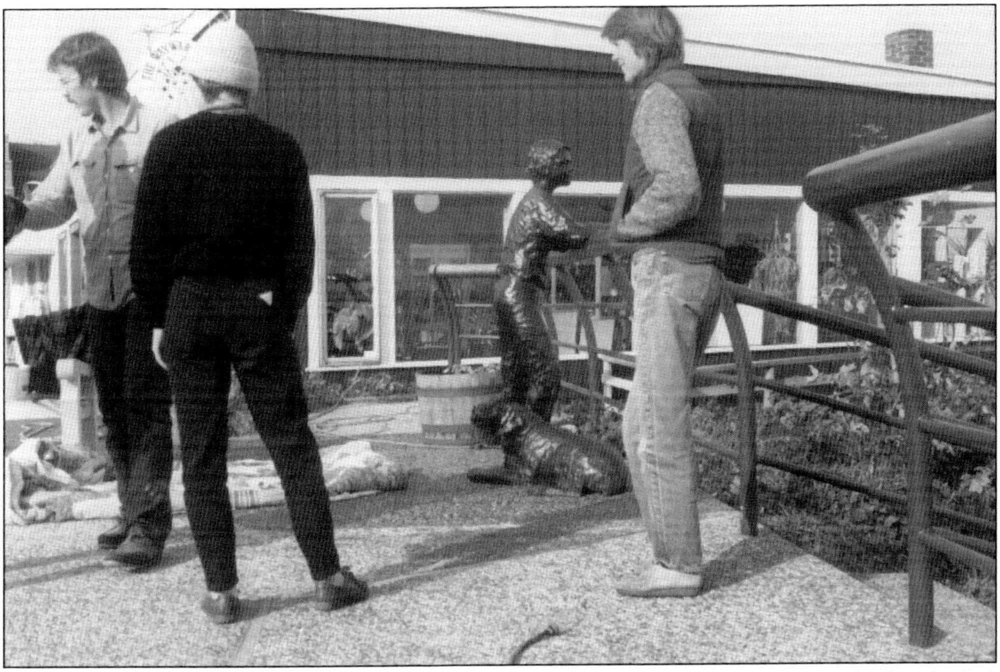

In November 1986, the *Boy* and *Dog* statues by Whidbey Island artist Georgia Gerber (right) were unveiled in Robert Smith Park, replacing the 20-year-old totem pole. Gerber's neighbor, Chris Adams, and her dog, Joshua, served as models for the statues. Gallery owner Ronald Childers spearheaded a drive that raised $4,500 in three weeks to pay for them. (Courtesy of Ronald Childers.)

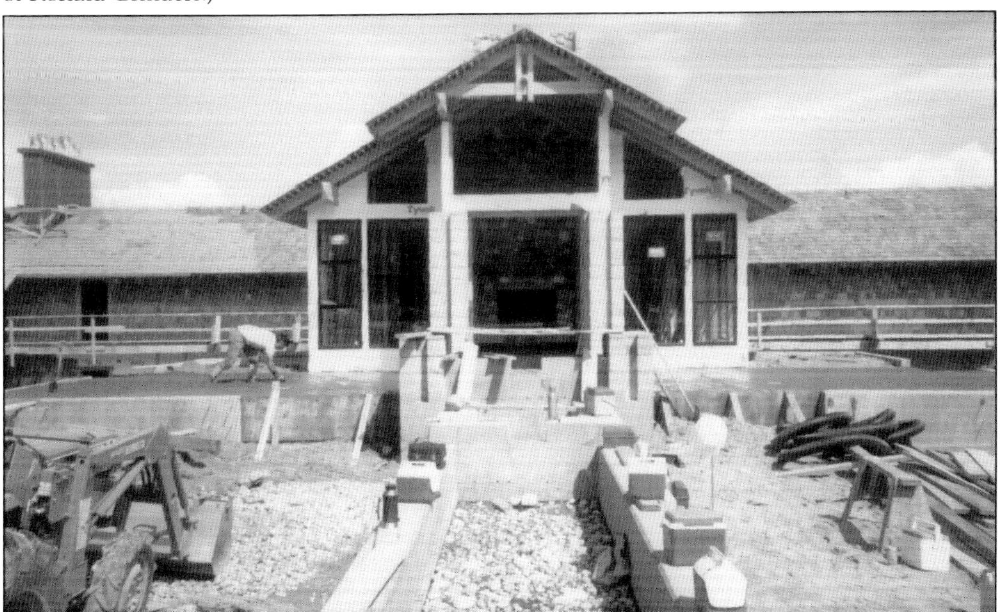

A major sign of the trend toward tourism as Langley's economic base was the construction on First Street of the 28-room luxury Inn at Langley by Paul and Pamela Schell and partners in 1989. The inn was built on the site of the former Howard Hotel. (Courtesy of Paul Schell.)

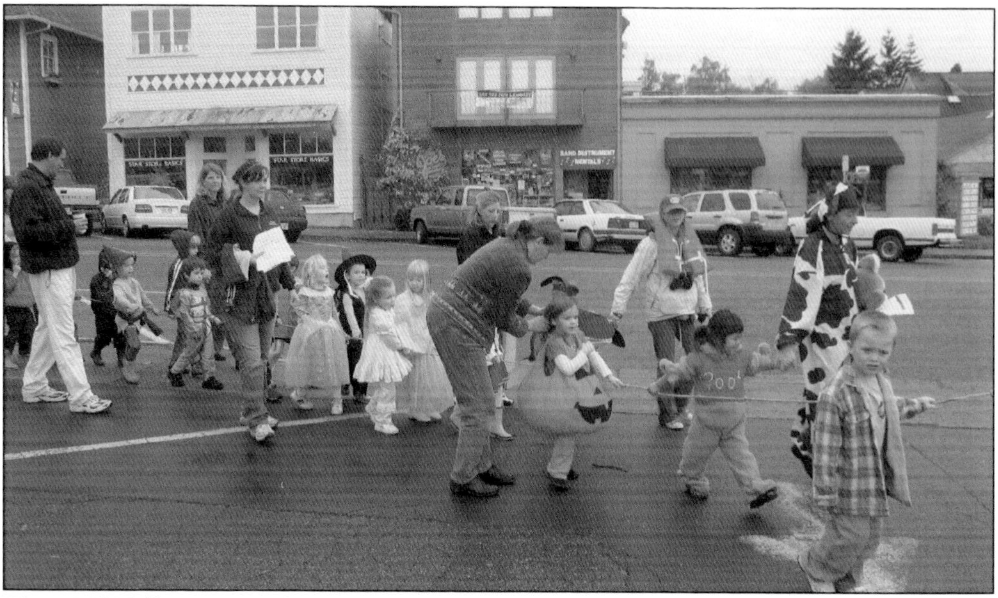

This 2005 Halloween parade features preschoolers from the South Whidbey Children's Center. The three two-story buildings beyond them, on the south side of Second Street, called the Second Street Project, were designed by local architect Ross Chapin and constructed in the 1990s. At far right, a walkway leads into a cluster of commercial and residential buildings known as the Langley Village, designed by Dale Elliot. (Courtesy of Robert Waterman.)

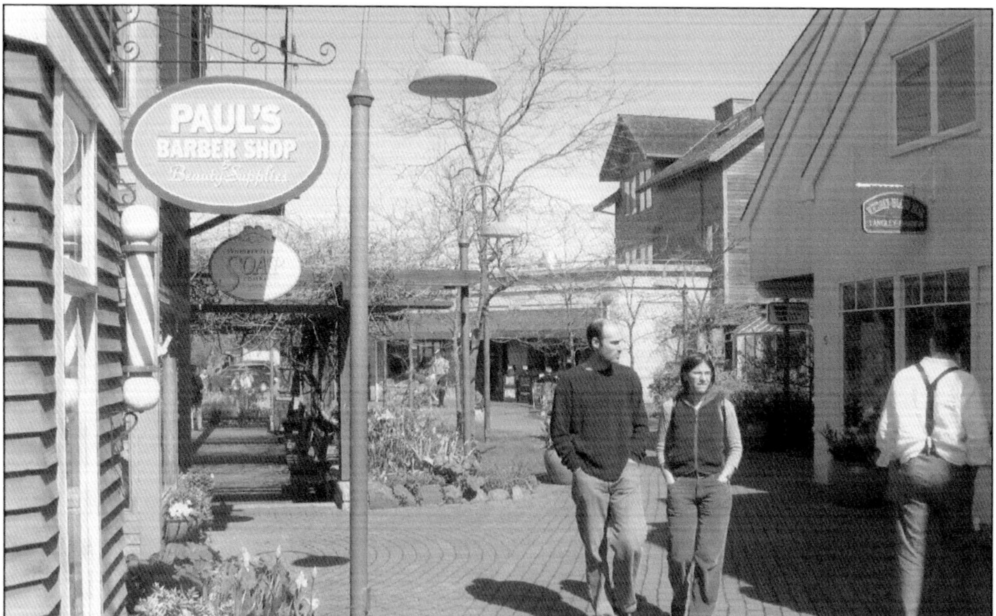

The Langley Village is an integrated collection of retail shops, services, and residential spaces. It was designed to offer a complement to Langley's historic First Street and was part of a cross-block project to provide pedestrian walkways connecting First to Third Streets. The Second Street Project and Langley Village helped define the character of the south side of Second Street. (Courtesy of Robert Waterman.)

Bibliography

Cherry, Lorna. *South Whidbey and Its People*. Vols. I, II, and III. Langley, WA: South Whidbey Historical Society, 1983–1986.

Hawes, E.M., and Lou Clark. *Island County: A World Beater*. Langley, WA: South Whidbey Historical Society, 1968.

Kellogg, George A. *A History of Whidbey's Island*. Coupeville, WA: Island County Historical Society, 1934.

Martin, David. *An Enduring Legacy: Women Painters of Washington*. Seattle: Whatcom Museum of History and Art, 2005.

McGinnis, William A. *The Langleyites of Whidbey Island, 1899–1921*. Willits, CA: William McGinnis, 1986.

Sherman, Roger M. *The Sinking of the* Calista: *Part I of a Maritime History of Central Whidbey Island*. Coupeville, WA: Roger Sherman, 1998.

White, Richard. *Land Use, Environment, and Social Change: The Shaping of Island County, Washington*. Seattle: University of Washington Press, 1992.

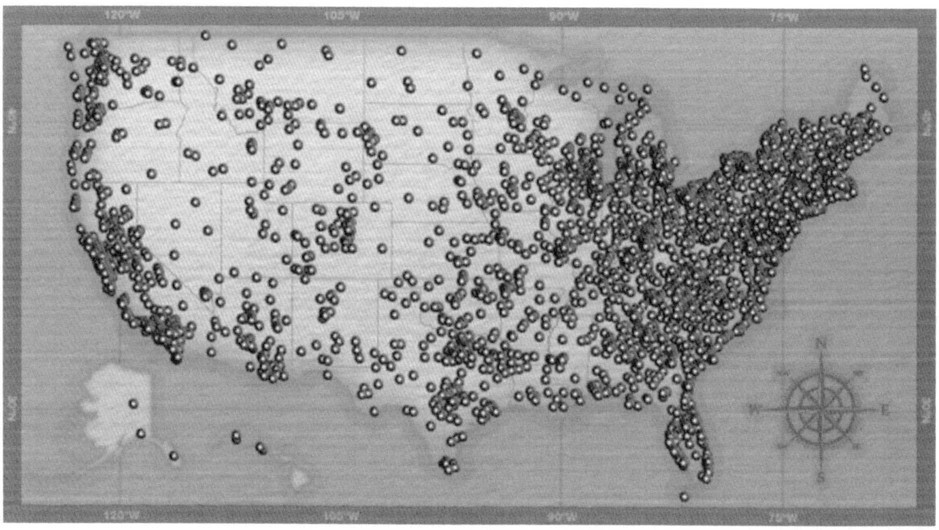

Consistent with our mission to preserve history on a local level, this book was printed in South Carolina on American-made paper and manufactured entirely in the United States. Products carrying the accredited Forest Stewardship Council (FSC) label are printed on 100 percent FSC-certified paper.

MADE IN THE USA